Britain Since 1918

Britain Since 1918

SECOND EDITION

Bentley B. Gilbert

St. Martin's Press   New York

DA
566
G54

© Bentley B. Gilbert 1980

First published 1967
Revised and updated 1980

All rights reserved. For information, write:
St. Martin's Press, Inc., 175 Fifth Avenue, New York, NY 10010
Printed in Great Britain
This edition first published in the United States of America in 1980

ISBN 0-312-09876-6

Library of Congress Cataloging in Publication Data

Gilbert, Bentley B   1924–
  Britain since 1918.
  Bibliography: p.
  Includes index.
  1. Great Britain—History—20th century.   I. Title.
DA566.G54   1980   941.082   80-19856
ISBN 0-312-09876-6

Contents

Acknowledgment

The writer wishes here to announce his debt to Lois Lentz, his editorial assistant, whose skill in unravelling syntax, typing, spelling, proof-reading, and discouraging interruptions by undergraduates has made this book possible.

Colorado Springs,   Bentley B. Gilbert
Colorado
27 February 1967

Preface

The first edition of this book, referring to the international payments crisis of October 1964, concluded that this event probably 'marked the end of the unhealthy prosperity of the fifties and demonstrated that the British citizens faced a second period of austerity and re-allocation of resources'. This was written in 1967 and seems justified completely by the melancholy events of the last decade and a half.

Modern history, certainly British history since the First World War, divides itself easily into periods of movement and of stagnation. The former may not be easy nor the latter unpleasant, nor indeed uneventful. Rather the distinction lies in the presence or absence of a clearly perceived national purpose. Obviously the struggle against Hitler evoked such resolution, although one could argue that only the Battle of Britain solidified it. In any case it continued through the Attlee ministry, an administration that appears in retrospect to have been one of the most astonishingly successful that Britain has known in this century.

Equally clearly this sense of commitment by the individual to the whole has been lacking in the past 15 years, which look now to have been almost barren of real achievement, the entry into the Common Market aside. Without this sense among citizens of corporate responsibility a government can accomplish little. Wilson understood this, as he understood many things, and continually enjoined his countrymen to display the 'Dunkirk spirit'.

Fairplay, tolerance and moderation are still the code that Britain lives by. They keep the country, as it has long been, a museum of civilized virtues. But generosity of spirit may be a weakness in an unreasonable world and the willingness to give way to the threat of violence, whether internal or external, whether economic or military, may produce a situation in which the civic balance that has made Britain what it is becomes itself a danger.

Most historians are pleased to be asked to produce a revised edition of one of their earlier works. To know that the publisher is still willing to trust one is satisfying. It provides the author the occasion to reread, and possibly to rethink, what he has written years earlier. It makes possible the rectification of mistakes before they are found out. And in fact it is occasionally possible to see that some things have turned out as he predicted.

In the additional chapters of this study I have tried to concentrate upon the issues in British society that seem to me still unresolved. Inevitably these are as much economic as political. The two have for the last 30 years been almost inseparable and continue to present the problems that Britain has faced since the First World War: declining productivity, trade union power, the balance of trade. But on the other hand, one senses that the goal of fair shares for all, the slogan of the 1945 Labour government, symbolized by the welare state, has been eclipsed, indeed made impossible, by trade union militancy. Ireland has of course re-emerged. Otherwise little has changed.

In concluding this preface I should like to note that many of the opinions that appear in the last chapters of this study, although entirely my own, were born in years of conversations and disputes with an old friend, the Managing Director of B. T. Batsford, Peter Kemmis Betty, before whose television, as a matter of fact, I watched the polling in the crucial general election of February 1974. In addition I must acknowledge that the leisure to begin writing was given me by an invitation to Chatham Hall in Pittsylvania County, Virginia, a place chartered the year the Great Commoner became Prime Minister, and which remains an enclave of mellow brick walls and ancient churches, horses, broad meadows and huge oaks, a green and pleasant land as more of England still ought to be.

Glencoe, Illinois   Bentley B. Gilbert
4 January 1980

Introduction

Britain celebrated the Armistice of 11 November 1918 for two days and nights, and might have continued for a third night had not the police begun to interfere with the grosser forms of rejoicing. The exultation was proportionate to the despair of the previous years. The First World War not only had decimated the manhood of the nation but it had stunned the survivors. No experience in previous conflicts had prepared Englishmen for the material sacrifice or the grey hopelessness of the 1914–18 years. There had been much heroism, but little excitement. Men had achieved personal glory in the cause of waste and miscalculation. The nation had survived but a world had died.

The military events of the First World War may be briefly told. While the British army ready for service in France was well trained and well organized, slightly fewer men were available than had been on hand to go to the Crimea in 1854. As a result, although the components of the regular army that were hurried over to France in the first weeks of the war served with notable gallantry, the British military contribution to the Allied land strength in the first two years was small. The principal British activities were in the naval blockade of Germany, in the mobilization of the resources of the British and French empires, and finally in specialized expeditions, of which the attempt to force a water route to Russia through the Straits of Dardanelles is the best known. This campaign, occupying most of 1915, centred in an attempt to establish a beachhead in the Gallipoli peninsula. Although fought with great heroism, consuming large amounts of resources and resulting in enormous casualties, the campaign was a failure.

The public reaction to the lagging British war effort, of which the

Gallipoli campaign served as an example, was a mounting discontent with the Liberal government of Herbert Asquith, who had been Prime Minister since 1908. While he unquestionably ranks as one of the greatest peacetime Prime Ministers of the twentieth century, as a war leader Asquith was ill-served by the very qualities—honesty, judiciousness, patience and tolerance—that made him a great man. A newspaper campaign against him and his government for an apparent lack of energy and drive in the prosecution of the war and indecision over the handling of the Gallipoli campaign caused a reconstruction of the government in May of 1915, resulting in a coalition with the Conservative opposition. Two changes that would be important for the future were the resignation from the Admiralty of Winston Churchill, who was accused in the press of responsibility for mismanagement in the Gallipoli campaign, and the appointment of David Lloyd George, the Chancellor of the Exchequer, to head a new Ministry of Munitions.

This office put Lloyd George in a position to supervise the organization of British industry for war. He realized earlier than any political leader in any country (with the possible exception of Walter Rathenau in Germany) that the war that had broken out in 1914 was a struggle in which the mobilization of industry and industrialists was perhaps more important than the mobilization of fighting men. He knew that in the long run the strength of the nation lay in its potential to produce the engines of war and thus the organization at home was as important as the organization in the field. In effect he understood what would later come to be called 'total war'.

For the immediate future, however, Lloyd George's short period at the Ministry of Munitions, which ended in July of 1916 when he replaced Lord Kitchener as Secretary of State for War, was as important for his own future as for the history of Great Britain. At the Ministry of Munitions the man who would become Prime Minister in December 1916 emerged. Here the Lloyd George whom the British upper classes had known as the socialistic radical and demagogue—the most dangerous man in England—suddenly became the organizer of victory. His superb gifts for harmonizing conflicting points of view and for seeing, almost by intuition, the heart of a knotty administrative problem, his cunning, his charm and his ruthlessness—attributes long known to the civil servants at the Treasury —now became familiar to the leaders of the British business world, who for the first time came in large numbers into government service.

The year 1916 witnessed also the beginning of the second phase of the Great War. The huge volunteer army that Britain had been training and equipping for two years was at last thrown into the conflict on the Somme, and there most of a generation of young men were killed. For all of the warring powers, 1916 was a year of catastrophe. But perhaps for Britain, uninvolved in any important war for a century and unused to the collision of great armies, the hideous losses of the Somme were more of a shock. There came the realization by the end of the year that the war was no closer to decision than it had been two years earlier. Added to the military disasters that began in 1916 on the Western Front, Russian army officers murdered the mysterious favourite at the Russian court, the monk Gregory Rasputin, and so set in train the events that would bring by mid-March 1917 the collapse of the Czar's government. During the rest of the year the Russian war effort dwindled and in the autumn, with the Bolshevik Revolution, Russia withdrew from the war. In the spring of 1917 the German campaign of unrestricted submarine warfare, beginning on 1 February, added to the discomfort of the citizens of the British Isles by causing severe shortages of clothing, food and fuel, all of which, combined with ever-growing casualty lists, made the winter of 1916–17 the grimmest period of the war. By this time men in all countries—Lord Lansdowne was the most important in England—were searching for ways to bring the seemingly endless and futile conflict to a halt.

It can be argued that, were it not for three events, the war might well have terminated with some form of a compromise peace in 1917. One of these was the German defeat of Russia, which raised temporarily German hopes for victory and alleviated slightly the effect of the British blockade. The second, of greater moral if not military effect, was the entrance of the United States in April of 1917. This made an Allied victory practically certain, provided Britain could survive the immediate effects of the German submarine blockade, which was the specific cause of the American entrance. The American military contribution toward the winning of the war was modest, but its potential in men and material was great and of critical importance in a war of attrition. As the American entrance raised Allied hopes, it correspondingly depressed German hopes. When the Germans realized that they would not be able to force a decision in France before a large number of American troops were in the field, they made peace as quickly as possible.

The third event, and for Great Britain unquestionably the most important in overcoming the disastrous war weariness that might have forced a compromise peace in the winter of 1916–17, was the character and personality of David Lloyd George, who, with the connivance of the Conservatives, unseated Herbert Asquith as Prime Minister on 6 December 1916. Invariably cheerful and optimistic, never discouraged, fertile with innovation, he used his personality— as did Winston Churchill in a different way in the Second World War—as a weapon of victory. Lloyd George did not, of course, have radio broadcasting with which to place himself before the nation, but he could and did continue the practice begun during his days at the Ministry of Munitions of personally appearing in war factories and public meetings. Always urging more effort, more sacrifice, he reminded the citizens and the workers that not the army but the nation was at war. At the same time he reorganized the government, superseding the large, unwieldy peacetime cabinet with a War Cabinet devoted to supreme direction of the war; small and intimate, it was perfectly suited to the Welshman's talent for personal negotiation and compromise. The reorganization of the cabinet, not entirely successful, was matched by the appearance of new ministries to organize civilian affairs as would be appropriate to a nation totally mobilized. Within days after Lloyd George took office, there were created Ministries of Food Control, of Labour, of Pensions, of Shipping, and perhaps most significant, in the spring of 1917, of Reconstruction.

The Ministry of Reconstruction symbolizes what may have been Lloyd George's greatest contribution as the leader of the nation in Britain's darkest hour. He understood intuitively, as he understood many things, that the old aims of the war had disappeared. Britain was no longer fighting for the integrity of Belgium, still less for Serbia. Nor was the nation presumably in search of enemy territory or of increased resources, or of national identification, as had been the aim of so many nations in the nineteenth-century wars. Nor finally could it be argued, as in the Second World War, that the Kaiser's Germany represented the recrudescence of tribal savagery that was Nazi Germany, the expunging of which itself provided a sufficient excuse for war. But the tremendous sacrifices of the struggle demanded some justification or goal other than the simple defeat of Germany. Hence almost immediately in a thousand ways, well before the publication of President Woodrow Wilson's Fourteen Points in January 1918, Lloyd George began to teach the British people that the immense conflict in which they were engaged was toward the goal of a better world—specifically a better Britain. Government planning would show the way in many fields, and of this the Ministry of Reconstruction was an important but by no means the only symbol. Inevitably much that was promised represented a continuation of his prewar programmes of social reform. The new Britain would offer economic security to the worker, better institutions for the care of the aged, better schools for the children. There would be new houses and improved health care. The old poor law, it was implied, would disappear. As the war moved toward its close, these plans took more and more concrete form, either as legislation or as part of the speeches of politicians, and finally as part of the platform of the coalition government in the general election immediately after the Armistice.

Thus in the last two years of the war, between December 1916 and November 1918, David Lloyd George presided like William Pitt over a national revival. By energy and wit, with a genius for negotiation and a talent, if not for administration, for the solution of administrative problems, he led Britain from the despair of 1916 to victory in 1918. Although his international prestige was overshadowed by that of Woodrow Wilson of the United States, his political position at home, in Parliament, and in the nation, appeared to be stronger than any Prime Minister's had ever been. 'He can be Prime Minister for life if he wants to be', remarked Andrew Bonar Law, the leader of the Conservatives. As it turned out, the disillusion of the nation with the peace would also mean disenchantment with David Lloyd George.

CHAPTER ONE

The End of the War to The End of Lloyd George: 1918-22

The almost hysterical celebration with which Britain greeted the coming of peace illustrated more than the nation's hopes for the future. The mood was of relief, the feeling that one must have upon release from prison, and of expectation. No one, for the moment, counted the cost. About 750,000 young men had been killed and twice that number wounded. This was nearly three times the military casualties of the Second World War. A whole generation of young men had died in the great battles of 1916 and 1917. Prime Minister Asquith's eldest son had been killed, as had the only son of Lord Grey, Foreign Secretary at the outbreak of the war. Nearly every household in the United Kingdom had lost a father, a son, a brother, or a sweetheart. From these men would have come the artists, the scholars, the political and business leaders of the next generation. For their loss Great Britain was immeasurably poorer.

The struggle had affected also those who survived. Erich Maria Remarque dedicated one of the great novels to come out of the war to that generation of men who, 'even though they may have escaped its shells, were destroyed by the war'. It is impossible to overemphasize the importance of the fact that almost without exception the nation's leaders through the period of this volume had spent four of the most impressionable years of their early life serving a nation at war, in the trenches, at home in the government, or, in several cases, in jail as a protest against the struggle.

But while the human cost of the conflict, however huge, was immeasurable, the losses to the British economic system and the destruction of the economic world in which Britain had been preeminent were all too easy to calculate, and in the long run no less important. The goods that were not produced and not consumed in the twenties and thirties because of economic depression, the millions of lives that were dragged out in hopelessness and physical misery in northern and Welsh cities where the mill or shipyard had closed, the grey agony of continuous unemployment, of year after year living on the dole, these also must be counted as costs of the war no less than if the worker had been murdered by a bullet or his worldly goods destroyed by a bomb.

For the historian the economic losses and dislocations from the First World War are perhaps its most important effect. They will be treated later in this chapter with reference to specific industries. Let it be said here only that the nation had seen the national debt go from about £700 million to £7,000 million, and the proportion of expenditure covered by current revenue drop from 100 per cent for the fiscal year ending 31 March 1914 to 31·9 per cent for the fiscal year ending 31 March 1919. Except for one budget during the Boer War the British government had never spent over £200 million in a single year. The average expenditure for each of the four years of the First World War was well over ten times this amount. In 1914 national income in the United Kingdom, that is the total amount of all wages, salaries, profits and rents—everything in fact except savings for the depreciation of plant equipment—amounted to £2,209 million. In the year ending 31 March 1916, the first fiscal year for which the budget had been drawn up during the war, the government spent £1,559 million. In the next three fiscal years government spending averaged £2,491 million or about £200 million more than the total national income in the last year of peace. Even allowing for considerable inflation in prices during the war and for a drastic reduction in individual consumption in the same period, it is clear that Britain paid for a large part of the First World War from savings not only of money but of accumulated wealth in plant facilities, natural resources, and goods. In effect the national productive apparatus, which had made Britain strong for 150 years, was allowed to run down without renewal and without replacement. It has been estimated that the nation used up 12·7 per cent of its national wealth in the four years of the First World War.

BRITAIN AND THE PEACE OF VERSAILLES

David Lloyd George's first act after the surrender of the German army was to ask King George V to dissolve Parliament and to order

Britain's first general election since December 1910. This election, the first in which the voting was completed on a single day and the first in which women voted, took place on 14 December, a little more than a month after the shooting had stopped in France. Its peculiar name, the 'Coupon Election', derives from the fact that the coalition government, made up of the Liberal followers of Lloyd George, the Conservatives, and a few members of the Labour party, appealed to the electorate as a group. Coalition Liberals and coalition Conservatives did not oppose each other in constituencies. Each coalition-sponsored candidate received a letter of endorsement from the leader of his party, which H. H. Asquith derisively referred to as a 'coupon'. Opposed to the coalition candidates were the Liberal followers of Asquith who had retired when Lloyd George supplanted him as Prime Minister in December 1916, the old Irish Nationalist party, the new Sinn Fein party—both of which fielded candidates almost exclusively in the other island—and the majority, practically the whole, of the Labour party, which had declared itself independent of the coalition at a special conference on 14 November.

The official coalition platform offered the electors a gigantic programme of domestic political, economic and social reform. Much of this was based upon the plans already worked out in the Ministry of Reconstruction for improving the working and living conditions of the people. Several acts in this direction, for the extension of public education, maternity and child welfare, had already been passed and a bill to establish a Ministry of Health, long projected by reformers, had been hastily introduced in the crowded last few days before Parliament was dissolved. In addition, the nation was promised, either directly or by implication, a large number of radical measures which had been discussed but not accomplished before the war—reform of the poor law, reconstruction of the House of Lords, and Irish home rule.

But this was only part of the coalition programme. The cost of the new Britain, fit for heroes to live in, would be paid by defeated Germany. Throughout the electoral campaign in a thousand ways, by specific promises, or more frequently by implication and by violence of language, government candidates and newspapers associated in the minds of the voters reconstruction of Great Britain and revenge upon Germany. Germany would pay and pay. Her pockets would be searched for the last farthing. She would be squeezed like an orange until the pips squeaked. How much of this artificially stimulated ferocity was the responsibility of David Lloyd George and how much was the work of popular newspapers is not clear. In the long run it is probably of no significance. The important thing is that many members of the overwhelming coalition majority in the new House of Commons, which assembled in January 1919, felt they had been elected upon a promise to punish Germany and were prepared to force the government to demand the harshest possible terms from the defeated foe.

The importance of the Coupon Election of 1918 for the general problem of peacemaking and for the condition of Britain after the war is that, intentionally or not, Lloyd George obligated himself to make reparation demands upon Germany that would continue and intensify the economic dislocations of the war itself. ('Heaven only knows what I would have had to promise if the campaign had lasted a week longer', he is reported to have said.) Paradoxically Lloyd George's electoral victory made him less of a free political agent than he had been before. He went off to Paris in January 1919, under orders to inflict a revenge that was directly contrary to the interest of the nation he served, a revenge that would go a long way toward making impossible social and economic reconstruction not only of Germany, but of his own nation as well. (In March 1919, attempting to moderate some extreme French demands and to support a rather too-idealistic position taken by the American President, Woodrow Wilson, Lloyd George received a telegram from 370 coalition supporters in the House of Commons reminding him that he and the government had pledged themselves during the election to force from Germany the cost of her aggression. The question at hand in Paris, therefore, was not whether or not Germany was liable, but simply how her liability would be discharged.)

Among the victorious major powers in the West, France had suffered the most. Nearly 13,000 square miles of her continental territory where lived one-eighth of her population had been overrun at some time during the war. Several of her most productive cities had been in German hands for four years and a number had been devastated by military action. Finally, during their withdrawal the Germans had deliberately destroyed certain natural resources, particularly coal. Her loss in manpower in proportion to her population had been considerably greater than Britain's. Despite the fact that the victory ensured she would now receive the provinces of Alsace and Lorraine, which Germany had taken from her in 1871, the French leader Georges Clemenceau could reasonably reflect that his nation, although victorious, was weaker in relation to Germany than it had been in 1914.

French policy aimed, therefore, at military security. She could not be sure of a repetition of the series of events that had brought most of the rest of the world into the conflict as her allies. Hence Germany must be so weakened that she never again would be a threat to France. How this weakening would be accomplished was a matter of some dispute among the French leaders themselves. French military leaders hoped to see the German provinces in the Rhine Valley detached from Germany and made into an independent state. This not only would weaken Germany economically and militarily and establish a buffer state between the ancient enemies, but also would provide an outpost for French influence east of the Rhine.

Secondly, as a means both of weakening Germany and of rebuilding France, the French intended to force Germany to pay huge war reparations. French political leaders had promised during the war that the devastated areas of the nation would be rebuilt after the end of the conflict. Both economic and moral justice dictated that Germany should pay for this. Reconstruction began soon after the Armistice and went on as the peace conference at Paris assembled. It was carried through swiftly, and expensively. (By the spring of 1921, 20,000 million francs had been spent.) But with Germany at the mercy of the Allies, no one counted the cost. It was unpatriotic to do so and implied tenderness for the defeated aggressor. The diplomatic effects of France's vast and hurried expenditures for the rebuilding of her devastated areas were great. By committing herself to huge short-term debts (that would be redeemed when German reparations began), the nation made it impossible for its leaders at Versailles even to negotiate on the subject of reparations. German payments were more than a moral obligation or a prize for victory; they were an absolute economic necessity.

France's need was a part of Britain's difficulties. In the negotiations at Paris Lloyd George and his colleagues could not consider forgoing reparations for their own country so long as France led the victorious continental powers in insisting upon high reparations for herself. The British delegation—besides the Prime Minister, Andrew Bonar Law and Lord Balfour—soon came to understand, if they had not known before, the importance of a revived and prosperous Germany. Such a nation would be valuable to Europe and a market for British goods, while a humiliated and impoverished Germany would be easy prey for Bolshevik revolution. Indeed one had broken out in

Berlin in January just as the peace conference assembled. Nevertheless, bound by their own promises at home and by France's absolute refusal to moderate any of her demands upon the defeated foe, Britain's representatives were unable to exert the authority that the prestige of the nation should have given them.

A second factor making difficult resistance to exorbitant reparations against Germany was the French, Italian, and Belgian insistence that without reparations they would be unable to pay the huge debt they owed the United Kingdom. This argument was more powerful because much of the money Great Britain had lent her continental allies, particularly in the last months of the war, had been borrowed from the United States. Britain's own ability to pay her debts and her resumption of her position as a creditor nation in the world seemed to depend upon reparations. Although the United States never acknowledged any legal connexion between reparations and war debts, the *de facto* connexion was nevertheless important. The British government had lent to Allied governments during the war about £1,825 million. She had borrowed from other governments, principally America and the British dominions, £1,340 million. Of this figure, about £850 million she owed to the United States government alone. These amounts, the first being more than twice the prewar total national debt, seemed astronomical at the time. None of the continental nations admitted it could afford the domestic rebuilding that the war had made necessary, plus the payment of the external debt contracted in the pursuit of victory, without large-scale cash assistance from Germany. Finally, these claims were reinforced by the Bolshevik repudiation of the huge foreign debt built up by the Czar's government.

In the peace settlement with Germany, none of the victorious powers achieved what it hoped to accomplish. Germany was, to be sure, superficially disarmed as France had desired. Her standing army was reduced to 100,000 men enlisted for 12 years' service—barely enough, as it turned out, to maintain domestic order. The army was forbidden to have tanks, aircraft, and heavy artillery, and the navy was forbidden to possess submarines or any vessel of greater than 10,000 tons' displacement. The general staff, the agency responsible for the frightening technical expertise that the German army always displayed and the repository of the Prussian military tradition, was ordered dissolved. Finally, she was required to accept the responsibility for the material losses of the war and to pay on this account a huge, but in 1919 unfixed, amount of reparations to the victorious powers.

But from all this France did not get the security she sought. The proposal for an autonomous Rhineland state was out of the question for her allies and was never seriously considered by the conference. Instead France had to content herself with the Allied occupation of certain towns to the east of the Rhine for 15 years and with the permanent demilitarization of the 'Rhineland', that is, all German territory west of the Rhine. In return for agreeing to these compromises of her military security, she was promised a perpetual alliance with Great Britain and the United States, to take effect in case of any attack by Germany. It is doubtful whether Premier Clemenceau took seriously this offer of a permanent military guarantee of his nation; there is some indication he did not. In any event, the United States Senate quickly made clear to President Wilson that a permanent American involvement in Europe was completely out of the question. Following this Britain announced that she also was no longer bound to France. Thus France received neither the strategic military advantages she deemed vital to her military security nor the political guarantees that she had been induced to substitute for them.

For Britain the treaty was an almost unmixed disaster. Caught between a revengeful domestic electorate and French hate and fear, Lloyd George and his colleagues had permitted, indeed participated in, the economic destruction of Britain's best prewar customer. Still worse, they had thrown away the opportunity to write a lasting peace. More than one political commentator has used Versailles as the supreme example of the unwisdom of permitting popular participation in diplomacy. Arguably the promises made to the British nation during the war were necessary to maintain the will to fight. The alternative would have been defeat. But even if this is so, the result was the raising of popular expectations far beyond any reasonable level of fulfilment. Somehow the peoples of Great Britain were led to believe that countries which had spent between one-eighth and one-sixth of their national wealth in wasteful conflict and had seen a whole generation of young men killed would somehow be better places to live when peace returned. They were made to expect that a defeated nation, which had suffered no less in men and money than they had themselves, would be able to accomplish almost alone the task of reconstruction for both victor and vanquished, and moreover would do this willingly. The surprising thing for the historian is not that such promises were made, but that they were believed for so long and that responsible leaders in Great Britain felt themselves called upon to act in accordance with popular demands which the leaders themselves knew to be unrealistic. The England to which the veterans of the First World War returned could not be a better place to live. It was bound to be a worse place. The war had not built more houses, nor made work in mines more secure, nor improved the market for Lancashire cotton or Jarrow ships. Neither was the upper class more understanding; the civil service was no more sympathetic. The result, inevitably, was disillusion and cynicism. A nation which had been taught to look forward to everything soon looked forward to nothing.

THE PROBLEMS AT HOME

Arguably, the war's most serious permanent damage for Britain was the destruction of the old self-adjusting system of economic institutions and usages of world trade that had been built up gradually through the nineteenth century. Britain's economic pre-eminence was based upon the free international movement of gold, an adequate supply of low-interest risk capital that could move without political control, and finally, upon an almost universal assumption that London was the market of last resort for the purchase and sale of practically any commodity. To be sure, in the decade before the war Britain's leadership in many commercial fields was being challenged. But the fact that many international sales contracts were financed in London even when the principals were not British and the goods of foreign origin and destination ensured that almost all trade of any kind brought profits to the United Kingdom. In addition, the highly specialized institutions for international banking and brokerage available in London served by themselves as an incentive for the purchase of British goods. British manufacturers were frequently able to offer better credit, acceptance, and delivery terms than those of other nations.

Coupled with the general decline of Britain's position as the world's banker and broker, and no less serious, was the loss of foreign markets for British goods. Between 1913 and 1923 the proportion of total British production sold on foreign markets declined from 23·2 to 19·9 per cent and Britain's proportion of the total foreign trade of the world fell by a similar amount. This decline may be better understood when it is remembered that at this time some of Britain's competitors, notably Japan, were rapidly increasing their trade. Secondly, behind these bare figures lie some large and basic changes in the pattern of British trade. Certain new industries, electrical goods and chemicals, for instance, grew rapidly in the period between the wars. But in the same two decades the three industries which before the war had been most important in Britain's commercial supremacy, alone producing nearly two-fifths of the nation's total revenue from foreign trade (£202,422,000 in a total of £525,254,000 in 1913), went into permanent and tragic depression. These were cotton textiles, coal mining, and shipbuilding.

Although the crisis came after the war, there can be no question that well before 1914 Britain's importance in the world's markets depended already on far too narrow a range of commodities. Of the three mentioned above, perhaps coal demonstrated best the vulnerability of the British export situation, and certainly this mineral would provide the most intractable of all industrial problems in the 1920s. In the last census before the war the mines employed about 1,111,000 men, more than any other industry except agriculture, about ten per cent of the nation's work force. Altogether in 1913 these men dug 287,430,000 tons of coal, of which 94 million tons were exported to earn £65 million. This amount was about ten per cent of the nation's total export revenue in 1913. The fact that an industrial state should earn so large a proportion of its foreign exchange from the sale of an unimproved natural resource tells much about Britain's position in international commerce. A technologically advanced nation ought to have found it more profitable to use its coal as power for the manufacture of more complex items of trade in which the labour component was smaller.

The effect of the war was to throw an industry already in a precarious position into ruin. In the first years of the peace, with the European coal industry disorganized, the international price of the mineral was twice its prewar figure. In 1920 Britain exported about 25 million tons of non-bunker coal to earn £99,600,000. This may be compared with 1913 when 73,400,000 tons of non-bunker coal had earned £50,727,000. Then, toward the end of 1920 Germany began to pay reparations to France in coal. By the end of the year a veritable river of coal, far more than France could use herself, was flowing into that nation from her defeated enemy. The result was that by the winter of 1920-21 the world price of the mineral had collapsed. The next year Britain exported almost exactly the same tonnage of coal as she had the previous year, but in place of £99,600,000, coal earnings in 1921 were £43 million. Although production and earnings revived temporarily in 1923 and 1924 as a result of the German strikes following the French invasion of the Rhineland, coal, after the war, was an industry in permanent decline.

It should be emphasized here that coal mining's difficulties were not solely the result of the war. Even without the conflict, the ordinary flux of economic activity and technological progress would have reduced its importance. By the beginning of the twentieth century, other sources of power were replacing coal. Electrical energy and the petrol engine were taking the place of the steam engine. Even the battleships built by the Royal Navy in the last years of peace had been designed to burn oil, and the government had acquired an interest in the Anglo-Persian Oil Company (now part of British Petroleum) to ensure an oil supply. Moreover, many of the best seams of coal in the United Kingdom had been exhausted, and during the war those that remained were ruthlessly exploited. After the war, therefore, the individual miner worked less efficiently than he had before. More men were engaged in the industry, yet less coal was produced. In 1913 the average miner produced 260 tons of coal. In 1923 he produced only 229 tons, a figure which itself represented a substantial increase from the years immediately after the Armistice.

As the coal industry was the victim of technological change and foreign competition based on cheap labour, so was the textile industry. Artificial textile fibres were replacing the natural fibres that Britain produced in huge quantities. Still more important, other nations entered the textile industry with up-to-date spinning and weaving machinery (in many cases bought in Great Britain) with which the century-old mills of Lancashire could not compete. This process of decay had begun before the war, but was immeasurably hastened by the conflict. Areas of distribution which Britain was unable to supply were entered by other nations. In this Japan was particularly active, taking over large portions of the gigantic Asian market. In addition, India, traditionally Britain's largest market, began to establish textile mills of her own. The course of the decline may be traced in the exports of grey, unbleached, cotton cloth, the largest single item in the trade. In 1913 Great Britain had exported 2,357,492,000 square yards of this material. By 1920 she was exporting fewer than 1,000 million square yards, and by 1923 had recovered a market for only 1,300 million square yards. More significant, she was receiving only about half as much money per yard in 1923 as she had in 1920. In some cotton commodities the market almost completely disappeared. Printed handkerchiefs and shawls, for one hundred years the mark of British civilization upon native women throughout the tropics of the world, practically ceased to be sold altogether. In 1913, 54,167,000 square yards of this material had been exported; in 1923 only just over six million square yards could be disposed of.

In shipbuilding the story was unhappily the same. During every one of the last five years before the war, Britain had at least one million tons of shipping under construction. In these same years, about half of the total tonnage built found its way into foreign hands, either as ships constructed specifically for foreign owners or subsequently purchased by foreigners. Through the war, Britain lost through enemy action about seven and three quarter million tons, amounting to three-quarters of the total tonnage of steam shipping under British registry at the outbreak of the war. But at the same time the replacement of vessels lost in the submarine blockade had gone on steadily, both in British yards and in the newly expanded yards in the United States. As a result, by the end of the war the British merchant marine was scarcely smaller than it had been before the conflict, and a good deal more modern.

As had happened with coal the years immediately after the Armistice were most prosperous. Orders for ships from both the United Kingdom and abroad poured into British shipyards. By 1920 the yards were building a larger tonnage of steam vessels than they had in any year before the war. But as also happened to coal the initial burst of activity quickly subsided, so that, whereas there had been 1,200,000 tons of shipping under construction in 1920, by 1923 there were only 380,000 tons, and income from ships built for export dropped from over £30 million in 1921 to under £10 million in 1923 and continued to drop thereafter.

The effects of the decay of these three industries constitute an important part of the political story of the 1920s, and for that matter of the 1930s. These industries were important, not only because they made up the old traditional staple of British prosperity, but because they employed large numbers of men and women. And because a large proportion of their produce went abroad, they were particularly vulnerable to foreign competition. Therefore the peculiar dislocations of trade that the war caused hit them harder. Not all of British industry was depressed in the twenties and early thirties. New enterprise in chemicals, in electrical goods and in motor cars maintained prosperity in the Midlands and the South-East. These supported the overall statistics of British exports and stimulated a migration of people to the South that reversed the trend of a hundred years. But in the Welsh valleys and in the cotton towns of Lancashire, along the Mersey, the Tyne, and the Clyde, the war's damage was permanent.

The old economic patterns could not be reconstructed. Moreover, the decay of these industries brought hard times to other forms of production and business activity that depended upon them—to steel, to the railways, and to the shopkeepers in the town where the local mill had closed. So began the growth of the 'Black Areas', localities of permanent economic depression where generations of young men reached manhood in the twenties and thirties without ever having known the security of regular employment. The memory of these conditions would not only affect British economic life after the Second World War, but political life as well. It would be reflected in an altered attitude toward the prewar period after the conflict. There would be no popular nostalgia for the thirties after 1945 as there was for the Edwardian period after 1918. The thirties were not worth going back to. But more important, the memory of these years would make the maintenance of full employment the most important single aim of government activity, more important than efficiency or profitability in industry, even more important perhaps than competitiveness in the world markets.

POLITICS AFTER 1918

The Coupon Election of 14 December 1918 resulted in an overwhelming victory for the coalition government. Together, the parties of the coalition controlled 478 seats, while the opposition was nearly wiped out. Most seriously hurt were the Liberal supporters of former Prime Minister H. H. Asquith, who were reduced to an impotent handful of 28. Even Asquith himself was defeated for the seat at East Fife he had held for 32 years, despite the fact that the coalition had not endorsed a candidate against him. The largest single group outside of the coalition was the new Irish party, Sinn Fein, which succeeded in destroying the old Irish Nationalist party. However, the goal of the Sinn Fein political effort had been the complete separation of Great Britain and Ireland, and almost immediately after the results were complete, early in January 1919, the Sinn Fein deputies met in Dublin and announced that they constituted an independent Irish Parliament, the Dail. Thus the largest single group left outside the government was the Labour party. Even though it held only 63 seats, it was now the official opposition. The fact that such a party, holding principles not only distasteful but almost incomprehensible to the majority of the British governing class, should constitute the normal alternative government, reminded men what a breach with the past the Great War had been.

Despite the numerical insignificance of the opposition, the government was weaker than it appeared. In many ways the national coalition that emerged from the Coupon Election was more reminiscent of eighteenth-century ministries—a combination of factions and interests clustered about a single strong leader—than it was of its more recent predecessors. Although David Lloyd George seemed to be more securely in power than ever, 70 per cent of the votes in the House of Commons that maintained him were Conservative. Besides this, many of the new Members of Parliament were businessmen who felt that the first task of the government, now that the war was over, should be to provide an economic climate in which Great Britain could revive her prewar industrial supremacy. Generally the new MPs had only limited sympathy for the measures of social reform with which Lloyd George had been associated in his years at the Board of Trade and the Treasury before the war. More important, they were suspicious of the promises he had made to the electorate before the Coupon Election. Indeed they were suspicious of the Prime Minister himself, who combined an almost disdainful lack of interest in the day-to-day affairs of the House of Commons with a seemingly hypnotic power over his Conservative colleagues in the cabinet that enabled him to elicit support for measures the party had long opposed. It is important to remember that the Tory revolt which finally shattered the reform programme of the coalition government originated not with the party chiefs, but with the rank and file. (A final result of the Conservative backbenchers' distrust of their own party hierarchy was the establishment, immediately after Lloyd George's resignation, of a permanent Conservative MPs' organization, the '1922 Committee'. This body aimed to ensure that the party chiefs were aware of attitudes among ordinary members of the House of Commons, and sought to be, in the words of one of its founders, 'a rein upon the leaders'.)

A factor of greatest importance in solidifying the cabinet's attitude on social reform was the fear that, unless the government acted promptly in favour of the public welfare, the capitalist system itself might be overthrown. In the old days Lloyd George had always looked upon social reform as the alternative to socialism. After the war he could plead that the appearance of Communism and of widespread working-class violence in Europe made reform even more necessary. It is almost impossible to overrate the importance of the fear of violence in the deliberations of government leaders in the months after the war. Looking from London at Central Europe, or for that matter at Ireland, it scarcely seemed that the war was over. The only change was that organized conflict carried on by national governments had become popular rebellion organized by secret societies. Beginning in the spring of 1919 the members of the cabinet received long and detailed weekly reports from the Home Office Directorate of Intelligence which transmitted to them, in surprisingly inflammatory language, the most intimate information about the activities of trade unions, veterans' societies, Sinn Fein, the Parliamentary Labour party and the Independent Labour party. The connexions of British working-men's groups with European revolutionary organizations were examined with special care.

Inevitably the continuous reports of public violence and private conspiracy affected cabinet decisions. All measures dealing with the popular welfare—gratuities for discharged soldiers, the release of men from work in arsenals, the amount of money to be spent on roads, unemployment insurance, or education—were examined not only in terms of whether they were socially useful, or indeed whether they would win or lose votes, but whether they would serve to allay the popular tendency to disorder. Fear caused the government immediately after the Armistice to cancel the rather complex plan it had devised for releasing men from the army only as rapidly as they could be absorbed into industry, and to institute instead a relatively simple scheme based on length of service—'first in, first out'. This change in policy, the result of riots at army depots early in January, meant discarding, after a few weeks' trial, a scheme upon which the government had worked for many months.

But even more difficult than discharging men from the army was caring for them after they were out. Here far more dangerously loomed the prospect of public disorder should large numbers of former servicemen be unable to find jobs. As a result, the government eventually permitted itself to become responsible for the maintenance of unemployed men even when they were ineligible for unemployment insurance. Those benefits, and later the ordinary insurance benefits, came to be called 'the dole'.

The dole began on 25 November 1918, as an out-of-work donation for discharged soldiers. For 12 months after their army discharge soldiers were entitled to a generous 29s. a week for 26 weeks plus an allowance for children. There was a further payment of 20s. for 13 weeks plus a dependants' allowance. Civilians under certain circumstances received reduced benefits. (In addition to these payments there were, for soldiers, a discharge gratuity based on length of service, a month's furlough, and the opportunity for retraining in various trades, overseas settlement, or settlement on unused agricultural land.) The importance of the out-of-work donation lies first of all in the fact that, once it began to support unemployed ex-servicemen, the government found it impossible to stop doing so. Hence the donation was continued through the winter of 1919–20 and again through the summer of 1920. Finally, with the extension of unemployment insurance to all working men in the autumn of that year, unemployed servicemen, many of whom had not qualified for coverage, were nevertheless absorbed into the scheme. Because they had not had the opportunity to pay the required number of contributions to make them regularly eligible for unemployed benefits, they were given a payment styled the 'uncovenanted benefit'. After the military out-of-work donation lapsed in 1921, the uncovenanted benefit was termed the dole.

A second lasting effect upon unemployment insurance of the precedent set by the veterans' benefit involved the provision for dependants and the level of the benefit itself. In the same way that the government had found itself bound to continue the system of unemployed relief for servicemen once it began, so also it was forced to maintain payments at the same rate to which the veterans had become accustomed, even when merging the out-of-work donation scheme with the existing unemployment insurance system. In the spring of 1921, with well over one million men without jobs, many of them ex-soldiers, the government was faced with the choice of seeing payments for soldiers reduced from the 20s. level of the out-of-work donation to the 15s. level of the unemployment benefit, or of raising the rate of the unemployment insurance benefit. It chose to do the latter. Under pressure from economizers, this benefit was quickly lowered again to 15s. in the summer of 1921, but counter-pressure from veterans' organizations, whose members had been accustomed to receiving extra payments for dependants, compelled the government to begin to pay extra unemployment benefits for dependants. In this way the principle of the graduated benefit first appeared in British national insurance.

The decision to bring into unemployment insurance all sections of the working population except agricultural labour was to some extent a response by the coalition government to the fear of an aroused proletariat. But the extension of insurance had been also an ideal of David Lloyd George since the passage of the original unemployment scheme in 1911. Except for the one million munitions workers who received insurance in 1916, unemployment insurance at the end of the war was confined, as it had been originally, to about a quarter of a million men, principally engaged in the building and engineering industries. These workers were for the most part well organized and highly skilled. Although there had been from the beginning an intention to expand coverage, everyone connected with the measure knew that unemployment insurance was actuarially a risky business. Its extension to unskilled and casual labour seemed almost impossible without other measures for the control of the labour market. Above all, it was absolutely vital for the insured to understand that in the last analysis their benefits had to be proportionate to their payments and that the state's liability toward the scheme was strictly limited.

The difficulties of the Unemployment Insurance Act of 1920 came not from its disregard of the safeguards of the act of 1911, but from the radically changed political climate. At the end of the war the unemployment insurance fund possessed a surplus of over £22 million. At least until the summer of 1920 the re-absorption of returning soldiers into industry appeared to be taking place without difficulty. Above all there was the reckless optimism that pervaded the minds both of government leaders and of the population at large. The old, prewar, cheese-paring ways of state activity were over. The nation had been taught to expect bold new departures; economic security for all was certainly one of them. And so the carefully safeguarded measure of 1911 that had promised 7s. a week for 26 weeks only after six months of contribution for men in selected occupations —considered at the time of its passage as a fantastic leap in the dark —was heedlessly extended to cover the whole working class except two groups not particularly liable to unemployment, agricultural labourers and domestic servants. The new measures included, as had the old, a six months' qualifying period for benefit, a 26-week maximum on benefits, and the important stipulation first introduced by W. H. Beveridge that, all other circumstances notwithstanding, no contributor could receive more than one week's benefit for five weeks' payment (later changed to one and six). The difference lay not in the drawing of the measure itself, but in the attitude of the people and of the government toward it.

In the nine years between 1911 and 1920 the assumption that unemployment insurance was basically state-aided self-insurance had dissolved. After the war both politicians and the nation at large tended to look upon unemployment insurance essentially as a government guarantee of maintenance for the working man, to which the recipient of benefit happened also to make contributions. Therefore, only weeks after the unemployment insurance became law, when the number of men out of work began to grow, the government without hesitation extended the period of out-of-work benefits for soldiers and agreed at the same time to give unemployment benefits to men who had not yet paid the statutory six months of contribution. Theoretically these 'uncovenanted benefits' were to be deducted from the amount of the man's eligibility once he again found work. The huge surplus in the fund left over from the war made the payments easy. No appropriation was required from Parliament. But, with the payment of uncovenanted benefits, a new concept of social welfare began. Once the benefits were started, they could not be stopped. The government's obligation to the citizen was paramount. The solvency of the insurance fund, which had seemed so important before the war, was irrelevant.

In its varying forms the problem of care for the unemployed remained perhaps the most important single domestic question confronting British politicians in the interwar years. By the end of 1921, the surplus in the insurance fund left by the war had disappeared, and in nearly every year for the next decade and a half the fund's debt to the Treasury grew larger as the government advanced millions of pounds to make up the difference between income from contributions and the ever-increasing cost of benefits. The necessity of supporting the unemployment fund stifled all proposals for the improvement of other social welfare institutions. It prevented any serious talk of the supersession of poor law relief or of the extension of health insurance. Only under the threat of national bankruptcy in the early thirties was the government able to summon the courage to re-establish the insurance scheme upon some semblance of the self-supporting basis contemplated for it. And it was not until 1937, after the economic stimulus of rearmament had begun an economic revival, that the Unemployment Assistance Board brought at least a workable compromise, if not a solution, to the problem of maintenance of the unemployed working man.

The other great promise of domestic reform made to the British nation during the war had been bettered conditions of ordinary life. This meant improvement in health and educational facilities, but above all improvement in housing. 'Homes for heroes' were specifically understood to be a primary national responsibility with the coming of peace. Housing legislation, particularly domestic sanitary regulation, had been among the earliest of all British social reform measures, dating well back into the middle of the nineteenth century. But the Liberals had accomplished little in this direction during the great burst of reform legislation before the war except for the ineffective Housing and Town Planning Act of 1909. However, David Lloyd George had been preparing a substantial programme of house building for agricultural labourers when his energies were diverted by the struggle over Irish home rule. After the war, with a four years' deficit in building to make up, the Prime Minister prepared to revive and expand his interrupted plans.

The story of the public housing experiments of the national coalition begins with the founding of the Ministry of Health. The consolidation of all public health and planning activities into a single ministry had long been a goal of social reformers. In 1917 a formal recommendation to this end appeared as a report of the Ministry of Reconstruction, presided over by the Prime Minister's friend, Dr Christopher Addison, who had been his adviser on health matters since the days of the passage of the National Insurance Act. The creation of the Ministry of Health was held up for nearly a year by a controversy about whether the new department should include among its functions the supervision of the poor law. Although most health reformers thought the poor law should be placed elsewhere, the political friends of the Local Government Board made clear they would prevent the creation of the Ministry of Health altogether unless the poor law were incorporated in it. Therefore, so as to provide token fulfilment of the government's promises on the subject before the election of 1918, the cabinet surrendered to the Local Government Board, and a Ministry of Health Bill was hurriedly introduced in the last days of the wartime Parliament. It passed quickly in the spring of 1919 and the new ministry, charged with responsibility for both poor law and housing, came into existence in the summer of that year, with Christopher Addison as its chief.

From the first, Addison had understood that his primary task was to deal with housing. In the summer of 1919 he obtained parliamentary approval for Britain's first public housing measure (as opposed to slum clearance and town planning), the Housing and Town Planning Act of 1919, usually styled the Addison Act. This statute ordered local authorities to prepare plans for building houses in their area and to submit them to the Ministry of Health for approval. Most important, it promised them an unlimited subsidy payable over the life of the house against all expenses incurred in building above the proceeds of the penny rate. Later in the year

Addison supplemented this act with a second measure permitting government assistance to private builders who wished to build houses of moderate cost that would be available for rent or sale to the working class.

In the next three years under the Addison Act, the state built or financed over 213,000 new houses, more than one-third of the calculated 'deficit' in housing that had appeared as the result of the war and far more than had been built privately in any similar period before 1914. Moreover, this was done at a time when building manpower was dispersed and the flow of building supplies disorganized. But it was accomplished at tremendous expense to the government. By the time of the Second World War, the government had paid under the Addison programmes more than £130 million in housing subsidies to aid local authorities in amortizing their costs. This sum was more than three times the amount spent under any subsequent government housing programme and over two-thirds of the total spent on all public housing in the interwar period.

The cost of houses under the Ministry of Health programmes caused an outcry in Parliament and in the country that quickly destroyed Addison's position in the coalition government, and which began also the disintegration of the coalition itself. On 1 April 1921, Lloyd George deprived Addison of the Ministry of Health and gave it to Alfred Mond, although he promised Addison privately that house building would be continued. Addison remained in the cabinet as Minister without Portfolio. In July it was announced that no more houses would be built under the Addison Act, and Addison resigned from the cabinet. Soon afterwards he joined the Labour party.

So ended the most ambitious, and by far the most expensive, of the coalition reform measures with which Lloyd George had hoped to redeem his promises of the war and also, unquestionably, to rebuild the Liberal party. The revival of the New Liberalism was a failure. The surprising factor in all of it is not that the Prime Minister was unable to bring into existence after the war the new world he had promised, but that he remained in office for nearly two years after the collapse of his plans.

IRELAND

Of all the long-term difficulties of British politics, none was more intractable, more ferocious, yet sadder; and none occupied fruitlessly more time of Members of Parliament, civil servants, and governmental leaders, than did the Irish problem. For centuries Ireland was the incubus of British politics, hostile and accusing, combining an appeal to arms with an appeal to conscience. Since the autumn of 1885, when W. E. Gladstone decided that the British government could no longer stand in the way of Irish self-government, until the final passage of home rule in 1914 under the terms of the Parliament Act, it had appeared that justice for Ireland would be the greatest accomplishment of British Liberalism. But when the Government of Ireland Act was finally signed by King George V on 17 September 1914, Great Britain had been engaged in the First World War for six weeks. As a result, the final enactment of the measure into law was accompanied by a suspending act that delayed its effect until the end of hostilities.

At the outbreak of the war John Redmond, the leader of the Irish Nationalist party in the House of Commons, had promised whole-hearted support of Britain's war effort for himself and for the Irish nation. But Irish enthusiasm soon dwindled. Because of clumsiness in British recruiting, of insensitivity in the handling of Irish volunteers of a sort that only a major-general with long colonial experience could be capable, of the admission to the cabinet of Sir Edward Carson, who had led the fight for the exclusion of Ulster from the jurisdiction of the Dublin Parliament, and most of all because of the emergence of a new revolutionary organization able to exploit these grievances, few men were enlisting from southern Ireland by the end of 1914. Within six months, enlistments from the south had fallen to almost nothing and, indeed, families whose sons did leave to fight in France suffered from the boycott.

The parliamentary phase of Ireland's drive toward independence came to an end over an event that grew entirely out of the war, unconnected with any of the traditional Irish political questions. This was the so-called Easter Rising of 25 April 1916. The rebellion was the result specifically of Irish fear that military conscription, which the British government was considering and which would be carried by Parliament within a week after the rising began, would be extended to Ireland. Also the Irish hoped to take advantage of Britain's preoccupation in Europe and of the possibility that their rebellion would receive military aid from Germany.

As a military event the rebellion was unimportant. It began on Easter Monday and was crushed by the end of the week. It was confined solely to Dublin where by far the most dramatic action occurred in the siege of the general post office in O'Connell Street (then

Sackville Street). About 100 British soldiers and 450 Irishmen were killed. Nevertheless, the Easter Rising was a disaster for Britain. It offered the last of many missed opportunities to solve the Irish problem. During the rebellion Irish prisoners taken by the British had been jeered and insulted by the Dublin population. But for the first two weeks after fighting stopped the repression was left to an extraordinarily unintelligent general, Sir John Grenfell Maxwell (who was made a Privy Counsellor of Ireland for his services). His summary execution of 15 of the leaders turned the sympathy of the Irish population toward the rebels.

Perhaps more tragic and more important was the failure of the government to use the excuse of the Easter Rebellion to give Ireland immediate home rule. Such a plan was brought forward at Lloyd George's suggestion and was discussed at length in the government. John Redmond agreed to permit the exclusion, perhaps temporarily, of the six northern counties of Ulster. Unhappily the Conservative leader in the House of Lords, Lord Lansdowne, without whose approval the measure never would receive the speedy and non-controversial passage it needed, began to demand further safeguards and the plan was dropped. With it went all chance of a parliamentary compromise solution to Irish problems. So died also the party of home rule, the old Irish Nationalist party of Butt, Parnell, McCarthy, and Redmond. Peace in Ireland was at an end, and between 1916 and 1918 Ireland was governed as a conquered province. Fifty thousand soldiers, badly needed on the Western Front, had to be maintained in the other island.

The near-monopoly position in south Irish politics that had been held for nearly three-quarters of a century by the Irish Nationalist party was now taken by a radical revolutionary political organization, which rejected the offer of autonomous administration of Irish domestic affairs provided by home rule. The new party, called Sinn Fein, insisted upon complete Irish independence. The Sinn Fein party had its origins before the turn of the twentieth century in the Gaelic League, one of several similar organizations that attempted to revive the study of Irish history, literature and language. Before the war Sinn Fein had been a relatively unimportant political organization led by Arthur Griffith, who founded it while he was editor of *United Irishmen*. As a group, Sinn Fein had taken no part in the 1916 rebellion, although some of the fighters of Easter Week had been members of that organization. With the decline of the Irish Nationalist party after the failure of the home rule negotiations of 1916, the

Sinn Fein organization began to gather support in all parts of south Ireland. Any doubts about the propriety of resistance to Great Britain that had remained in the Irish public mind were removed in March 1918, when as a result of growing German pressure on the Western Front the British Parliament passed a military service bill, raising the age of compulsory service in Britain to 50 and extending compulsory military service to Ireland. The wave of hatred that swept over the island as a result of this action not only made certain that no conscripts would be taken among Irishmen, but that any Irish politician or party connected with the British Parliament would be considered an enemy of the nation. Not surprisingly, in December 1918 Sinn Fein candidates swept every constituency in south Ireland except four, and in January 1919 about 30 of the 73 elected—being those who were not then in jail—assembled in the capital and proclaimed themselves the parliament of the Irish nation, the Dail. They announced that Ireland was entirely separate from Great Britain and that they were the legal Irish government. They appointed ministers to an Irish executive, instituted courts to which Irish litigants were expected to resort, and bade all levels of the Irish civil and military administration serve only the new government.

By March 1919, armed attack had begun on the British administration, mostly by means of the ambush of policemen in villages or in the countryside. The British retaliated with the arrest of Irish leaders and by the end of the year Ireland was the scene of a fierce, if undeclared and unadmitted, civil war. By this time also the Anglo-Irish conflict had assumed the character it would maintain for the next three years, that of partisan or guerrilla warfare, of terror and counter-terror. The first reprisals by the British forces occurred because of an attack in September by Irish volunteers upon a small party of British soldiers attending church. Although the aim had been the capture of weapons, one of the soldiers was killed. At the coroner's hearing witnesses declined to testify and the jury refused to return a verdict of wilful murder, saying simply that the victim had been killed from a bullet wound caused 'by some person unknown'. This verdict, rather than the attack itself, caused the soldier's comrades in the Fermoy garrison to attack the houses of the members of the jury.

As the fighting in Ireland grew from sporadic outbreak to full-scale civil war, the coalition government searched for a parliamentary solution to the Irish problem. The result in 1920 was the Fourth Home Rule Bill, which set up separate parliaments for the six counties of Ulster and the 26 counties of the south. There would be also a deliberative body for national affairs provided by a Council of Ireland whose members were representatives of the two parliaments at Belfast and Dublin. The powers of the two parliaments were to be essentially those offered in the three previous home rule bills— control over all domestic affairs, but excluding any jurisdiction over defence, foreign affairs, finance, and religion.

In the south the Government of Ireland Act was treated with contempt. The time for home rule was long past. The 26 counties used the requirement of the election as a means for electing a new Dail. The north accepted the idea of a parliament at Belfast, but rejected from the beginning the proposal for a Council of Ireland. In any case this requirement was dead because of the failure of the south to accept the bill. Nevertheless, the Fourth Home Rule Bill created the present Northern Ireland Parliament at Stormont and George V's speech at its formal opening in June 1921 paved the way for a compromise in the south where methods of warfare had passed beyond the conventions usually observed by civilized men.

Through the first year of the war, generally until the spring of 1920, the Irish forces, who styled themselves the Irish Republican Army, had the better of most encounters with the British authorities. Because the British government wished to maintain the fiction that the members of the Irish resistance movement were essentially criminals who could be dealt with through the ordinary apparatus of the police, they were reluctant to use military forces to maintain law and order, even though about 60,000 troops were in fact stationed in south Ireland. Particularly in the countryside, in the villages, and for the work of seeking out the centres of Irish resistance, the British intended to rely, so far as possible, on the regular Irish police force, the Royal Irish Constabulary. In March 1920, to carry the heavier burden of duties that the Irish resistance entailed, and to make up for the reluctance of Irishmen to join, the RIC began for the first time to advertise for recruits in Great Britain. In the second half of the year with unemployment rising, the £3 10s. per week paid by the RIC appeared quite attractive, as did to former servicemen the prospect of adventure. In its early period of expansion in the second quarter of 1920, there had not been enough RIC uniforms to supply the new recruits, who were issued instead the regular army khaki supplemented by the forest green, almost black, RIC cap. This unusual combination of uniforms earned for the constabulary the rather jeering title of 'Black and Tans', a name which had long been applied to the famous foxhounds of South Tipperary and East Limerick. In July 1920 the regular Royal Irish Constabulary was supplemented by a special corps of about 1,500 men, the Royal Irish Constabulary Auxiliaries, who were recruited exclusively from among ex-officers in Great Britain and who were paid twice the salary of the RIC. The Auxiliaries also were frequently styled Black and Tans, although their force was entirely separate. They wore military uniforms and Glengarry caps instead of the billed RIC cap, and their duties were principally the harsh ones of the maintenance of counter-terror.

From the summer of 1920 until the summer of 1921, Ireland was a land of murder and reprisal, of night ambush in remote country lanes, and gangland-style execution in crowded city streets. Hostages were taken and 'shot while trying to escape', while British officers were dragged from their beds in Dublin hotels and shot before the eyes of their panic-stricken wives. The agony had to end. Public opinion in Great Britain, not to mention the rest of the world, was horrified as reports of atrocities piled upon one another. More important, influential Liberal newspapers, led by the *Manchester Guardian*, attacked the government's handling of the Irish situation. The break came on 22 June 1921 in the speech of George V who had insisted, at considerable personal risk, that he open in person the Northern Ireland Parliament. The speech had been written principally by the South African leader Jan Christian Smuts and approved by the leaders of the British government. It urged peace and conciliation in the friendliest terms. Irish as well as English hearts were touched.

George V's speech inaugurated a series of negotiations between Irish leaders and the British government. The difficulty was that the leaders of the Irish resistance movement were divided among themselves. The political head of the Irish Republic, in that he was President of the Dail, was Eamon De Valera, who was opposed to any settlement on terms other than complete independence. On the other hand, Michael Collins, the military leader of the Irish Republican Army, and Arthur Griffith, the founder of Sinn Fein and Acting President of the Dail during De Valera's several money-raising trips to America, were willing to accept dominion status for Ireland. After a long series of conferences in the autumn of 1921 with De Valera absent, Griffith and Collins signed on 6 December an 'agreement' in which Ireland was promised the status within the British Commonwealth held by Canada while the six counties of the north would remain a part of the United Kingdom.

Griffith and Collins may have known that for them the Irish war was not yet at an end. The agreement of 6 December was immediately repudiated by De Valera. Although all British organs of administration and a large number of British weapons were handed over to the Irish provisional government, De Valera proclaimed rebellion against his former comrades. Thus until the end of May 1923 Ireland was racked by a second civil war. In the struggle Collins himself was shot from ambush and Griffith died from overwork. But the Irish Free State came into existence in December 1922, and the present republic is their monument.

By this time David Lloyd George had gone out of office. Discontent with the Irish agreement was one of the principal Conservative indictments against him. He had spent an important part of his political capital to give part of Ireland independence even though events would show that he had not solved the Irish problem.

LLOYD GEORGE'S DISMISSAL

The life of David Lloyd George's coalition government ended with a meeting of Conservative Members of Parliament at the Carlton Club on 19 October 1922, which voted to withdraw the party's support from the Liberal Prime Minister. The next day Lloyd George resigned.

Discontent had been bound to appear in a coalition in which the Conservatives, who made up by October 313 of the 454 coalition MPs, yet served, and were dominated by, a Liberal Prime Minister whose supporters were scarcely one-third their number. Nevertheless, the Conservatives remained quiet until the coming of economic depression in the winter of 1920–21. So long as times had been good and there was work for all, high prices and government extravagance could be forgotten. But with the collapse of the postwar economic boom, opposition to high taxes and government prodigality burst forth. So ended the possibility of any reconstruction and reorganization of the British economic plant or of British social services. If the period of Lloyd George's coalition government were to be divided into phases, the first, the constructive phase, should terminate at the end of 1920. The most serious criticism to be made of Lloyd George's peacetime government is that he failed to do what he could to modernize Great Britain when he had the opportunity—that is, the money and the political support. With the coming of the postwar depression, the collapse in prices, and the vast increase in unemployment, he allowed himself to be diverted from his projected social reforms. He used government poverty and the necessarily huge expenditures in unemployment benefits to excuse his failure to accomplish those things he had neglected earlier in the days of prosperity, when his political power was unchallenged.

Economic malaise would darken most of the two decades between the wars. It affected politics most quickly and immediately in relation to the coal industry. The age of steam that had made Britain great in the nineteenth century had in fact been an age of coal. As has been pointed out, the industry traditionally employed about one-tenth of the male labour force in the United Kingdom and in the years before the war coal had become, dangerously, the largest single item of British exports (although all forms of textiles taken together earned more money). During the war the mines had been nationalized, not, it should be noted, to make production more efficient or to help pay for new machinery, but to prevent the mine owners from profiteering from war-swollen coal prices. Government operation focused attention on the hopelessly inefficient capital and managerial structure of the industry—many small mines with narrow coal seams, mining companies and owners both demanding a profit from the coal, leaving little money for technological improvement. Consequently, in the spring of 1919 while coal prices were still high, the cabinet appointed a strong royal commission including representatives of the miners and of the mine owners, as well as a number of economists, to investigate the organization of the industry. In June this commission (chaired by Sir John Sankey, who later became Lord Chancellor) rendered four conflicting reports. All but one admitted that the coal industry was sick and needed reorganization. Upon how this was to be accomplished, through the maintenance of private ownership or through some degree of nationalization, there was no agreement, although a majority of the commission was for some form of government ownership.

The important effect of the Sankey Commission lay not in the solutions it proposed, but in the elucidation of the problem that faced the coal industry, which would remain until nationalization was finally accomplished in 1946. Far too many mines could never make a profit if the miners were paid anything approaching a living wage. But, on the other hand, neither could owners be induced to introduce the necessary technological improvements, even in mines that might make a profit with modern machinery, so long as the industry was threatened by the surplus capacity of many small marginal mines.

On the other side, however, was the unwillingness of the unions to permit any pits to close. Finally there was the competition on the world market from coal mined in better foreign pits by workers paid less than British miners, coupled with the continual technological change from coal to other forms of primary fuel.

On the rather weak grounds of the disagreement among the members of the commission, in the autumn of 1919 Lloyd George rejected all recommendations. Even though he had promised earlier to accept the commission's report, he announced that the mines would continue to be operated under public ownership. In these days the government could afford to postpone a solution to the difficulties of the coal industry. Coal prices were higher than they had ever been and the fear of a coordinated strike by the miners, the transport workers, and the railwaymen—the 'Triple Alliance'—made it desirable to buy off labour discontent at any cost. Under the same threat of a general strike the railwaymen had made an exceedingly advantageous wage settlement with their employers late in 1919.

The rapidly rising cost of living in 1920, besides resulting in increased wages for railway workers, won for the miners in October a special government subsidy of 2s. per shift, to run until 31 March 1921. (At the end of the war the average level of industrial wages was about 100 per cent above 1914. By the end of 1920 it had risen to 170–180 per cent above 1914. Meanwhile, prices that were about 120–125 per cent above 1914 at the end of the war had climbed in November 1920 to a peak of 176 per cent above 1914. In effect by the last months of 1920 the rise in wages almost exactly matched the rise in prices.) Almost immediately after this concession international coal prices collapsed, so that a ton of coal was worth about half as much as it had been six months before. The government, which had been able to avoid any loss on the coal mines it operated by putting the earnings of the good mines into a pool from which wages for the poor mines were paid, discovered that in January 1921 it lost £4,750,000 in coal mining. It now hastily decided, along with a number of other ill-considered economies, to act upon the oft-deferred plans for handing the mines back to their owners. The date set for denationalization was 31 March. The mine owners announced that when the mines were returned to them they would institute varying but drastic reductions in wages. The unions announced that if wages were reduced, the miners would strike. (The wage of a miner in South Wales would, for instance, have been halved.)

The strike began on 1 April. The miners' great weapon, one with which they hoped to coerce the government rather than the mine owners, was a sympathetic strike—they called it a 'General Strike'—by the railwaymen and the transport workers' federation. However, on the excuse of the miners' intransigence in their negotiations with the owners, the other two great unions called off at the last moment the strike that had been due to begin on Friday, 15 April. This date, 'Black Friday', became a day of mourning in the labour movement. Its memory, and the shame connected with it, would be an important factor in labour solidarity during the general strike of 1926 and thereafter.

Eventually the miners lost their struggle. They fought on alone until the middle of June. When they returned, wage levels in some places were little more than half what they had been, although in others the decline was much smaller. Their only victory was the promise of a government subsidy of £10 million, to last until autumn.

By the time the coal strike ended, unemployment was approaching the two-million mark, more than double the rate of six months before. For practical purposes it would not fall below one million again until 1939. In government everything now was subordinated to the needs of economy. Except for maintaining the unemployment benefit (many of the workers covered by the new bill of 1920, it will be remembered, had not had time even to qualify under the six-month waiting period before they were thrown out of employment), virtually all plans for reconstruction and reform were dropped. In July it was announced that no more houses would be built under the Addison housing programme. The extensions of public education under the Fisher education act were no longer mentioned, nor was the reconstruction of the poor law. Proposals for the extension of national health insurance to workers' dependants and for the enlargement of the benefit to include specialist services were forgotten. The railways were unceremoniously handed back to private enterprise, not electrified as had been planned, but reorganized into four regional networks. (About the only other change was the dropping in 1922 of the second class, leaving only the first and third. This class had been instituted in the nineteenth century to separate gentlepeople's servants from the ordinary working class. Fewer people now travelled with servants.)

Although Lloyd George was now far separated from the radical wing of British politics and from his own social reformist background, he retained a strong hold upon the ordinary, conventionally minded English voter both in the working class and out of it. The Conservative whip, Sir George Younger, was terrified in the spring of 1922 lest the Prime Minister choose to call an election at that time. The result, Younger was sure, would be increased strength for the coalition leader. This might well have been the case, although any victory would have been solely a personal one for the Prime Minister. It is hard to believe that the ordinary working-class voter by that time would have chosen the Liberals over Labour as the party of social reform.

Yet it was not for actions in domestic affairs, but in foreign affairs, that the Conservatives finally renounced their allegiance to the coalition. The story of British foreign policy since the Versailles peace conference is in its main lines the story of the breakdown of the good relations with France that had existed since 1905, and of British retreat into a form of diplomatic isolation. This evolution was the result of several events only slightly connected with each other. First, there were the differences of opinion between Britain and France already discussed about the treatment of defeated Germany. Besides these there were widely divergent national attitudes about the Bolshevik government in Russia. France gave considerable aid to the Soviet Union's enemies, particularly to Poland, enabling that nation to extend her eastern boundary far beyond what the British Foreign Office believed ethnic and racial considerations entitled the Poles to hold. In Great Britain, working-class opinion was almost unanimously opposed to giving any aid to the enemies of Russia. Dockers refused to load ships carrying supplies to the British expedition at Murmansk and to Poland; a general strike was threatened.

Most dangerous was the growing ill-feeling between Britain and France over conditions in the Middle East where war had broken out between Greece and Turkey. The last of the treaties to be signed at Paris, not concluded until 10 August 1920, was the Treaty of Sèvres with Ottoman Turkey. By this time Turkish republicans had begun a rebellion brought on in large degree by the humiliating terms of the treaty. One of the important beneficiaries of the treaty would have been Greece who now, fearing that she would lose some of the advantages gained by the Allied victory, began military operations against the Turks to compel them to accept the treaty. By the end of 1920 the Greeks had occupied extensive regions of Asiatic Turkey and by 1921 were threatening the republican capital of Ankara. In this adventure Britain had supported the Greeks and the French had supported Turkey. In October 1921 the French in fact had signed a separate treaty with the new Turkish republican government under the leadership of Mustapha Kemal.

Unfortunately for the Greeks, by the autumn of 1921 the Turkish armies, inspired by nationalist patriotism, began to gain an advantage. Toward the end of the year Britain was reducing its material (although not its diplomatic) support of the Athens government. By September of 1922 Turkish armies had driven the Greeks from the Asiatic mainland and were advancing toward the Straits of the Dardanelles. This movement threatened a small Allied force stationed in the neutral zone that had been established along the entire south shore of the Straits. The Treaty of Sèvres, theoretically still in effect, had provided that the Straits would be internationalized and the adjoining territory demilitarized. On those grounds the troops were there under a perfectly valid international agreement which the new, unrecognized Turkish government was attempting to revise by force of arms. At this moment, the French and Italian forces which occupied the area with the British were withdrawn. A small British force at Chanak opposite the Gallipoli peninsula was left to face the victorious Turks alone. It seemed that war might break out between Britain and Turkey.

The possibility of war, even with Turkey, evoked no enthusiasm either in Great Britain or in the Empire. Although a sensible truce was arranged with Turkey by the middle of October and although the Conservative members of the cabinet, excepting Lord Curzon and Stanley Baldwin, were firm in their support of the Prime Minister, the Conservative rank and file in the House of Commons had had enough. In the past they had been held back by only two factors. First there was the fear that the alternative to the coalition might not be their own party but rather the Labour party. Second, they were unsure of the position of the only possible alternative Prime Minister, the Conservative leader Andrew Bonar Law, who had been Lloyd George's Leader of the House of Commons and Lord Privy Seal. To be sure he had resigned in March 1921, but so far as anyone knew on the sole grounds of health. The burst of Labour indignation at the possibility of war over the Straits had laid some of the fears of socialist victory and so removed the first hindrance to action. Nevertheless, the rebellion that occurred at the Carlton Club on the evening of 19 October—a meeting called originally to obtain party permission for a general election under the coalition banner— was totally unexpected both by a number of Conservative leaders within the cabinet and by Lloyd George himself. Andrew Bonar Law, who was dying of cancer although he did not yet know it, preserved the unity of his party by agreeing to become Prime Minister, and by a vote of 87 to 187 the Conservative party determined that it would fight the next general election as an independent organization. Lloyd George surrendered his office the next day. Although the king's biographer reports that the Prime Minister told George V he would be invited to return, he never was.

CHAPTER TWO

The Baldwin Age, Part I: 1922–31

THE POLITICAL SITUATION

The administration formed by Andrew Bonar Law on 24 October was a curious blend of elderly men, largely noble, past their political and physical prime, and young men, a number of whom were enjoying the experience of cabinet membership for the first time. A 'Government of the second eleven', Churchill called it. With the exception of Curzon, who resigned from the previous ministry just before it fell because of Chanak, and Bonar Law himself, the leading Conservatives of the coalition, Austen Chamberlain, Lords Balfour and Birkenhead, and Sir Robert Horne, were absent. As a reason for this, it should be remembered that the Carlton Club meeting of 9 October had been a rebellion in the literal sense—an attack by the rank and file of the party upon its officers. Those members of the cabinet who remained loyal to Lloyd George did so at the risk of their careers, and one writer, perhaps overstating the case, suggests that Austen Chamberlain forfeited the prime ministership by a speech defending the coalition.

Perhaps the most sensational appointment, soon to be of critical importance in view of Bonar Law's rapidly declining health, was that of Stanley Baldwin as Chancellor of the Exchequer. Baldwin had been in Parliament since 1908, but his progress had been slow. In 1917 he was appointed Joint Financial Secretary to the Treasury in order to do official entertaining for Bonar Law, who detested that side of political life. His only other experience in departmental administration had come from a year at the Board of Trade in 1921–22. He was by no means brilliant, nor was he energetic, and indeed it may be that his laziness was the cause of several unhappy political events that a less self-indulgent minister might have avoided. Yet

Baldwin proved to be an immensely popular political figure until very nearly the end of his life. He gave the impression of possessing a vast store of common sense, and he did in fact have a substantial amount of real political shrewdness. He was publicly honest, as Lloyd George had not been honest. His motives for action usually were clear, and he was willing to explain them with disarming frankness so far as he understood them. He perfectly suited the average Englishman's growing distaste for the excitement, the daring, and what now seemed to be the dangerous innovation, of the Lloyd George administration. In this sense also he represented a reaction to the disappointment in the hopes that had been raised by the war.

But as Baldwin represented the old-fashioned, bluff, honest, Victorian Englishman who was a bulwark against the growing frivolity and cynicism of the twenties and the despair of the thirties, he was also the wrong man to be the leading British politician in the interwar period. As Lloyd George had looked to the future, Baldwin looked to the past. He set himself to retrieve the world that was gone, and which he must have known could not be recaptured. He offered the British voters an illusion of peace because he knew that was what they wanted. In this sense, therefore, he was perhaps less honest than David Lloyd George, and more dangerous to the country he served.

Bonar Law's tenure as Prime Minister and Baldwin's as Chancellor of the Exchequer lasted until 22 May 1923, not quite seven months. Only two events of that interval need be noted. A general election on 15 November returned, rather against the party's expectations, a Conservative majority of 77 over all other parties combined, the first independent Conservative victory since the Khaki Election of 1900. The election had been fought on the absurd Conservative slogan of 'Tranquillity'. Possibly the result was a measure of the national mood. Not a programme but a yawn, Lloyd George called it.

Then, in January 1923, Baldwin and the Governor of the Bank of England, Montagu Norman, went to America to negotiate a settlement of the British war debt to the United States. Here they presented the American commissioners with a statement of the interlocking facts of war debts and reparations, that Britain's ability to pay her debt to the United States was largely contingent upon her own debtors' ability to pay her, and that these nations could pay Britain only so far as they received reparations from Germany. As if to illustrate this argument, on 11 January 1923, while negotiations were in progress, French troops, to the dismay of Great Britain, occupied Essen in the Ruhr Valley to enforce the payment of reparations.

By the spring of 1923, Bonar Law clearly was no longer able to carry out the duties of the Prime Minister (he had nearly lost his voice from cancer of the throat), and on 20 May he resigned. He asked specifically not to be required to give King George V advice about his successor. As a result, although other factors may have influenced his choice, the king leaned heavily upon the advice of Lord Balfour. Somewhat to his own surprise, Baldwin was asked to form a government.

Baldwin's appointment as Chancellor of the Exchequer in the previous administration had been principally the result of the lack of alternative candidates for the post, since the best-known figures of the Conservative party still regarded the overthrow of the national coalition as a betrayal. His appointment as Prime Minister a little over six months later, after a relatively undistinguished tenure at the Treasury, was at least partly the result of the same lack of talent among the Conservatives. The most obvious candidate for leadership was Lord Curzon, who had accepted the post of Foreign Secretary in Bonar Law's government. In doing this he had incurred the cordial dislike of many of his former colleagues and had therefore made himself unlikely to be an agent in reuniting the party. Other factors favouring the choice of Baldwin for Prime Minister were Curzon's defects of temperament and his membership in the House of Lords.

Baldwin's first period as Prime Minister was hardly longer than Bonar Law's, just eight months. Nor was it much more fruitful. Dominating Baldwin's mind, as it dominated the minds of all Englishmen in the time between the wars, was the problem of unemployment. It hung like a cloud over all considerations. It deflected thought and stifled plans. How to provide work? Baldwin's answer, derived apparently from a visit to the United States in 1892 just as the McKinley Tariff took effect, was a return to import duties for Great Britain. He had decided that the high level of taxation and wages in his country made impossible commercial competition with nations that at once subsidized their exports through an artificially depressed standard of living at home and prohibited imports by tariff barriers. An important segment of the Conservative party agreed with this point of view and had strenuously advocated the revival of tariffs since 1903 when they were proposed by Joseph Chamberlain. The Lloyd George coalition had instituted some duties ostensibly as war measures, and tariffs had been proposed frequently enough during the election of 1922 to elicit from Bonar Law a promise that he would not attempt to establish them without a further reference to the voters. Baldwin felt himself bound by this promise and determined to dissolve a Parliament hardly a year old and fight a second election on the issue of tariffs. A second reason for the election may also have been the desire to reunite the Conservatives. Among the coalition dissidents were several important tariff reformers.

In the general election of 6 December 1923 the Conservatives received 38,000 more votes than they had in the election the year before. But whereas they held 344 seats at the dissolution of the House of Commons, they now returned only 258 members, while the Liberals returned 159 and the Labour party, to the astonishment and terror of many Englishmen, seated 191. The Conservatives held more seats than any other party, but were a minority in the House of Commons as a whole. The unbelievable was about to happen. The Conservatives would be unseated by Labour.

THE LABOUR PARTY

The British Labour party, which had been born at the beginning of the century, came of age as a mature political group only during the war. Although about 50 working men gained election to the Parliament of 1906, they did so only at the sufferance of the Liberal party. Within the House of Commons, Labour's effect upon the policies of the New Liberalism was slight. The Liberals were well aware of the need to win back the working-class voter, who appeared now to be exercising his franchise in the Labour interest, but they had little need for, and indeed tended to disregard, the Labour party MPs at Westminster. However, after the split in the Liberals that came with the formation of the Lloyd George coalition in December 1916 and with the increasing wartime importance of the working man, the party's status in the House of Commons grew. Labour was allotted a place in the War Cabinet, and Labour leaders both in and out of Parliament were regularly consulted on plans for reconstruction.

The Secretary of the National Executive Committee of the Labour party from 1912 was Arthur Henderson, a man widely respected in Parliament and regarded during his lifetime and since as one of the most capable of the senior Labour party leaders. He had been the first Labour man to reach cabinet rank, being appointed president of the Board of Education at the time of the reconstruction of the Asquith cabinet in May 1915. In December 1916 he had taken a place in the coalition War Cabinet. Eight months later he resigned because of the government's refusal to permit British delegates to attend a socialist peace conference in Stockholm. (He was succeeded by G. N. Barnes.) Free from political responsibility, Henderson, early in 1918, set about reconstructing the Labour party.

Until the last year of the war, the structure of the Labour party reflected the rather haphazard conditions of its organization. It had no national organization beyond the Annual Conference, which determined broad lines of policy, and its National Executive Committee. Worse, it had no local party structure except the branches of the various trade unions and socialist societies in affiliation with the party that happened to have a branch within a given parliamentary constituency. As a result there was virtually no way for a prospective candidate who was not a trade unionist or a member of some other affiliated organization to obtain sponsorship as a party-candidate. Henderson's chief work in 1918, carried out in cooperation with James Ramsay MacDonald and Sidney Webb, was to begin the establishment of a network of constituency organizations. These would possess separate representation from the trade unions upon the National Executive Committee, and membership in them would be available to any voter sympathetic to Labour party principles. They would sponsor candidates independently although, as it worked out, candidates first selected by constituency organizations frequently were adopted later by a local trade union.

Henderson's other achievement for the Labour party during 1918 was in securing the adoption of a comprehensive statement of party dogma and policy. This document, drafted by Sidney Webb and entitled *Labour and the New Social Order*, was important both because it remained the basic Labour platform until the general election of 1950, and because it frankly proclaimed Labour to be a socialist party. The new constitution proposed a guaranteed minimum standard of living for all citizens, nationalization of industry, heavy taxation of large incomes—with, to the terror of the middle class, a capital levy—and urged the use of the nation's surplus wealth for raising the general level of culture and education. While the statement bore little resemblance to the doctrines of continental Bolshevism, it seemed frightening enough to a generation that nine years before had seen revolutionary implications in a duty of one halfpenny in the pound on the capital value of undeveloped land and minerals.

The Labour party's accomplishments in the election of 1918 were hardly remarkable. It seated only 63 candidates, not a significant increase of its prewar strength. In view of the effort that had gone into the election, the creation of 292 constituency associations and the fielding of 388 candidates, there might have been some cause for discouragement. Nevertheless, the Coupon Election marked a turning point in the history of the Labour party. Numerically weak as it was, it had elected more MPs than the handful returned by the Asquithian Liberals who constituted the other opposition party. Thus, so far as the concept of an 'official' opposition had developed, this group was now the Parliamentary Labour party.

Unfortunately the PLP was able to make little use of its new prestige. The coalition majority was overwhelming, and the prestige of the men among the Asquithian Liberals, however small their numbers, overshadowed the Labour party leadership. Labour's position on the front bench was further weakened by the fact that several of the party's most experienced parliamentarians, G. N. Barnes and J. R. Clynes among others, had chosen to remain in office when the party withdrew from the coalition after the Armistice, and so were dropped. At the same time, other leaders—Henderson and Ramsay MacDonald—had lost their seats in the election.

During the period of the national coalition, Labour party policy both in and out of Parliament generally supported the extension of social legislation, opposed repression in Ireland, and particularly opposed British intervention in Russia. With the coming of the depression at the end of 1920, as the government's willingness to spend money on welfare projects ended just when unemployment began to grow in cities of the North and East where many Labour MPs found their seats, the party's interest came to centre on domestic problems concerned with the provision of work. 'Work or Maintenance' became their cry.

The election of November 1922 saw great Labour gains. The party nearly doubled both its popular vote and its membership in Parliament. This outcome was not altogether unexpected. It had secured a net gain of 13 seats during the four years of the Lloyd George coalition, and had lost only one seat of its own. Therefore, with the increase of November 1922 behind them, the party welcomed the second trial of strength proposed by Baldwin 13 months later, particularly on the issue of tariffs. For most Labour politicians, and for most Labour voters, tariffs simply were a trick that would raise the cost of living and increase employer profits. Work came from trade, and the more freedom in international commerce, the more trade. The arguments advanced 35 years later that a protected economy was necessary for social and economic planning were scarcely heard, although some Fabians had been thinking along these lines since the early days of tariff-reform agitation at the turn of the century.

The Labour victory of 6 December 1923 which brought Ramsay MacDonald to office as Prime Minister (he had been returned to Parliament in November 1922) was a highly qualified one. With 258 seats, the Conservatives remained the largest party in the House of Commons, and any Labour government had to depend on the Liberals, who were now technically reunited through the attack on free trade. There were many Labourites after the election who questioned whether the party should accept office under these circumstances. But most leaders agreed that if the party were to be accepted as the normal alternative custodian of power, it should accept office when offered simply to gain experience in the management of affairs of state. This was true, even though the necessary coalition with the Liberals would be likely to stifle much of the socialist legislative programme. Hence, on 22 January 1924, Mac-Donald accepted the king's invitation to form a government. (In the manner of nineteenth-century Prime Ministers, Baldwin did not resign until after he was defeated by the new House of Commons when it reassembled.)

The Labour record in office was hardly glorious in terms of fulfilling the promises made in *Labour and the New Social Order*. But in the long run, the party's unadventurous and undynamic first period of responsibility perhaps redounded to its credit. The budget of Chancellor of the Exchequer Philip Snowden, although he was a member of one of the most radical of the party's constituent organizations, the Independent Labour Party, could hardly have been questioned by even the most careful disciple of Gladstonian finance. The government made no serious cuts in defence expenditure and its only important contribution to domestic social legislation was a housing bill pushed through Parliament by its popular and highly successful Minister of Health, John Wheatley. The Wheatley Housing Act put the local authorities back into the business of building houses where they have been ever since. Unlike the Addison Act, Wheatley's measure offered a strictly limited subsidy toward the cost of council-owned dwellings, payable only upon units let at rents that the working class could afford.

MacDonald's most significant departures from the policy of previous governments were in the field of foreign affairs. He retained the Foreign Office for himself and used his tenure to break down the British isolation from continental affairs that had been increasingly apparent since the war. He could not end the animosity that had grown up between Britain and France, the 'Rupture Cordiale', but he did devote his considerable negotiating talents to gaining German acceptance of the Dawes Plan, so enabling the French to end their two-year occupation of the Ruhr Valley. He thus paved the way for the German return to the European family of nations, symbolized by the signing of the Locarno Treaty in 1925. He was also the only Prime Minister of the interwar period who could be considered an unqualified supporter of the League of Nations. Here he sought to overcome French reluctance to place her security in the League's hands by offering to join other European League members in a specific guarantee, the 'Geneva Protocol', which would at once promote disarmament and provide a mutual guarantee of all European frontiers against aggression. The Protocol took Britain further into European affairs than the Conservatives wished to go and was dropped when they returned to power.

Meanwhile, Labour had been preparing a far more radical change in British foreign policy, the resumption of normal relations with Russia. This decision, the most controversial step of MacDonald's administration, had repercussions in the domestic field that contributed largely to the fall of the Labour government at the end of 1924. Great Britain had extended formal diplomatic recognition to the Soviet Union soon after Labour came to power. But besides Labour's doctrinal interest in recognizing the first workers' republic, the party looked on Russian trade as a step toward solving the problem of unemployment. However, a revival of trade was impossible without the extension of large credits to the Soviet Union, and many Englishmen considered the extension of credits impossible so long as Russia ignored the huge obligations contracted before the revolution by the Czarist government. One could not lend to a nation that did not pay its debts.

Over the proposal for a loan to Russia the working agreement between the Liberals and the Labour party broke down. The Liberals, particularly the Lloyd George wing, were unwilling to support a loan until the Soviet Union made some promises about the Czarist debts. In addition, Labour's advocacy of a loan made the party seem unduly tender toward Bolshevism and reinforced the many unsupported charges that there existed a connexion between foreign revolutionary movements and the domestic Labour party. With the support of the Liberals falling away, MacDonald determined to gamble on a third general election within two years which he hoped would bring him an independent majority. The polling day was set for 29 October. On 25 October there appeared in *The Times* and in the *Daily Mail* a letter purportedly signed by Gregory Zinoviev, the 'President of the Presidium' of the Comintern, and Arthur McManus, the British Communist Party representative on the Comintern, to the Central Committee of the British party. The letter specifically referred to MacDonald's attempts to re-establish commercial relations with the Soviet Union and to the controversy that this policy had aroused. It suggested that reactionary circles in Britain would attempt to break off the agreement, and urged British communists to undertake seditious activity, particularly infiltration of the armed forces. The letter caused widespread indignation and Conservative newspapers and some Conservative politicians affected to see in it a revolutionary conspiracy. (In a clear appeal to anti-Semitism the *Mail* printed a most unflattering drawing of Zinoviev and pointed out that his real name was Apfelbaum.)

The genuineness of the letter is doubtful, but in any case it could hardly have surprised many Conservative party leaders who sought to make use of it. Since 1919 the Home Office Directorate of Intelligence had laid dozens of similar documents before cabinets of which many of them had been members. Perhaps in the long run it is of little importance whether or not the document emanated from Moscow, and indeed it is doubtful whether it affected many voters' decisions. Quite possibly the election had already been lost by Labour. The importance of the 'Red Letter' is, first, that it provided the Labour party, and MacDonald, with an excuse for losing the election, and second, less clearly but perhaps more powerfully, it confirmed the Conservatives in the rectitude of their anti-Communist, anti-radical, and, by implication, anti-Labour posture. The appearance of the letter lowered the tone of British politics and diminished temporarily the respectability that had begun to accrue to Labour through its extreme conventionality in office. It added a new element of class vindictiveness to the struggle between the parties.

BALDWINISM, 1924-29

The election of 29 October brought the Conservatives firmly into power with 419 seats to Labour's 151. Nevertheless, for Labour the election was hardly a disaster. Although it lost about 40 seats in the House of Commons, it polled a million more popular votes than it had in December 1923, while the Conservative popular vote increased by less than half this number. The chief sufferers were the Liberals, whose popular vote was cut nearly in half, and whose representation in the House of Commons was reduced by three-quarters. Clearly the voters disliked the Liberal party's part in destroying the Mac-Donald government, and distrusted the highly conditional support Labour had received. Even though the Liberals regained in 1929 many of the votes they lost, and held again the balance of power between the parties, the election of 1924 must stand with that of 1918 as one of the major steps toward the near-extinction of the party at the national level. (Asquith himself was defeated at Paisley. He accepted a peerage in 1925 as Earl of Oxford, and the next year retired from the leadership of the party.) With a majority now double that of the parties in opposition, Baldwin returned to office, to remain for five years.

The new cabinet demonstrated the reconciliation with the coalition Conservatives, who had remained outside Bonar Law's government. Austen Chamberlain became Foreign Secretary. Lord Birkenhead took the India Office and in April 1925 Lord Balfour succeeded the dying Curzon as Lord President of the Council. The surprise of the new government, however, was not so much the reunion with the coalition Conservatives, most of whom had returned to the opposition front bench during MacDonald's administration, but the appointment of Winston Churchill as Chancellor of the Exchequer. Churchill appeared to have many disabilities. He was a radical Liberal in debt to Lloyd George, who had brought him back from the political wilderness in 1917 after his dismissal over the Dardanelles. He had been a leading member of the national coalition. But perhaps most important, he was an apostate Conservative who had left the party in 1903 over tariffs. Churchill's estrangement from the Liberals began soon after the fall of the coalition, and in March 1924 he had offered himself at a by-election as an 'independent anti-socialist' against candidates of the other three major parties. (He is not quite candid about this in *The Gathering Storm*.) Here he had much support from former coalition Conservatives and from Lord Beaverbrook, whose influence on him would be important throughout the rest of his life. He was defeated by only 43 votes. At the general election in October, he stood as a 'constitutionalist' for Epping and was elected by an overwhelming majority. He did not formally join the Conservative party until late in 1925.

Churchill's appointment to one of the highest posts in the cabinet came as a surprise to him, as well as to the world. There is a well-known story that Baldwin, in his casual way, asked whether he would like to be 'Chancellor'. Churchill, thinking the Prime Minister-designate meant the Chancellor of the Duchy of Lancaster, accepted this minor office with enthusiasm. He was badly suited for the Exchequer, and Baldwin's choice of him—with two experienced and capable chancellors, Austen Chamberlain and Robert Horne, available—illustrates the Prime Minister's tendency to allow personal, subjective, almost mystical considerations to influence him in the most important decisions. The choice apparently was solely Baldwin's, made without consultation, on the single criterion that Churchill represented, so far as was known, free trade. The issue had not figured in the 1924 election, although many Conservatives still considered tariff protection a matter of greatest importance.

Churchill's appointment deserves comment here both as an illustration of the character of Baldwin and because of Churchill's future importance, but its great contemporary significance lay in the fact that it put at the head of the British government's financial affairs a man whose inexperience in the matters with which he dealt made him almost totally dependent upon the advice of those who served him. As a consequence, Churchill permitted himself to be convinced, principally by the City of London banking community headed by Montagu Norman, that Great Britain should return to a freely convertible gold standard. This act, as will be seen, had disastrous consequences for the nation and for the world. It was advantageous for some parts, by no means all, of the City. It resulted in hardship for many manufacturing and exporting enterprises, and for the working men who were employed in them. Although from the perspective of nearly half a century economists have severely blamed Churchill for not stiffening the cabinet's resistance to the proposal, it must be admitted that within the context of the time the decision to make the pound convertible into gold at the old parity was perfectly consistent with the temper of Stanley Baldwin and with the mood of the British nation, which he almost invariably understood.

Baldwin's second ministry is always described by historians as the time when Britain finally recovered from the shock of the Great War, when the nation returned to stability. 'Tranquillity' is a word frequently used. This is true in a superficial sense. In Europe, Germany seemed at last to have thrown off the political and economic malaise of the first half of the decade of the twenties. The signing of the Locarno Pact in 1925 presumably signified her free acceptance of the boundary provisions of the Versailles treaty and gave Austen

Chamberlain and the Baldwin government one of its greatest achievements in foreign affairs, although the groundwork for this policy had been laid during MacDonald's administration. At home the tensions between the classes and the fear of working-class revolution diminished somewhat, despite the general strike of 1926. Without question Baldwin was genuinely popular among all social levels of the nation. Unemployment remained well over a million, about 11 per cent of the insured working population, but the rapid growth of new industries, particularly in the South, obscured the hardship in the North and in Wales. Yet even if the last half of the decade of the twenties was a time of tranquillity, it was not one of safety. The old world was gone and many of the institutions which the nation sentimentally remembered and which Baldwin seemed to symbolize were nearing collapse. A large part of Baldwin's political strength lay in his power to evoke nostalgia. He could speak fondly of the old workers who sat on the bench at the gate of his father's iron works, exempt from regular tasks but drawing their pay. He could predict grandly the resurrection of empire solidarity and loyalty that would come with an imperial tariff or the revival of London's commercial preeminence that would accompany the return to gold. Nevertheless, as the twenties waned, Great Britain and the world were sliding toward economic and political catastrophe. Baldwin could not arrest this rush toward destruction, but he made it pleasant.

During his political career, Baldwin was involved in three great crises—the general strike of 1926, the run on the Bank of England and the flight from the pound in 1931, and the abdication of Edward VIII in 1936. His actions in each of these events can be severely criticized, not precisely for dishonesty of motive nor for ruthlessness of intent, but rather because he approached each crisis as though he personally could do nothing to prevent it. With full knowledge he allowed each to develop and then, instead of using the powers of the government to solve the problem that brought on the crisis, he used them simply to bring an end to the crisis itself.

Baldwin was lucky, as he frequently was, that the general strike came in 1926. Unemployment was no lower, indeed somewhat higher, than it had been in the previous several years. But the hard edge of violence that had always seemed hidden just below the surface of all dealings between employers and employees had been smoothed by increasing production, falling prices, and a slightly increased purchasing power of wages, all of which had occurred since 1924. Nevertheless, conditions in mining areas were worse than they had been two years earlier. After the disastrous strike of 1921, the British coal industry in 1923 and 1924 had enjoyed a brief period of prosperity that was caused ironically by the dilemma of French-German reparations. As has been mentioned, the German payment of reparations in coal in 1920–21 had caused a slump in world coal prices that plunged the British industry into hard times. Then, in 1922, to enforce the payment of further reparations, the French occupied the valley of the Ruhr, and German coal miners, along with all other workers in the area, went on strike. The result was a sudden rise in world coal prices and renewed prosperity for the British miner. In May 1924, supported by the Labour government, the miners had been able to make an advantageous wage agreement with the owners. But soon afterwards the Germans accepted the Dawes Plan and the French began to withdraw from the Ruhr. By 1925, German mines were again back in full operation and world coal prices tumbled. At the end of June 1925, with the termination of the previous year's wage agreement, the owners announced a large decrease in wages and an increase in hours from seven to eight. Again the miners threatened to strike, this time having in hand resolutions of firm support from the Transport and General Workers' Union, the National Union of Railwaymen, and from a large number of other union councils. The strike was due to begin on 31 July. At the last moment, the government bought time by a subsidy in aid of wages that would last until 1 May 1926. At the same time, it appointed a royal commission, the Samuel Commission, to investigate the coal mines and, more to the point, began to make preparations for the maintenance of essential services in case of a general strike.

The miners were attempting again, as they had in 1921, to coerce the government and the community. A general strike would have no more effect on the mine owners than a strike of the miners alone, but it would bring the whole weight of labour to bear on the population at large. This threat had been effective in the grim days of 1919 and 1920 with Europe convulsed by Bolshevik rebellion and hundreds of thousands of demobilized soldiers, many still in uniform, tramping the streets. Labour expected that it would be effective again. Unquestionably many of the trade union leaders, who supported the coal miners in their threat of a general strike and who urged them to reject all compromises offered by the government, believed that the strike would never occur because before the crisis the government would seek compromise as it had done so many times before. But in the calm afternoon of Baldwinism, the fear of violence that had so dominated the government in the first years of the decade had evaporated. Baldwin had many faults, but he was not easily frightened. And there were no men in his government continually urging all possible concessions to labour as T. J. Macnamara and Christopher Addison had done in the national coalition. Instead there were Churchill, Amery and Birkenhead demanding resistance. Hence in the nine months' interval purchased by the Treasury subsidy to miners' wages, the government quietly went forward making detailed plans on the assumption that a general strike would take place, while the trade unions did nothing on the assumption that it would not.

The miners were reinforced in their intransigence by the report of the Samuel Commission, issued on 10 March 1926, which proposed nationalization of mining royalties, that is, the government purchase of the right to receive the rent paid for each ton of coal to the owner of the land upon which the mine was located. (Mining companies in Britain virtually never owned the land they mined. Mining royalties eventually were purchased by the state in 1938.) The Committee also recommended a large number of other administrative improvements, amalgamation of mines, and a national wage board. With these recommendations in their favour the miners, in the last few days before the subsidy ran out, refused all concessions, expecting that at the last moment the government would capitulate and perhaps continue the subsidy. In the long run, this policy would force the nationalization of the industry.

On 30 April the subsidy and the miners' temporary wage agreement expired together, and, as the miners had rejected the owners' proposal for a new agreement based on the wages of 1921, the mines closed at midnight and the workers were locked out. The question now was whether the rest of the trade unions would strike in support of the miners, and the next three days were occupied with negotiations between the government and leaders of the Trades Union Congress. For a moment it appeared that a temporary agreement might be reached permitting the mines to reopen with a short period of government subsidy, but due to a misunderstanding, or again perhaps simply laziness on Baldwin's part, the arrangements were never completed. In summary, Baldwin did little to try to head off the general strike, and at midnight on 3 May it began.

The strike was not really general; somewhat less than three-quarters of the total Trades Union Congress membership of 4,300,000 men went out. Principal industries affected beside mining were transport, building, steel, heavy manufacturing, and printers. (An unauthorized strike of printers against the *Daily Mail,* which had been publishing inflammatory editorials calling the strike a revolutionary conspiracy, was the immediate cause of Baldwin's decision to bring an end to negotiations for a temporary agreement.) The general strike lasted from 3 May until 12 May. These nine days were treated by the general population of the United Kingdom as a holiday. The middle classes were united against the strike, and working men themselves were by no means uniformly favourable to it. There was little violence, although there might have been more had the strike lasted. The shortness of the period ensured also that there were few shortages of food supplies. The ordinary recollection of the event is of a well-to-do lady taking tickets on a bus, or of a university undergraduate fulfilling a boyhood dream as a locomotive driver. Similarly, Winston Churchill accomplished a lifelong ambition by being permitted to edit the United Kingdom's only national newspaper, the *British Gazette.*

The strike came to a quick end, first because of the immense prestige of Baldwin, who believed, and who was able to convince most of the British nation (including no doubt many of the strikers themselves), that the whole affair was illegal. Secondly, the T.U.C. leaders—Arthur Pugh, the President of the Congress, J. H. Thomas of the Railwaymen, and Ernest Bevin of the Transport and General Workers—were themselves moderate men who perhaps had believed secretly, as certainly many of their followers had, that the strike would never come to pass, and who were appalled when it did. They were well aware that a general strike was at bottom a revolutionary tactic, and that the European syndicalists had always considered it so. The use of this dangerous weapon of political coercion to settle a very traditional, if important, economic grievance was not only bad strategy, it was un-British. The affair had to be ended.

On the technical excuse that the miners had rejected the report of the Samuel Commission, as indeed had the owners, and under the assumption that the government would begin again negotiations with the miners, the T.U.C. declared the strike at an end. The miners, again deserted by the rest of the labour movement, fought on alone until autumn. On 19 November hunger forced them back to work. But by this time a number of the less productive mines had closed, and about 200,000 of them remained not only unemployed but unemployable in their chosen occupation.

Baldwin emerged from the strike with his personal reputation greatly enhanced. The *Spectator* compared him to Pitt, the Saviour of the Nation. However, the effect of the government victory certainly was to increase in the next few years the friction between the employing and the working classes, and to decrease the popularity of the Conservative party. Within the next 34 months, the Conservatives lost a net of 13 seats to the Liberals and Labour, while in the first 18 months of office, before the strike, they had lost a net of two seats.

The immediate parliamentary reactions to the general strike, considering that many Members had called it an act of rebellion, were relatively mild. Government policy hardly seemed to be deflected. In a way, perhaps, this is an example of the gravest criticism to be made of Baldwin's general performance as Prime Minister, of his tendency to do nothing unless forced to. After having handled the crisis well, as he conceived it, he remained unconcerned about the very real grievances that had brought it on. The miners were left at the mercy of the coal owners. The government, although compiling a fairly respectable record in social legislation, took no steps to reorganize the desperately inefficient and uneconomic structure of the coal industry, or to revive industry in the depressed areas generally, while at the same time, under the plea of financial stringency, it cut back, in 1927, on the Wheatley housing programme and reduced the state's contribution to national health insurance.

The principal piece of legislation emanating directly from the general strike was the Trade Disputes and Trade Unions Act of 1927. Specifically, this act made illegal any strike that had some object other than the simple economic benefit of the members of the trade union concerned, and made illegal any strike calculated to coerce the government—in effect, general strikes. By itself, this part of the act was ethically defensible. A government must govern, and any public activity that hinders it in the discharge of its responsibility is by definition revolutionary. However, the second section of the Trade Disputes Act was of a different nature. It had no connexion with the general strike and was concerned solely with normal trade union political activity. This provision stipulated that union contributions to political funds could not be taken from their general treasury and must be taken from a separate fund collected for the purpose. Since 1913 unions had been specifically permitted to employ funds for political purposes, providing a majority of the members approved, and subject to the provision that any given member might prevent his dues from being so used if he wished. In effect, he could 'contract out' of the political contribution. The act of 1927 reversed this procedure. Instead of contracting out, union members now had to 'contract in'. This rather small change had considerable effect. Pressure from his fellows or sheer lack of interest might prevent a man from contracting out, but the same lack of interest, plus the fact that withholding a political contribution no longer made him conspicuous, might prevent a person from contracting in. As a result, between 1927 and 1946 when the Labour government repealed the act, there was a considerable drop in union funds available for political activity. In this sense, the Trade Disputes Act was a clumsy piece of class legislation designed simply to favour a party whose members received few contributions from trade unions, but many from businesses and businessmen. It was fiercely resisted by the Labour party within Parliament, whose members on one occasion walked out of a debate in a body, and was most unpopular with working men generally, certainly contributing to the Conservative defeat in 1929.

SOCIAL LEGISLATION AND THE GENERAL ELECTION, 1926-29

The Conservative government between 1926 and 1929 had no particular legislative plan or set of administrative goals. They were bound by no dogma, as had been the Labour government in 1924, nor even by the ideal of national reconstruction and improvement that had been announced, if dishonoured, by Lloyd George. 'Baldwinism' was not a policy; specifically it was the absence of policy. But it does not follow that the last three years of Baldwin's second government were altogether without achievement. The cabinet contained a few men of considerable talent, even if several were in the wrong posts. One, in a post admirably suited to his very substantial administrative gifts, was Neville Chamberlain, the Minister of Health and younger brother of the Foreign Secretary. As the years passed, Baldwin came more and more to lean upon Chamberlain, so that, when the Prime Minister retired after the coronation of George VI in 1937, the younger man's succession was taken for granted. Chamberlain was completely loyal to Baldwin, having agreed to enter the cabinet of 1924 much to the embarrassment of his older half-brother, Austen Chamberlain, who was at that time charging Baldwin with betrayal of the coalition. He provided the administrative drive and the businesslike respect for facts that Baldwin, himself technically a businessman, lacked. Indeed it is arguable that Chamberlain's success as an administrator of cabinet departments and his confidence in his own abilities were his undoing as Prime Minister.

Chamberlain was responsible for most of the useful achievements in social legislation that provide the few adornments of Baldwinism. Although far more carefully thought out than the enactments of previous governments since the war, his programme showed little originality in conception. Of the three acts to be discussed here—widows' and orphans' contributory pensions in 1925, the reform of unemployment insurance in 1927, and the abolition of the boards of guardians in 1929—the first is perhaps the most important. In summary, Chamberlain's pension measure established a contributory pension scheme tied to national health insurance so that every contributor to health insurance was also a contributor to pensions. The measure provided a pension of 10s. for a contributor's widow in case of his death, and a pension of 7s. 6d. for orphans. From the new scheme the contributor himself received a pension of 10s. at the age of 65, that is, five years earlier than pensions began under the old non-contributory programme of 1908. The significance of Chamberlain's plan lies in the fact that it put an end to the expansion of the non-contributory pension programme which had originated as the first large measure of the New Liberalism and added pensions to the growing number of welfare institutions that were handled by means of insurance. Unquestionably one of the motives for the Conservatives' interest in contributory pensions was the fear that the next Labour government might undertake to expand the existing scheme on a non-contributory basis. But their interest went deeper than this. A contributory pension programme had been the official Conservative alternative to the Liberal pension act in 1908, and in addition had first been proposed in 1891 by Neville Chamberlain's father, Joseph Chamberlain. In the Widows', Orphans', and Old Age Contributory Pension Act the Minister of Health could feel that he was accomplishing a goal not only of his party, but of his family.

Chamberlain's attempt to deal with the chronic problem of unemployment was far less successful. In July 1925 the insurance fund had a debit balance of nearly £8,500,000, which represented an increased indebtedness of £1,500,000 since the previous year. Many workers had never been in employment long enough to qualify under the ordinary terms of the act since the extension of coverage in 1920, and many more had exhausted their 26 weeks of regular benefit. The 'uncovenanted benefit', or 'dole', that they now received was paid strictly at the pleasure of the government and was in essence a measure of the political strength of the British working class. One of the first acts of the Conservative cabinet had been to appoint a departmental committee under Robert Younger, Lord Blanesburgh, an eminent judge, to examine unemployment insurance with the aim of finding a means by which the scheme could become self-supporting and end its dependence upon Treasury advances. The Blanesburgh Committee report, rendered in January 1927, became the basis of the Unemployment Insurance Act of 1927. It recommended sweeping away the multitude of protections that had been incorporated in previous acts for the safety of the insurance fund. Henceforth, unemployment insurance would be given for an indefinite period instead of for a specific number of weeks (the 15 weeks of standard benefit of the Acts of 1911 and 1920 had been increased to 26 weeks in 1921). Also discarded was the old rule that no contributor could receive more than one week's benefit for each six weeks of contribution. The committee's argument was that uncovenanted benefit had made these rules a dead letter. The committee recommended that the only requirements for benefit should be, first, that the claimant had been in insurable employment for at least thirty weeks within the previous two years and, second, that he should be 'genuinely available for work'. For the next two years only there would be a new 'transitional benefit' to enable those not presently drawing the standard benefit to qualify under the new rules.

The Blanesburgh report was based on the assumption that unemployment in Great Britain had reached a peak and would henceforth grow less. In this it reflected the general atmosphere of unfocused optimism that was the essence of Baldwinism. But in this also lay the eventual disaster that resulted from the Blanesburgh recommendation. Unemployment did not grow less in the next few years; rather it increased. However, with the act of 1927 the government lost all control over payments for unemployment expenditure. Uncovenanted benefits, although given generously, had been discretionary with the Minister. Now they became a matter of statutory right. Worse, for the solvency of insurance, in 1929 it was found necessary to increase the period for transitional benefits, and by May 1931 410,000 men, almost one-quarter of the unemployed, were drawing transitional benefits. For the ordinary unemployed, transitional benefit was no different from the old uncovenanted benefit. It became the new dole. Finally, by an act of 1930, the requirement of 'genuinely available for work' was discarded. It was felt to be a useless and unfair test when both the unemployment insurance officer and the unemployed men were aware that no work existed. The result, after the requirement was changed, was an immediate increase of about 60,000 in claimants for unemployment benefit. As a cause of the incredible growth in unemployment insurance costs that would contribute so much to foreign bankers' distrust of British finance during the crisis of 1931, the Blanesburgh Committee report is of basic importance.

The third of Chamberlain's major social welfare projects, the Local Government Act of 1929, gave effect to proposals a quarter-century old for the reform and reconstruction of the poor law, England's most ancient institution for dealing with the unfortunate in the community. The modern poor law dated from 1834, when the Poor Law Amendment Act of that year completely overhauled the Elizabethan statute. The basic change in 1834 was that henceforth an applicant for aid was assumed to be a type of criminal whose need for relief derived from his own laziness. He would be given aid, therefore, only under semi-penal conditions in a workhouse. The underlying premise in this was that state relief for the poor ought to interfere as little as possible with the normal working of the labour market. If relief were given too generously, men would withhold their labour from productive tasks. This was the so-called 'deterrent' principle of poor relief. But by the end of the war, at least, it had become clear that, whether or not this conception of poverty had been valid in 1834, times now were radically changed. With between eight and 15 per cent of the labour force continually unemployed, it was impossible to assume that all working men without jobs were lazy. More important, the chief clients of the poor law were now, and had been for many years before the war, not the able-bodied workmen, but the aged, especially the aged sick, and widows and orphans—in effect, those groups in society for whom the possibility of work practically did not exist. Yet, while the absolute requirement of the workhouse for relief, 'the workhouse test', had long since disappeared except for able-bodied working men, many of these unfortunates, particularly the aged, were forced to stay in workhouse infirmaries simply because they could not take care of themselves and there was nowhere else for them to go. Finally, although the legal disabilities of pauperism had virtually disappeared after the Representation of the People Act of 1918—except that a pauper could not be a member of a board of guardians or a parish council—the category itself, and the stigma, remained.

The problem had also an economic aspect. The pressure of thousands of applications for relief in areas where economic hardship was particularly prevalent threatened to bankrupt many of the 625 poor law unions in England and Wales. This was a special problem in certain areas where working men had come to control the local boards of guardians and where, as in London, extreme economic hardship and luxury existed side by side. In the metropolitan borough of Poplar, for instance, which reported more paupers than any other union in the United Kingdom, the borough councillors permitted themselves to be sent to jail rather than cut the scale of relief or increase local rates. The argument, one with which working men everywhere could sympathize, was that the extreme wealth of other London boroughs should be tapped to pay for the hardship of the East End. In effect, poor law administration throughout the United Kingdom was breaking down. It had to be modernized and given to larger, more efficient, units of government. Most important, it had now to coincide with the opinions of poverty held in a nation where the working men who suffered the hardships of unemployment constituted also the majority of the voters.

Considering the age and the state of decrepitude of the various institutions that made up the English system of poor relief, the Local Government Act of 1929 made surprisingly few changes. Rather, its importance lies in the fact that it opened the door to change. It made possible almost the entire reconstruction of the poor law by administrative order should the major local authorities desire to do so. Specifically, it did two things: it abolished the boards of guardians and passed their responsibilities to county and county borough councils, who would handle poor relief through a subcommittee of the council's public assistance committee. Secondly, the act provided that the major local authorities who received these new powers might alter the administration of the poor law, removing from it various functions not necessarily associated with poor relief, for instance medical facilities, and give them to the appropriate committees of the council. These powers unfortunately were little used in the next ten years except in the case of hospitals. Some progressive and wealthy authorities, particularly London (which received at the same time control of the contagious disease hospitals operated by the Metropolitan Asylums Board) and Middlesex, used the powers to begin to build a substantial system of municipal hospitals. The existence of such institutions run by local authorities and supported out of taxes would be a matter of great concern during the planning of the National Health Service at the end of the Second World War.

The general election of 30 May 1929 came late in the five-year parliamentary term. In 1928, with the Representation of the People

Act, the Conservatives had extended the right to vote to women between the ages of 21 and 31, who had been excluded in the act of 1918. This measure, the 'Flapper Vote', meant putting off the election until 30 May so that new registers could be prepared. Baldwin fully expected to win, and was already considering his new cabinet. Neville Chamberlain, the coming man, certainly deserved the Exchequer; but if he were put there, what would become of Churchill?

The election campaign itself was dull. There were no pressing issues, indeed no reason to call the election other than the statutory requirement. Unemployment was the problem, but no one claimed a solution for it except David Lloyd George, who had at last been elected leader of the Liberals. The Conservatives campaigned almost solely on Baldwin's image as an English domestic institution. Huge pictures of him were posted everywhere, and underneath were inscribed the words 'Safety First', not a significant improvement over the previous slogan of 'Tranquillity'. Labour attacked the Conservative economies in the health service and in housing. The Liberals talked of a comprehensive national plan to cure unemployment.

The returns reflected an almost even division of sentiment in the country. Labour elected 288 Members of Parliament, the Conservatives 260, the Liberals 59, with eight seats going to minor parties. Labour was in the position of the Conservatives in December 1923. They held more seats than any other party, but not a majority, and the balance of power was held again by the Liberals. Although the Conservatives had polled over 500,000 more votes than they had in the previous election in 1924, clearly the great majority of new voters, over seven million, had voted for the Liberal and Labour parties. But also, the Conservatives had been hurt by the disproportionately large size of many of the normally safe constituencies. There had been no boundary changes since 1911 and the distribution of parliamentary seats failed to reflect the vast movement of population from North to South. Constituencies that usually returned Labour MPs were on the whole smaller than similar Conservative constituencies. On the other hand, many Labour votes were wasted in absolutely safe constituencies in distressed areas where Labour candidates ran up huge majorities. Baldwin resigned immediately, not waiting to meet Parliament as he had in 1924. Ramsay MacDonald became Prime Minister a second time on 5 June 1929

THE GOLD STANDARD

The economic malaise of the twenties and the world depression at the end of the decade grew from the First World War and from the disruption of economic activity, particularly the requirement of reparations, caused by the peace settlement. Britain was especially susceptible to all these economic difficulties, not only because of the damage of the war, but because of her singular tendency in the twenties to pretend that the war had never occurred. While other European nations, and indeed the United States, were trying to insulate their economies against the damages of the 1914–18 period by the erection of protective tariffs, by credit controls, and, in many cases, by devaluation of their currencies, Great Britain remained obstinately free trade and in 1925, against the advice of most progressive economic thought, revalued its currency to its old parity with the dollar.

From the beginning of the decade the constant French pressure for German reparations payments made itself felt in Great Britain, particularly in connexion with the chronic difficulties of the British coal industry. Before 1921 the payments made under the terms of the Versailles treaty had been in anticipation of the final bill on reparations that was to be drawn up by a specially appointed commission. The Reparations Commission notified Germany on 28 April 1921 that the total amount of reparations was to be £6,600 million, of which Britain would receive 22 per cent, plus the Belgian war debt. (The commission added that German payments to that time had not been sufficient to cover the costs of the Allied occupation, and as a result Germany was still liable for the full amount.) After protests, Germany was informed that reparations were a first charge on all physical assets of the nation, and that, if the first year's payments were not immediately forthcoming, the Allies would occupy the Ruhr Valley. Following this, Germany agreed to meet the stipulated schedule of payments.

But through 1921 and the early months of 1922, German reparations payments caused a noticeable strain on the international exchange ratio of the mark. Each payment was accompanied by a large drop in the value of that currency. Finally, in July 1922, Germany requested that she be required to make no more payments until January 1925. With this request, the basic disagreement between England and France on the treatment of Germany reappeared. France insisted upon the enforcement of reparations payments in every detail. For political and military reasons she desired a bankrupt Germany but she would indeed be much distressed herself if

Germany did not pay, for she needed German money to redeem the obligations she had incurred in her own reconstruction. Britain, on the other hand, wanted a prosperous Germany that could resume the purchase of British goods. French security and British economic necessity met head-on. Finally, in January 1923, after a second German request for a moratorium on reparations payments, French troops with detachments of Italians and Belgians occupied the whole Ruhr and Lippe region as far east as Dortmund. With this action began the German economic collapse that contributed directly to the rise of Nazism.

The German population in the occupied areas, with the support of the Berlin government, countered the French invasion with a policy of passive resistance. In an area that produced 80–85 per cent of Germany's coal and about 80 per cent of her steel and pig iron, not a mine or a mill worked. As a result, the occupation was ruinous to both countries. The French, who had hoped to take Ruhr production for reparations payments, found that the cost of the occupation and the economic uncertainties that proceeded from it were causing severe economic hardships at home. For the Germans, the loss of production and taxes from the Ruhr, and more disastrously the burden of supporting nearly ten per cent of their population in idleness, proved to be more than the economy could bear. The immediate consequence of the French invasion and the German passive resistance policy was an incredible drop in the value of the German mark. The decline of the mark had begun during the war and was hastened by the German attempts to pay reparations in 1920 and 1921. By the end of 1922, just before the French invasion, the mark had already dropped to an exchange value of about 28,000 to the pound. By October 1923 German currency had become practically worthless, 1,083,600,000,000,000 marks being offered for the pound at Berlin and 1;720,000,000,000,000 marks in Cologne. But as the value of the mark sank the German will to continue the passive resistance also declined, and in October 1923 the government officially declared the policy at an end.

Thus the French invasion was a nominal success. It forced the Germans finally to attempt the payment of reparations. On the other hand, the cost politically, economically and morally was tremendous. The savings of the German middle class were almost completely wiped out. Insurance policies, bank accounts and bonds literally were worth less than the paper upon which they were printed. A political consequence was that the newly impoverished middle class became an easy prey for Nazi ideology, which promised stability, a firm government and revision of the Versailles 'Diktat'. The economic effect most immediately important to England was that the ordinary reservoirs of German capital were dried up. In the next few years German industry, and more particularly German banks, had to depend upon borrowing abroad for their capital. Their particular source was, of course, the London money market, although they also borrowed heavily in the United States. By 31 March 1931 Germany owed abroad a total of 5,636 million marks. Of this amount, about 37 per cent was due the United States and about 20 per cent due the United Kingdom. This represented a far greater increase in borrowing than normally would have been needed for Germany's foreign trade, and suggests what many English bankers discovered to their sorrow: that German banks were using English capital for their ordinary domestic business.

Another consequence of the inflation not immediately apparent in Great Britain, but which would affect that country greatly in the next decade, was that it had enabled German industrialists to pay their debts in worthless marks and so to emerge from the inflation completely debt-free while possessing, in many cases, modern machinery which had cost them practically nothing. In the same way, by inflation, the government had in effect repudiated its war borrowing. Thus the German entrepreneur emerged from the Ruhr occupation unburdened by costs of interest and far better able to compete with the British industrialist weighed down both by a heavy capital structure and by the high taxes he paid to a government still attempting to discharge its war debt. In these circumstances one may legitimately question the wisdom of the British decision to increase the value of the pound, making it more expensive in terms of foreign currencies, and increasing proportionately therefore the price of British goods.

The determination to return to the gold standard did not originate in the Baldwin government. The Cunliffe Committee on Currency and Foreign Exchanges had recommended this step in an interim report even before the end of the war. But the return to gold fitted perfectly into the nostalgic ethos of Baldwinism. For many, this *was* reconstruction. The decades immediately before the First World War had been the 'golden age of the gold standard' when the Bank of England regulated not only the credit facilities of Great Britain, but to a large extent those of the entire world of international commerce. That the pound should be convertible into gold so that it would again be the world's trading currency was more than a matter of good economics. Somehow it involved national prestige. The pound again must be able to 'look the dollar in the face'. The difficulty was that in order to make a currency freely convertible into gold, a nation's banks must hold large stocks of the metal. Before the war this had been no problem. British individual and institutional investors were owed large debts by foreign merchants and governments that were payable either in gold or in currencies convertible to gold. But since the war this had changed. Britain was no longer a creditor country. She was a debtor country. If she were to get gold in order to restore the pound and to regain her place as the world's major banking centre, which was the overriding goal of the restoration of the pound, Britain would have to borrow capital abroad. And to attract gold from other investments that foreign speculators might make, she would have to pay a high rate of interest upon it.

In order, therefore, to make Great Britain an attractive place for the investment of foreign money, interest rates in the 1920s were deliberately kept high. They were maintained even though in the first half of the decade Great Britain was going through a period of economic depression and of disastrous unemployment. As has been discussed in Chapter One, Great Britain most of all needed the reconstruction and the renewal of her economic plant after the wastage of the war. Because a high bank rate and consequent high interest rates made the borrowing of money artificially difficult, British industrial expansion went ahead more slowly and fewer new opportunities for employment came into being than otherwise would have been the case. In effect, the British manufacturing and productive world was penalized at the expense of the British financial and banking world. British industry, it has been remarked, was attempting 'to drive uphill with the brakes on'.

In Europe, on the other hand, most nations, either by accident or on purpose, were devaluing their currency. If this drove up prices, it also made easy the borrowing of money for the expansion of plant facilities and other economic enterprise. That Britain's deliberately deflationary policy was not reversed at some time between its inauguration toward the end of 1920 and April 1925, when Churchill finally announced the official return to a convertible gold standard, is a measure of the political influence of the London financial community and the Bank of England. No Chancellor of the Exchequer during the period, even Philip Snowden in MacDonald's government, who was both an expert economist and a convinced socialist, was able to withstand the arguments of the more conventional financial experts headed by the Governor of the Bank of England, Montagu Norman.

The City had concluded, remarks Sydney Pollard in his excellent study of economic policy during the interwar period, 'that its own prosperity, security and comfort, at no matter what cost to the other sectors of the economy, was the only way to benefit the British economy as a whole'.

Accordingly, in 1925 the pound returned to its old parity to the dollar of 4·86 to one. Temporarily the British banking community had prevailed. On the other hand, the advantages also were temporary and precarious. Much of the money Britain was now lending abroad was not her own; it was itself borrowed. It was what has come to be termed 'hot money', that is, funds which are simply attracted to a nation with a high interest rate and which leave when the interest rate falls or when danger threatens. The old reserves upon which the London money market had traditionally depended, debts owed by foreigners to London bankers and acceptance houses, were now exceeded to the extent of some £250–300 million by British debts owed abroad, and London's short-term foreign liabilities were estimated by June 1931 to amount to some £760 million. In addition the high cost of British currency which caused British goods in world trade to be priced, at John Maynard Keynes's estimate, ten per cent above foreign prices, made difficult both the expansion of production and the expansion of foreign trade necessary to improve England's export-import balance and so to regain the old prewar creditor position. In effect, the very steps taken to regain for Britain its old place as the world's banker destroyed any likelihood that the nation could recover the manufacturing pre-eminence upon which its financial strength really depended.

THE WORLD DEPRESSION AND THE CRISIS OF 1931

Labour returned to power at the beginning of June 1929, at what turned out to be the most inauspicious moment possible for the reputation of the party. Although its relative position in Parliament was stronger than had been that of the previous government in 1924, it was nevertheless a captive of the Liberals, who again held the balance of power. But worst of all, the accession of the second Labour government coincided with the world economic depression which not only swept away the cheerful heedlessness of Baldwinism, but which in addition so divided the Labour party that most of its parliamentary effectiveness disappeared.

MacDonald's government resembled his previous one. It was a combination of intellectuals and trade union leaders. However, this time MacDonald gave up the Foreign Office to Arthur Henderson, a man whose honesty and solid talents he tended to underrate. Snowden returned to the Exchequer. So far as Labour had a party platform during the election, it promised the restoration of the Conservative cuts in the social services and in housing. In 1930 a beginning was made by the passage of a comprehensive and large-scale slum-clearance programme and by the abolition of the requirement that a man applying for unemployment insurance benefit had to prove that he was 'genuinely seeking' work that both he and the unemployment officer knew did not exist. At the same time the government appointed a strong royal commission to investigate the entire problem of unemployment and to make recommendations for the insurance programme in the hope of bringing an end to the desperate series of expedients and improvisations that had constituted the history of the scheme since 1920.

Before the committee could report, indeed almost at the time it was appointed, came the beginning of the economic blizzard that would cut across all Labour programmes. The world depression, opening with the disastrous collapse of stock values on the New York Stock Exchange in the last week of October 1929 and ending only with the outbreak of the Second World War, divides the interwar history of nearly every European, North American, and Oriental industrial nation. It can be accounted a major reason for the Japanese expansion into Manchuria in 1931, for the rise of Hitler in 1933, and for the Italian invasion of Ethiopia in 1935. The depression brought an end to the era of Republican, business-oriented politics in the United States that had lasted since the election of Abraham Lincoln in 1860, and seemed for a time to threaten the American capitalist system itself. Finally, in Great Britain it destroyed for ever the illusion that the old prewar, unregulated, London-based, international economic world could somehow be revived. But curiously, while the effect of the depression in nearly all other democratic nations was to cause the election of radical parties, either of the right or of the left, in Britain it reinforced the place of Stanley Baldwin and the Conservatives.

The economic difficulties that led up to the crisis of 1931 began three years earlier with a slowing down of the movement of investment dollars from New York to London. This was caused first of all by the extreme profitability of investment in the soaring stock market in New York, and secondly by an increase in the United States Federal Reserve rediscount rate (bank rate), by which the government had hoped to check the borrowing of money for investment in the stock market. This deliberate tightening of the money market represented a reversal of previous policy. Hitherto, particularly since 1927, American interest rates had been kept low, partly to facilitate the movement of capital to England. But the American pre-occupation with stock-market speculation not only ended the flow of dollars to Great Britain (by late September 1929 the Bank of England discount rate was at the near-panic level of six and a half per cent), but to other European countries as well. These countries were now forced to turn to London or Paris for credit. In 1928 and 1929 British lending in Europe, particularly in Central Europe, rose rapidly. These investments made the stability of the British financial community dependent to an important extent upon the prosperity of Central Europe. British bankers could pay their debts to their foreign creditors only if their own debtors remained solvent.

At the end of October 1929, in a series of dismaying plunges, each of which wiped out hundreds of millions of dollars in stock values, the great crash began. Its immediate effect upon Great Britain was first to redirect some American investment abroad, and so to make somewhat easier the extremely tight credit situation in London. But these advantages quickly disappeared as other American investors, attempting to increase their liquidity, began to withdraw gold from London. In 1930, London lost £64 million in gold to New York and another £95 million to Paris. (France had deliberately undervalued her currency as Britain had overvalued hers. In effect, a given amount of gold would buy more francs and hence more goods in France than the same amount of gold would buy in pounds and similar English goods.) Still worse, in June 1930 President Hoover of the United States signed into law the Hawley-Smoot Tariff Act, the highest in American history, virtually excluding many imports from the American market. Other nations passed similar legislation. The result was that British exports that had been worth £729 million in 1929 dropped to £571 million in 1930 and £391 million in 1931. The index of industrial activity fell proportionately. It was 118 in 1929, 108 in 1930, and 86 in 1931. As factory output slowed, unemployment increased. In 1929 registered unemployment stood, as it had through-out most of the decade of the twenties, at about 1,200,000, or slightly more than ten per cent of all workers covered by unemployment insurance. By 1930 this figure leaped up to 1,975,000, or 16 per cent of the insured labour force. By 1931 it had increased nearly the same amount again, to 2,700,000, or 21·3 per cent of insured workers.

The decline of international trade and the increase of unemployment affected British finance and contributed to the crisis of 1931 in two separate ways. First, the rapidly growing claims for unemployment benefits put an almost killing strain on the always hard-pressed unemployment fund, and the fund's debt to the Treasury grew from £39 million for the fiscal year from March 1929 to March 1930, to £115 million for the fiscal year ending in March 1932. At the same time, parliamentary expenditures for benefit (mainly the 'transitional' benefit) increased from just under £12 million for the year ending March 1929 to almost £50 million for the year ending March 1932. In the two fiscal years between March 1930 and March 1932, total payments from the unemployment insurance fund, which had tended to average about £50 million since 1921, soared to over £101 million for the first year and almost £123 million for the second. One result of these expenditures, when combined with a decline in government revenue—even though Snowden as Chancellor of the Exchequer had increased income taxes—was a threatening series of budget deficits. (The national debt also increased, although not so rapidly as the tremendous expenditures on unemployment would suggest, because the deficit in the unemployment fund was not counted as part of the national debt.)

The second financial effect of the combination of falling exports, industrial stagnation, and unemployment was the appearance of a rapidly growing imbalance in Britain's trade. Imports fell far less slowly than exports, and the difference between the amount Britain spent abroad and the amount she was able to earn abroad had to be made up by gold. Thus the nation was at once exporting gold as capital for investment abroad—throughout almost the entire year of 1930—and exporting gold or, technically, claims upon sterling that were redeemable in gold, to pay for the surplus of imports over exports. Eventually a crisis was bound to come. The amount of pounds, redeemable in gold, held by creditors of Great Britain, far exceeded the amount of gold available to pay them off. The nation was in the position of a family that had been long living beyond its means. Any whisper of the family's threatened insolvency would bring all creditors at once, and potential bankruptcy would become an actuality.

The crisis began in May 1931 with the suspension of gold payments of the central bank of Austria, the Kredit-Anstalt. This bank itself was eventually able to avoid disaster, but as it had operated as a central bank and held deposits for other banks, not only in Austria, but throughout South Germany, its suspension of payments involved the solvency of all other institutions whose money it held. Thus, like a plague, the defalcation of one bank spread an infection to all others to which it was in debt. Within weeks banks throughout Germany were closing their doors as their depositors began to clamour for money. The run on the German banks affected the confidence of the creditors of British banks. Too many of the large loans made in Germany during the past five years represented money that Britain herself had borrowed. The security of the British financial community was now in question. If German banks could not make good on their own liabilities, British banks might default on theirs. Thus on 15 July, the day after the German government ordered all banks in that country closed, a run began on British banks which continued even after the German banks reopened on 18 July because of a partial moratorium placed by the German government on foreign payments. As creditors of British banks now began to demand the redemption in gold of bills and notes they held, the managers of British banks turned to the Bank of England, whose duty it was to guard the solvency of the British banking community. By the last week of July, the Bank of England was giving up gold to English merchant banks at the rate of £2,500,000 a day. The City had no other resources. The old reserve of foreign debts owed to London that could have been collected in gold and which, before the war, would have been the second line of defence, no longer existed. England herself was now not only a debtor nation but also one with an unfavourable balance of trade. By the end of July, the huge advances made by the Bank of England to the British financial community were threatening the reserve of the Bank itself, and at the end of the month it was forced to borrow £25 million each from the Bank of France and from the Federal Reserve Bank of New York.

The second stage of the crisis began on 31 July. On that day, with singularly bad timing, the government published the report of the Committee on National Expenditure, which had been appointed in February and was headed by Sir George May, previously Secretary of the Prudential Insurance Company. The May Committee's findings were a shock to Parliament and to the country. It estimated a government deficit of £120 million and, most important of all for a Labour government, proposed to meet this deficit largely by economies in government spending totalling £96 million, of which two-thirds, or over £66 million, would be found through wholesale cuts in the maintenance of the unemployed.

The May Committee's report quickly destroyed whatever confidence might have accrued as a result of the announcement of the large loans to the Bank of England. After a brief respite in the first week of August, the flight from the pound continued with gold withdrawals going on at such a rate that it was soon clear the new reserve would be exhausted by the end of the month. The question no longer was saving the credit of some private British banks which had made over-large loans abroad. Now the concern was to save the Bank of England itself and, by implication, the credit of Great Britain. In effect, by the middle of August, the crisis had become a political rather than a financial one. This was essentially the counsel given to the MacDonald government by the Bank of England directors. The crisis was less a matter of confidence in the stability of British financial institutions than in the intentions of the British government. Foreign banks, the representatives of the Bank of England intimated, had suggested that they would come to the aid of the Bank again only if the government itself gave indications of prudent and conventional finance, of the trimming of wasteful expenditure on social services, specifically of carrying out the recommendations of the May Committee.

The demand that the government take upon itself the responsibility for the institution of widespread economies in the social services so that foreign bankers would come to the aid of the Bank of England appeared to many Labour politicians as nothing more than an invitation for the party to commit suicide. From 20 August until 24 August the cabinet fought without reaching a compromise. Some members were willing to accept small economies, but a substantial minority led by Arthur Henderson were opposed to all cuts. On the 23rd, news was received from New York that the likelihood of a further loan was small unless Parliament enacted some recommendations of the May Committee. MacDonald immediately asked for the resignations of the members of his cabinet, conferred with the leaders of the opposition, and on the 24th announced to his former colleagues that there would be a coalition government with himself as Prime Minister.

So the second Labour government came to an inglorious end. The rank and file felt betrayed by their leaders, whom they now expelled. The leadership, principally MacDonald and Snowden, must have felt that the party had demonstrated that as yet it was unready to accept the responsibility of power. The effects on British history for the next ten years were lamentable. The Labour party was deprived of its best-known and most capable public figures except Henderson and J. R. Clynes. Unfortunately both of these men lost their seats in the general election called by the new government at the end of October. As a result Parliament, through one of the most critical periods in British history, functioned with a feeble, and almost leaderless, opposition. Criticism of government policies had to come from within the swollen majority itself.

CHAPTER THREE

The Baldwin Age, Part II: 1931-37

THE NATIONAL GOVERNMENT, 1931-35

The national government that took office on 24 August 1931 included, besides MacDonald and Snowden as Prime Minister and Chancellor of the Exchequer, Stanley Baldwin as Lord President of the Council and at the Ministry of Health Neville Chamberlain, who succeeded Snowden at the Exchequer in November. At the Foreign Office until November representing the Liberals was Rufus Isaacs, the Marquess of Reading. When the proposal for tariffs divided the Liberal party, Reading was succeeded by Sir John Simon, and a new group of coalition Liberals, the so-called 'Liberal Nationals', came into existence. (The 'Liberal Nationals', who since the Second World War have disappeared into the Conservative party, must be distinguished from the 'National Liberals', who were the Lloyd George wing of the Liberal party in the 1916–22 coalition.) Even though the party held surprisingly few of the great offices of state at the time of the formation of the cabinet, the directing force behind the new government almost from the beginning was the Conservatives. Stanley Baldwin was Prime Minister in everything but name.

Although the previous cabinet had received intimation on 23 August that further loans were unlikely unless the government immediately introduced economy legislation, the formation of the national government on 24 August brought, only four days later, an announcement of a new loan of £80 million from New York and Paris. The loan, it was noted, was not to the Bank of England, but to the British government itself. The reductions in expenditure that would balance the budget were not given to Parliament until nearly two weeks later on 10 September and were specified to take effect on 1 October. Snowden's emergency budget provided for decreases in spending of slightly over £70 million. Of this amount, exactly half, £35 million, came from decreases in unemployment benefits, which were cut by ten per cent, and from increases in contributions. Another large amount, over £15 million, was found by reducing the pay of school teachers, the fighting services, and the police. The reductions in pay of the fighting services caused a refusal of duty of the sailors of the Atlantic Fleet at Invergordon.

The 'mutiny' at Invergordon—not really a mutiny, more of a strike—had important consequences. After the establishment of the national government, the loan of 28 August, and Snowden's determined money-saving on 10 September, many journals, even the most well-informed, such as the *Economist*, assumed the panic was over. But clearly it was not. Besides the German financial crisis, which seemed incurable, there grew a general feeling of uneasiness as back-bench members of the Conservative party began to talk of an immediate general election on the question of a return to tariff protection. For many government supporters import duties were the only possible solution. They would help cure Great Britain's unfavourable balance of trade and so strike directly at the root of the gold problem. But they caused discontent among coalition Liberals and Labourites still wedded to free trade, and so seemed to weaken the national government. Invergordon, however, was the final blow. The 'disorders' were announced on 15 September. In the next four days, Treasury credits to the Bank of England amounted to £44 million, over half the total of the latest loan and nearly a quarter of the total amount of gold that left Great Britain during the entire crisis. On the 19th, Bank of England officials reversed all they had been saying for the previous decade and advised the government to declare at an end the Bank's obligation to sell gold at a fixed price. British consulates overseas were informed secretly of this decision the same day, and on 21 September the nation abandoned the convertible gold standard.

So the great decision was taken. The surprising thing was not that a large number of foreign bankers disapproved, or that the pound fell quickly in international markets to about three-quarters of its former value, but that in Great Britain the change scarcely was noticed. Domestic prices remained almost unaltered. (Indeed, between 1931 and 1936, the nation enjoyed its last period of price stability.) Until the coming of the Second World War, the pound was allowed to find its own level in the market. Its price reflected the demand for it by holders of foreign currencies, which demand itself was a result of the movement of capital in and out of Great Britain, of Britain's purchases and sales in international trade, and of the operation of the Exchange Equalization Account. Because, temporarily at least, British currency was cheaper in terms of foreign currency, British exports were proportionately lower priced and imports higher priced, and the tremendous imbalance of trade that had been behind the crisis of 1931 disappeared within two years. Probably the important result of leaving the gold standard was less that the British pound was no longer convertible into gold than that British currency was now devalued. In international terms, British goods were now markedly inexpensive. Until the devaluation of the American dollar in 1934, the purchasing power of the dollar for British goods was greater than it had been in 1913. Some of these advantages, however, were largely theoretical. Foreign nations facing depression at home raised tariff barriers against British goods, and, although export trade revived, it was subject now to restrictions and controls previously unknown.

This development leads to the last and perhaps the most important effect of the crisis of 1931, the ending of the nearly century-old policy of free trade that had been the symbol of Britain's commercial supremacy. The possibility of introducing some measure of protection had been an important reason for the Conservative backbench demand for a general election, which had appeared within days of the formation of the national government. On 21 September, the day that Britain went off the gold standard, the 1922 Committee formally resolved that an immediate general election should be held on the issue of the tariff. On 7 October, Parliament was dissolved, and on the 27th the election occurred. As both the Liberal and Labour members of the coalition were divided among themselves on the question of tariffs, the members of the government and their supporters could offer no agreed platform to the electorate, and could unite only in attacking the Labour opposition and playing upon the fears of the electorate. They asked for support to try any expedient—MacDonald called it 'a doctor's mandate'—that would contribute to the return of prosperity. To the Conservatives, to the Liberal followers of Sir John Simon, and to Ramsay MacDonald, this meant tariffs. To the Liberal followers of Herbert Samuel and to Philip Snowden, it meant anything else.

The result was an overwhelming victory for the government, but again, as in 1918, most of the candidates elected were Conservative by party affiliation. Of 554 supporters of the government, 473 were

Conservative, 33 were Samuelite Liberals, and 35 were Simonite Liberal Nationals. Only 13 so-called 'National Labour' men were elected. One of these was the Prime Minister. More than ever, MacDonald was a prisoner of the Conservatives, bound to take the blame for unpopular decisions not his own, impelled by vanity to cling to a powerless office. The Labour opposition contested 515 constituencies and received 6,600,000 votes, more than in any election except 1929, and yet seated only 52 candidates. Also in opposition as Independent Liberals were David Lloyd George and three members of his family.

The general election had made the national government Conservative in everything but name. No matter what the other members of the government felt, the Conservatives, under the leadership of Baldwin, Neville Chamberlain, and Walter Runciman, a former Liberal, determined to go forward immediately with protection for British markets. In November, as soon as Parliament met, a bill was rushed through to prevent the 'dumping' of foreign goods that would inevitably occur in anticipation of the general tariff. And in February 1932, with the Import Duties Act, Britain joined again the ranks of protectionist nations.

The act specifically exempted goods produced in the Empire. Tariff reformers had always argued that among its other advantages a tariff ought to be used to promote imperial consolidation by preferential lowering of duties upon goods produced in the colonies and dominions. It followed that the imposition of a tariff ought to be accompanied by a general agreement of British nations to work out the granting of reciprocal economic privileges. Accordingly, for a month in July and August of 1932, a conference of the British dominions met at Ottawa to set the rules for increasing imperial trade. Although Chamberlain, for whom tariffs represented a personal triumph of considerable proportions, had said at the Ottawa conference that the British Empire now had been 'born afresh', the leaders of the British delegation there, J. H. Thomas, a National Labourite, Chamberlain and Baldwin, soon discovered that the economic interests of the dominions and the mother country were by no means entirely complementary. The dominions were, to be sure, anxious to retain the British market for their foodstuffs and industrial raw materials, but all of them had emerging industries that they felt bound to protect. As a result, the conference was unable to arrive at a friendly and self-regulating general agreement for some form of imperial tariff union, and Britain had to content herself with a series of bilateral agreements with individual members of the Commonwealth. As a result of these agreements, some of the Liberals and Philip Snowden resigned from the MacDonald cabinet.

The effect of tariffs and imperial preference was more beneficial to the Empire than to Britain herself. British purchases from the Empire grew substantially; her sales to the Empire increased far less. In a period in which the prices of all kinds of raw materials were low, impact of tariffs on consumer prices was relatively small. The people hurt by protection were not the British buying public, but the old suppliers of British food, Argentina, for instance, and Denmark. At the same time the nation was able to use the weapon of its large domestic market to obtain favourable terms for the sale of British exports. (Between 1929 and 1938, the percentage of British imports bought from within the Empire grew from 25 per cent of all imports to 40 per cent. Exports to the Empire in the same period grew from 39 per cent of all exports to 45 per cent.)

As important as the beginnings of the political redirection of trade abroad were the possibilities offered by a protected market for undertaking economic planning at home. Planning took the form of what was in those days called 'rationalization' of industry, the closing down of redundant plant capacity and the amalgamation of industrial firms into larger units. This occurred particularly in steel and shipbuilding. The formation of larger steel companies and the construction of new steel plants in an industry with notoriously old-fashioned ideas was particularly the result of the increased profitability of steel-making that derived from tariff protection. British steel production was over 13 million tons by 1939, about 40 per cent more than ten years earlier. In shipbuilding rationalization meant closing and taking out of production obsolescent yards whose surplus capacity depressed prices for all. At the same time the government began to grant subsidies and easy loans for the building of new ships. While these resulted in a notable increase in British tonnage launched in the next few years, unemployment in shipbuilding remained large, 24 per cent in 1937. In towns where a local shipyard was closed—Jarrow, for example, where Palmer's yard was dismantled in 1934—scarcely a man in town received a regular wage.

In agriculture, government intervention was still more direct. Agricultural marketing boards had been established by Christopher Addison during the second Labour government. They received new powers and engaged directly in controlling the production and price of milk, bacon, potatoes and hops. In addition, producers of many commodities were given direct subsidies. This policy had the combined advantages of not antagonizing dominions who sold competing products to British markets and of bringing prosperity to the British farmer, while permitting the retail price of the domestic food subsidized to remain low.

Paradoxically, the one area of government activity most energetically pursued in the 1920s, housing, was nearly disregarded in the thirties. In each of the last five years before the war, well over 300,000 dwellings were built. This was nearly twice the number constructed annually in the 1920s. But whereas in the twenties nearly two-thirds of the houses and flats constructed were provided either by the local authorities themselves or by private enterprise with state assistance, in the next decade only a little more than a quarter received assistance from the state. In contrast to the American government and many others, Britain undertook little public construction of any kind. The task of reconstructing the nation's roads and public buildings and of rehousing the English working class was unfortunately not accomplished in the thirties when labour was plentiful and the cost of materials low.

The failure in this field is the more surprising in view of the cheapness of money. Certainly one of the most important catalysts of the economic revival that began in Great Britain after 1933, as well as an important promoter of the rationalization and modernization of the British industrial plant, was the availability of domestic risk capital. The situation was altogether unlike the previous decade when money had gone abroad to find investment and when the interest rate, to support the pound, had remained consistently high. Government economic policy in the 1920s, such as it was, had been oriented toward banks and the financial community. In the 1930s the needs of industry at last made themselves felt.

The advent of cheap money, as important as the tariff in aiding the remodelling of British industry, was a product of the departure from the gold standard. This fortuitous circumstance appears to have been practically unexpected. No one seems to have remembered that, as it was no longer necessary to maintain a gold backing for the pound, it was not necessary to attract gold to London by a high interest rate. Henceforth the international value of the pound would depend on the demand for that currency itself. This the government could control, in the short run anyway, by judicious purchases and sales of its own currency. Therefore, in 1932, the bank rate dropped to two per cent where it remained uniformly, with a short aberration in 1939, until 1951. The advantages were many. The government found it cheaper to service the national debt; manufacturers could borrow for new plants; builders could speculate in new houses.

The people who suffered were the unemployed. The rationalization of industry did not create new jobs. Frequently it destroyed old ones. The fall of prices caused the average wage throughout the period from 1933 to 1939 to be worth approximately ten per cent more than in 1929, but this did little for a man who earned no wages at all. On the other hand, it may help to account for Baldwin's continuing popularity. In the late thirties the majority of Englishmen were certainly better off than they had been a decade before. The sales of household goods, of houses, of motor cars, all attest to the spread of middle-class prosperity. The unemployed were still there, 1,300,000 of them at the time the war began, but they were scarcely visible. Although they gave huge majorities to their local Labour and Communist candidates, the very concentration of unemployment diminished its political effectiveness. Their spokesmen, such as Ellen Wilkinson and Aneurin Bevan, were vigorous and articulate. Unhappily they were few in number and no one listened to them. The absolute power of the cabinet in the House of Commons, the fatness of the Conservatives' parliamentary majority, and the absence of a committee system in which a determined minority could make itself heard made the unemployed feel not only disregarded, but forgotten. Even the distressed areas were renamed euphemistically 'Special Areas'. The disease that went uncured in the thirties left scars that had not healed after the war, and would continue into the sixties to affect the political behaviour of the trade unions and of the Labour party.

THE REAPPEARANCE OF FOREIGN AFFAIRS

As the great depression altered for ever the old presupposition of the British economic world, so also it affected British foreign affairs. Between 1929 and 1933, the postwar world became a prewar world. Before, European diplomacy, particularly British diplomacy, had been concerned with the rehabilitation of Germany. Britain had taken the lead in arranging the Locarno Pact of 1925. Germany's admission to the League the next year and the maiden speech of her Foreign Minister, Gustav Stresemann, on 10 September 1926, all seemed to indicate a genuine German desire for recognition as a peaceful nation. So far as there was fear and uncertainty in the world for Englishmen, it emanated from Russia. Certainly in the early years of the twenties, revolutionary Bolshevism had appeared to be a serious menace. But after the death of Lenin in 1924 and the elimination of Trotsky the next year, the Soviet Union's concern with the promotion of international disorder declined. Stalin's slogan of 'Socialism in One Country' and the inauguration of the five-year plans at the end of the decade manifested Russia's concentration on her domestic affairs.

Since the accession to power of Benito Mussolini in Italy in 1922, Italian foreign policy had shown, to be sure, a new vigour and truculence. But the Italians in the twenties were certainly far less of a problem to British diplomats than the French, and Mussolini's ability to organize Italy's traditionally undisciplined political and economic affairs (every Englishman knew that Italian trains now ran on time) evoked widespread admiration. Fascism seemed to be able to force a cooperation between capital and labour that strengthened society for the good of all. In the late twenties, with memories of the fear of domestic revolution and of the general strike still fresh, the corporate state appeared to have many advantages. In 1929, to the admiration of the world, Mussolini was able to make a peace with the Vatican and so end the long-standing estrangement between the Pope and the Italian state that dated from 1870.

With the depression everything changed. The response to economic hardship in virtually every nation of the world except Great Britain was political radicalism. Moderate democratic governments were overthrown and authoritarian governments found themselves forced to violence, usually in the form of military aggression. Within four years, the European alignments that would lead to the Second World War had appeared.

The trouble began in the Far East with the occupation of Manchuria by Great Britain's first modern ally, Japan. The Japanese had governed Korea since 1895 and after the Treaty of Portsmouth with Russia in 1905 had held special rights in the semi-independent, but Chinese-dominated, province of Manchuria. These rights consisted chiefly of political control of the naval base at Port Arthur at the southern tip of the Liaotung Peninsula and, more important, control over the operation and policing of the South Manchurian Railway that ran from Port Arthur to the city of Harbin in Central Manchuria. Here it connected with the Chinese Eastern Railway that was in fact the cross-Manchurian section of the Russian Trans-Siberian Railway which had its eastern terminus at the city of Vladivostok. In 1922, under pressure from the Pacific dominions and the United States, the bilateral military alliance with Japan was ended, and

Britain joined eight other powers with holdings in the Pacific in a mutual guarantee of Chinese territorial integrity and of the right of all nations to trade in China on equal terms—the so-called 'open door policy'.

No nation was more vulnerable to international trade depression than Japan. Her problems were those of Great Britain multiplied. She did not have the accumulated foreign investment nor the reserves of domestic wealth available in Great Britain. Her people lived far closer to the subsistence level, and any decline in the foreign consumption of her exports meant immediate hardship at home. For Japan the 1929 depression was a quick disaster. Exports that had amounted to 2,149 million yen in 1929 fell to 1,147 million yen in 1931. By 1931 also, nearly one-quarter of the industrial labour force was unemployed.

In the Far East, Japan had always looked for foreign markets that she could control politically. Here she had come into conflict with the United States and Great Britain, who supported free economic access to all oriental markets, especially China, and also with Russia, who sought economic and political control in competition with Japan. Potentially the richest market in the Far East, as Britain had known for a century, was China. Especially in Manchuria were reserves of industrial raw materials, particularly coal and iron, and a potential monopoly market that could be of greatest use to Japan.

The Japanese occupation of Manchuria technically was caused by the explosion of a small bomb that damaged very slightly part of the road bed of the South Manchurian Railway. On the twin contradictory excuses that China was attempting to make real her nominal sovereignty over Manchuria (which was true) and that on the other hand she was unable to protect properly Japanese property, the Japanese army, virtually without permission from the home government, occupied the city of Mukden. By the end of the year the Japanese had *de facto* control of all Manchuria.

The explosion on the South Manchurian Railway that began the Japanese occupation of Manchuria occurred in the midst of the British currency crisis, just two days before the devaluation of the pound and three days after the announcement of the 'mutiny' at Invergordon. Not surprisingly, the public and leading journals of opinion were little interested in the conquest of Manchuria. But China, awkwardly, insisted on bringing the matter before the Council of the League of Nations, which responded on 10 December by appointing a commission of inquiry, headed by the Earl of Lytton, to investigate the situation in the Far East. Once the commission was established, the League declined to take further action until the commission reported. The report was published in October. It showed considerable sympathy for the Japanese point of view, but nevertheless, when the League finally adopted the Lytton Commission findings in February 1933, Japan resigned from the international organization, and the League took no further action.

The League's failure to give effect to the recommendations of a commission of inquiry that it had itself appointed marked a turning point in the diplomatic history of the interwar period, just as the crisis of 1931 divided the phases of British domestic history in the same decades. Behind the Covenant of the League of Nations lay the assumption that all nations really desired peace and that war represented an aberration from the normal course of events. Although no one mentioned it yet, the ideal of collective security had disappeared. The postwar assumption that all first-class nations were equally interested in the maintenance of peace, the stability of international frontiers, and the settlement by peaceful means of international disagreements was clearly gone. In the eight years between September 1931, when Manchuria was occupied by Japan, and September 1939, when Japan's undeclared war with China merged into the general European war, world diplomacy moved from an occupation with the preservation of peace to the prevention of war. Instead of being concerned with the adjudication of international disagreements, which were presumed to cause conflict, Britain and France now were busy with the construction of diplomatic arrangements that would deter or appease a potential aggressor. The League of Nations still existed as a forum for appeals to international public opinion, but it meant nothing more. The world was divided between the totalitarian nations, who either wanted war or who were willing to use the threat of war as a weapon of diplomacy, and the Western European and American democracies, who were trying to avoid conflict at all costs.

HITLER

Any study of Britain's diplomatic history in the decade before the Second World War and of the nation's reaction to the appearance of German Nazism must take into account three basic assumptions— one might almost call them emotional responses—that were shared by the leaders of the country and by the nation at large. These were, first, that Germany had been treated unjustly in the peace settlement after the First World War and that the Treaty of Versailles was not worth defending. In this attitude there was a residue of the ill-feeling toward France that had built up in the twenties.

Secondly, by no means confined to Britain, there was a determination that the hideous experience of 1914–18 must not be repeated. A second world war was unthinkable. Added to this in Britain was a very broad strain of old-fashioned pre-First World War socialist pacifism. This attitude was particularly prevalent in the Labour party and was symbolized perhaps best by George Lansbury, who had succeeded Arthur Henderson as leader of the party in October 1931. Finally, although contempt for the settlement after the last war and fear of the consequences of the next were certainly determining factors in public opinion in the early thirties, the attitudes of the British people toward foreign affairs were perhaps more conditioned by fear of the cost of rearmament, ignorance of what Nazism meant, and most of all, by the overpowering importance of economic problems at home.

Adolf Hitler was appointed Chancellor of the German Republic on 30 January 1933, as the· League of Nations debated the Lytton report and when unemployment in Great Britain was close to its interwar peak. Hitler's accession, like the invasion of Manchuria itself, was almost completely a function of the great world depression. Despite constant appeals to German nationalism and promises to wipe out the stain of the Versailles humiliation, the Nazi party representation in the Reichstag had dropped from 32 in 1924 during the Ruhr invasion to 12 in the election of May 1928. But with the coming of the economic depression, the Nazi vote, as well as the Communist vote, soared. By the summer of 1932 the Nazis controlled 230 seats in a Reichstag of 611, coming closer to an absolute majority than did any party at any time under the Weimar Republic. These statistics illustrate an important fact about Hitler's coming to power. He had a better right to the chancellorship, and represented, so far as they expressed their feelings through votes, more nearly the wishes of the German people, than had any of his predecessors. In the years that followed, English newspapers frequently referred to the Nazi 'seizure of power'. This is true only in the technical sense that once Hitler was installed, he used the power he possessed in unconstitutional ways. His entrance to the Chancellorship came through perfectly normal parliamentary channels. The illegality occurred after he came to power, not before.

These circumstances had great influence on British public opinion and on the attitudes toward Hitler in the first months of his tenure.

The Nazi programme principally was viewed as a means of attacking the depression. Forcing cooperation between workers and employers and dissolving German trade unions into the Labour Front were not actions that an ordinary middle-class Englishman who had lived through the general strike could consider wholly bad. Even Winston Churchill, who realized the danger of Hitler earlier than most, remarked in his memoirs that he saw nothing objectionable in Hitler at the beginning. Moreover, there was in Mussolini's apparently successful programmes in modernizing and cleaning up Italy a ten-year-old example of Fascism of which many Englishmen approved.

Herein lay the germ of appeasement. Between 1933 and at least March 1939, British governmental leaders and, still more important, leaders of opinion outside the government, approved of the attempts to arrive at an 'understanding' with Germany. It was possible, the argument went, to deplore Nazi totalitarianism and its treatment of the Jews while admitting at the same time that Germany had genuine grievances about her treatment of the past 20 years. One might or might not approve of Hitler, but one could hardly deny that so long as the Allies themselves refused to disarm, as had been envisaged in the Treaty of Versailles, German demands for military equality had some justice. And certainly the principle of self-determination, in which the Allies professed to believe, dictated that the territories forcibly taken from Germany after the war ought to be returned if the populations living in those territories clearly wished it. Explicit in all this was the assumption that the settlement after the First World War had been unfair; it was not worth going to war to maintain. The only thing more terrible than war itself was an unjust war.

Finally, among the ingredients of the British attitude toward Nazism must be included the appeal made by Hitler on the basis of anti-Communism. Arguably this was more influential among the middle class than among the working class, and certainly it was more important in France than in Great Britain. Nevertheless, in decisions of foreign policy, on the matter of seeking an alliance with Russia or on choosing sides in the Spanish Civil War, many influential Englishmen, when offered a choice between Fascism and Communism, appear to have inclined toward Fascism.

The question of German equality in armaments had arisen well before Hitler came to power. In 1931, before the 15-year period stipulated in the Treaty of Versailles had run out, the small Allied garrisons in the Rhineland and along the east bank of the Rhine were withdrawn. The next year the Bruning government received a promise that general European disarmament would soon be discussed. Britain herself was anxious to obtain a general agreement on disarmament quickly. She was convinced that German equality ought to be achieved not by the rearmament of that nation but by the reduction of the armies and fleets of other nations. Accordingly, in February 1932, under the presidency of Arthur Henderson, a general disarmament conference of some sixty nations met in Geneva. Here Britain pressed for a phased programme of disarmament; France was unwilling to disarm until some effective system of international security had been achieved. Germany continually insisted that the Allies were already obligated to disarm, to which she added the implication after Hitler came to power that, since the victorious powers had not carried out the terms of their own treaty, Germany also was no longer bound by it.

Suddenly, on 14 October 1933, with the charge that the intransigence of other nations would always prevent her achieving equality in armament, Germany withdrew from the disarmament conference, and a few weeks later announced her impending resignation from the League of Nations. Although the other nations attempted to continue meetings in the spring of 1934, everyone knew that world disarmament was hopeless without agreement between France and Germany. Finally, on 11 June 1934, after a bitter statement by Arthur Henderson plainly charging France with the chief responsibility for its failure, the disarmament conference adjourned permanently. Germany now began to rearm openly, and in February 1935 reintroduced universal military conscription, admitted the existence of an air force, and formally denounced the disarmament clauses of the Treaty of Versailles.

While Germany was busily rearming, Britain dawdled. Political pressure against rearmament was overwhelming. Not all of it was genuine pacifism. Domestic arguments against British rearmament held that 'collective security' through the League of Nations was a reasonable alternative. Frequently also, there was fear of the cost of rearmament, particularly in view of the reductions in social services that had occurred in the last three years. Certainly this was the cause of the surprising outcome at the famous East Fulham by-election on 25 October 1933, just ten days after Hitler's withdrawal from the Geneva disarmament conference. Here a Conservative advocate of rearmament was defeated by an avowed pacifist in an election in which a Conservative majority of 14,521 was replaced by a Labour majority of 4,840. (Most journals commenting on this event at the time accounted for the swing by the fact that the Liberals who had supported the national government in October 1931 were now supporting Labour. In 1935 the seat returned to the Conservatives.)

Whatever were the real causes of the turnover of votes at East Fulham, the event had a profound effect on the mind of Stanley Baldwin. The lesson of Fulham, he said three years later in November 1936, was that the country was pacifist.

What chance was there within the next year or two of that feeling being so changed that the country would give a mandate for rearmament? Supposing I had gone to the country and said that Germany was rearming and we must rearm, does anybody think that this pacific democracy would have rallied to that cry at that moment? I cannot think of anything that would have made the loss of the election from my point of view more certain.

As the result, except for some plans to increase the air force, British rearmament was put off for two years, until March 1935. By this time, Germany had announced military conscription. 'Collective security' through the League of Nations was dead. (This deal continued to provide a useful excuse for those who opposed rearmament but did not wish to appear heedless of their country's safety.)

For a moment it appeared that the Nazis' own reckless acts might make British rearmament unnecessary. On 25 July 1934, soon after the final adjournment of the disarmament conference, National Socialists in Vienna murdered the Austrian Chancellor, Engelbert Dollfuss. Their intent was to overthrow the Austrian government and force a unification of the country with Germany. This action was frustrated by the Austrians themselves, but more particularly by the quick reaction of Mussolini, who hurriedly sent a number of Italian divisions to the Austrian frontier. For Italy, no less than for Britain and France, a growing, expanding Germany was a menace. Moreover, under Mussolini, Italy had been spending large sums on weapons and presumably was a worthwhile ally. Hence the last half of 1934 saw a growing friendship first between France and Italy that quickened in January 1935, when the citizens of the Saar Basin voted almost unanimously to break off their connexions with France and return to Germany, and became still warmer in February with German conscription. In the spring of 1935 Britain was drawn in, and on 11–14 April the three new friends met at Stresa to attempt to work out some common position against the German menace. Although Mussolini had expected little from the Stresa Conference and had no intention of permitting himself to be used as an instrument of French or

British policy, the formation of the 'Stresa Front' represents the peak of cooperation against Germany among the old First World War allies, and its collapse marks the real beginning of the Rome–Berlin Axis. Finally, in attempting to maintain an atmosphere of cordiality with Italy, Britain and France carried out the first clearly defined act of appeasement.

Britain herself made the first breach of the Stresa Front. On 18 June Sir Samuel Hoare, who had succeeded Simon as Foreign Secretary eleven days before, and the German Ambassador to Great Britain, Joachim von Ribbentrop, concluded a naval agreement in which Britain recognized the right of Germany to build battleships —she was building them anyway—up to 35 per cent of British tonnage. Although after the treaty many British admirals no doubt breathed more easily in the thought that a naval race similar to the one before 1914 had been avoided, the agreement was roundly denounced abroad. It seemed to be an act of supreme opportunism. It was the first sanction among the former allies of Germany's violation of the Treaty of Versailles and it had been concerned with weapons of peculiar interest to Great Britain. It was regarded as a signal for all nations to scramble to make such terms as they could with Hitler. Whatever the Stresa Front had been worth before, it was worth less now.

Meanwhile Mussolini, growing increasingly contemptuous of the determination of his former allies to resist aggression against any territory other than their own, was preparing for the invasion of Ethiopia. Italy had been manufacturing grievances against the ancient African nation since December 1934. At the Stresa meeting Mussolini had informed, or thought he had informed, Britain and France of his intentions to expand into that nation. Through the summer of 1935, while Britain was almost wholly preoccupied with the Silver Jubilee of King George V, Italian pressure built up against Ethiopia. Ethiopia sought to bring her position as a potential victim of aggression before world opinion by appeals to the League of Nations, and although people throughout the Western world were touched by the unfortunate position of the small kingdom threatened by forces of aggression, little was done. Finally, on 3 October 1935, Italian military and air forces moved into Ethiopia. Now, spurred by a particularly firm speech from Hoare, the League acted. Within a week the council and the assembly had declared Italy an aggressor and had voted economic sanctions against her. Technically, all members were obligated neither to buy from Italy nor to sell to her a number of important raw materials—rubber, tin and various other metals, but excluding oil. Unfortunately, these obligations did not extend to non-members of the League, most important of whom were Japan, Germany, Russia and the United States.

The quick action of the League in applying sanctions to a declared aggressor was a political triumph for the Baldwin government. The summer of 1935 had seen the publication of the 'Peace Ballot', a gigantic attempt at unselective mass polling organized by the British League of Nations Union. (A year later the *Literary Digest* poll in the United States, which was organized along somewhat the same lines, predicted the overwhelming election of Alfred Landon over Franklin Roosevelt.) The important conclusion of the Peace Ballot, among several other questions, was that ten and a half million of eleven and a half million responses supported the use of economic sanctions against aggressor nations. Now, just four months later, the government had responded to this overwhelming vote of confidence in the League of Nations by using that agency to deter aggression precisely in the way its founders and the majority of the British population intended that it should be. It was an ideal time to renew the four-year-old Parliament, and so, on 25 October, less than three weeks after the League council had declared Italy an aggressor, Parliament was dissolved and the general election fixed for 14 November.

In the campaign, all the advantage lay with the government. Although unemployment was still high, Chamberlain could claim with justice that four-fifths of prosperity had returned. (It might have been fairer to say that four-fifths of the nation was prosperous.) But the key issue was foreign affairs. Here the government had the best of two worlds. It had made collective security through the League a reality as the pacifists and anti-rearmers desired. At the same time it had pleased the more bellicose segment of the nation by refusing to sanction totalitarian aggression.

Predictably the election returned a large majority for the Conservatives. The party elected 432 Members of Parliament, but Labour increased its popular vote by nearly two million and returned 154 candidates. Because 33 of the new majority were Liberal Nationals and eight were National Labour, the government was still technically a coalition, although Baldwin had succeeded the rapidly failing Ramsay MacDonald as Prime Minister on 7 June. In any case the differences between the Conservatives and the Liberal Nationals had practically disappeared.

Even though the election had been fought, and won, on the government's firm support of the League and its apparent new-found vigour in foreign policy, there were many in the cabinet and out of it, led by Sir Samuel Hoare, who felt that the Stresa Front and friendship with Italy should be maintained at all costs. If the guarantors of the Treaty of Versailles were to remain united, it was argued, Britain and France must agree to a compromise over Ethiopia that would permit the withdrawal of sanctions before Mussolini became angered. Hoare proposed a partition of Ethiopia, giving the lowlands to Italy and leaving the highlands and the capital at Addis Ababa to Emperor Haile Selassie. On 7 December, with full knowledge of the cabinet, Hoare went to Paris, presented his plan to the French Premier, Pierre Laval, who approved of it strongly, and then went on to Geneva. There the Ethiopians would be presented with a demand for the partition of their country. They could accept it and retain some portion of their old sovereignty, or reject it and lose their entire nation. Then, as frequently happened in France under the Third Republic, the news of government plans leaked to the press. British opinion reacted in an explosion of anger and scorn. Hoare, who was unable to return immediately from Geneva to explain himself because of an ice-skating accident that broke his nose, was disavowed and allowed to resign. He was succeeded at the Foreign Office by Anthony Eden.

The furore over the Hoare–Laval agreement destroyed any possibility of the maintenance of the Stresa Front, but in a larger sense it also ended for ever whatever usefulness the League retained as a protector of small nations. It appeared to the world that not only the dictators but the Western powers were unwilling to play fairly with the League. Britain and France had saved neither Ethiopia nor Italy's friendship, although for the next three years Neville Chamberlain pursued the will o' the wisp of accommodation with Mussolini. In the process the two nations brought upon themselves the contempt of the world. The first overt attempt to buy off the dictators had been a disastrous failure.

THE CRITICAL YEAR—1936

The course of events that led up to Britain's declaration of war upon Germany on 3 September 1939 can be divided at 1936. Before 1936 Germany was principally concerned with the attainment of equality in armaments. After 1936, her aim was territorial expansion, the bringing of all Germans into a single political unit. For Britain, the year marks the end of two contradictory policies, each of which contributed to the lack of success of the other. On one hand Britain was attempting to organize Europe against Germany. At the same time she looked for agreement with Germany on the matters of armament and defence. In 1936, specifically after 'the German remilitarization of the Rhineland, British rearmament began in earnest, if slowly, and the previous search for an agreement on armament became a search for an agreement on the territorial size of the Third Reich. In 1936 also France abdicated her position as the chief enforcer of the Treaty of Versailles and permitted virtually all her diplomatic decisions where Germany was concerned to be made by Britain.

Hitler watched the inept conspiracies of Britain, France and Italy with much interest. In 1935, he had gone from success to success. On the crest of the prestige accruing from the overwhelming vote of the Saarlanders in January to return to Germany, he began the public rearmament of his nation. Then in June he had received a partial sanction of his actions in the Anglo-German Naval Treaty. He knew Mussolini feared and distrusted him and had no desire to share the European continent with an all-powerful Germany. Yet he could reasonably hope also that the clumsiness of the Allies might drive Italy toward him. Meanwhile he could use their preoccupation with the Ethiopian invasion, moving ahead rapidly in the early months of 1936, to his own advantage. A recent French diplomatic move had given him the excuse he needed to act.

Early in 1934, Louis Barthou, one of the most active and energetic of a rather undistinguished line of French foreign ministers in the 1930s, began negotiations with the Soviet Union for a mutual assistance pact against Hitler. Unfortunately, in November 1934, Barthou and King Alexander of Yugoslavia were assassinated in Marseilles during a state visit. Barthou was succeeded as Foreign Minister by Pierre Laval, who became Premier in June 1935, and who had far less interest in the Russian agreement than his predecessor. Whether it was from fear of antagonizing Hitler, as has been suggested, or simply from dislike of Communism and the Soviet Union, which is more likely, Laval delayed nearly a year, until November 1935, before submitting the pact to the French Chamber of Deputies, and did little to speed its progress once it was before that body.

Through the autumn and winter of 1935–6, while the world watched the Italian attack on Ethiopia, Hitler behaved with unusual discretion and forbearance. Germany took no part in the sanctions against Italy, and the German press, practically alone in the world, refrained from denouncing the Italian aggression. These favours were remembered by the Italians who, as has been noted, were not normally disposed toward friendship with the Germans. In the first months of 1936, as the Russo-French mutual assistance agreement was making its leisurely way through the French Chamber of Deputies and Senate and the League of Nations was debating the advisability of applying oil sanctions to Italy, even though the conquest of Ethiopia was nearly complete, Hitler prepared to take what was perhaps his largest peacetime diplomatic gamble.

By the terms of the Treaty of Versailles, the Rhineland, that part of Germany lying west of the Rhine along the borders of France, Luxembourg, Belgium and the Netherlands, had been permanently demilitarized. Germany had confirmed the demilitarization voluntarily in the Locarno Treaty. Indeed, since the spring of 1935, she had been proposing an extension of Locarno to cover violation of international boundaries by aircraft. Early in March, Hitler reiterated his interest in peace and the extension of European security in a special interview with the French press, and on 7 March promised to make known Germany's position on the 'Western Air Locarno'.

Instead, on Saturday 7 March, with photographers present and newsreel cameras turning, about 20,000 German troops crossed the Rhine bridges into the forbidden Rhineland. In the afternoon, in a bombastic speech before the Reichstag, Hitler justified his action as a protection against the planned encirclement of Germany. Specifically, he cited the Franco-Russian mutual-assistance pact as a violation of the spirit of Locarno. He pointed out that the world did not appreciate the dangers of Bolshevism, that Germany was therefore doing a service to the world as a protector against the barbarian East, and concluded by saying that he was now ready for 'real, honest, and equal European cooperation . . .' excluding Russia. He offered to sign non-aggression pacts with France and Belgium if they felt themselves threatened by his action. He would now re-enter the League of Nations, if the League would sever its connexions with Versailles, and proposed again the extension of the Locarno guarantee of all frontiers to violations by air.

The remilitarization of the Rhineland took the world completely by surprise, although, since the beginning of the Nazi period, army barracks in the Rhineland had been occupied by some 30,000 'special police'. France, for whom danger was the greatest and for whom the demilitarization of the Rhineland represented one of the few remaining securities against a revived Germany, declined into a state of virtual nervous shock. Although it is now known that German forces had orders to withdraw in case of French mobilization, France was unwilling to act without the solid support of Great Britain, and this was not forthcoming. Baldwin confessed that Britain was not in a position to enforce the Versailles treaty. Lord Lothian's well-known statement that the Rhineland was after all only Germany's 'back yard' probably represented the popular consensus. Hitler's reiterated promises that he had no further territorial ambitions received considerable notice in the papers. (During the war Hitler remarked in the course of a dinner-table conversation that he had received 'great assistance' from the *Daily Mail* on the 'reoccupation of the Rhineland and the naval programme'.) After all, the reoccupation of one's own territory could hardly be termed aggression. The public that had so recently driven Sir Samuel Hoare from office for the appeasement of Italy declined to react upon this far more dangerous violation of the now despised peace settlement.

Perhaps the most serious result of the Rhineland occupation was the great enhancement it gave Hitler's prestige and the corresponding weakening of the resolution of other countries. The summer of 1936 saw the beginning of the formation of the Rome–Berlin Axis. This was facilitated by the diplomatic cooperation of the two dictators in Spain, where civil war broke out in July, and by Hitler's promise to respect Austria's independence. Later, in the so-called 'October Accord', Hitler recognized the newly founded colonial territory of Italian East Africa. At almost the same time he signed the Anti-Comintern Pact (directed theoretically at the Communist International, rather than at the USSR) with Japan, which nation would invade the main body of China in the summer of the next year. In October also Belgium denounced her defensive alliance with France and proclaimed her neutrality in all international disputes. An important result of this decision was that the coordination of Franco-Belgian defensive arrangements, the linking of the great fixed works of the French Maginot Line with the Belgian emplacements along the Albert Canal and the Meuse River, were never accomplished.

At the beginning of 1936, Germany, for all practical purposes, had been diplomatically isolated in Europe. By the end of the year, the coalition of Axis powers that would fight the Second World War had been born. The same period saw the final destruction of the institutions and ideals of the twenties, the League of Nations, the Locarno spirit, collective security, which had been intended to secure peace for all time. The victors of the First World War had been separated, and France in the next three years relinquished virtually all diplomatic initiative to Great Britain.

The Spanish Civil War began on 17 July 1936, with the rebellion by a number of units of the Spanish Foreign Legion in Morocco. Generally, the rebels represented conservative, clerical, aristocratic and militaristic elements in the nation who sought to overthrow what they regarded as the excessively republican, democratic and socialistic government that had controlled Spain since 1931. Hence, in the Spanish Civil War, the loyalist and leftist elements represented the government, while the rightist, technically conservative, elements were the revolutionaries.

In the beginning, the rebellion was purely a domestic affair growing from internal difficulties, but Spain soon became a testing ground for foreign weapons and a battlefield where the ideologies of Fascism fought democratic idealism and Communism. It was, in effect, a microcosm of the Second World War. The Spanish rebels soon began to receive war material from Germany and Italy and before the war came to an end in the spring of 1939, nearly 100,000 Italian soldiers also were employed. More slowly and in much smaller amounts, the loyalists, or government forces, received material aid from Soviet Russia with some help coming from voluntary groups in other countries. In addition, as the ideological aspects of the conflict grew clearer, substantial numbers of Western European and American volunteers from liberal and socialistic organizations, including about 2,000 men from Britain, came to fight for the Spanish government.

The fact that the republican government was receiving aid from Soviet Russia tended to taint it in the eyes of British, particularly Conservative newspapers, although all public opinion polls in Great Britain showed that the Spanish rebels and their leader, General Francisco Franco, had almost no sympathy among the population at large. (Two opinion polls taken in March and October 1938 showed that 57 per cent of the population in both cases hoped that the government would win. Franco received seven per cent in the first poll and nine per cent in the second.) But at the same time there was real nervousness in the government, lest a loyalist victory mean that a Communist nation would emerge at the western end of the Mediterranean, while the Conservative press almost uniformly held that a government dominated by General Franco would seek to find some traditional Spanish accommodation with Great Britain. Rarely had British opinion been so divided on any subject of foreign policy. Justice, morality and human dignity seemed to reside with the government, who found articulate spokesmen in such writers as W. H. Auden; the American, Ernest Hemingway; and in George Orwell, whose *Homage to Catalonia* stands as one of the great narratives of battle to come from the Spanish Civil War or any war. On the other side, diplomatic expediency and national economic interest seemed to dictate a policy of hands-off, or 'non-intervention' as it was called. At bottom, the question for the British government was not whether it should aid the loyalists or the rebels, but rather whether it should aid the loyalists or refrain from helping anyone. The decision, the easy decision too frequently taken by Baldwin, was to do nothing. This meant non-intervention.

At the end of August 1936 the International Non-Intervention Committee was born. Specifically, the committee was to enforce an agreement signed by Britain, France, Germany, Italy and Russia, all of whom promised to refrain from sending aid or otherwise interfering with the warring factions in Spain. The committee set up a headquarters in London in September, but not until the next spring, after persistent obstruction by the representatives of Germany and Italy, was it able to agree upon a scheme of enforcement. Even so, non-intervention was always a fiction. It never meant that war material did not enter Spain; it simply meant that the loyalists got no official help from the Western democracies, while the rebel forces received ever-increasing amounts from Germany and Italy. It satisfied those in Britain who wished to maintain a pose of neutrality and to avoid the danger of a straightforward confrontation between the Western democracies and dictators while ensuring also that General Franco eventually would win the war.

The civil war dragged on until the end of March 1939, when Madrid surrendered to the rebel forces. The incredible brutality and cruelty, particularly to the civilian populations of towns occupied by the rebel forces, might have become a serious embarrassment to the British government had not other events by this time diverted public attention.

THE ABDICATION OF EDWARD VIII

The abdication of King Edward VIII on 11 December 1936 constitutes the third great crisis of Stanley Baldwin's political life. In this affair, for which there were no precedents to guide him, and yet in which everything was governed by tradition, where public profession and private policy were frequently contradictory, in which he had to anticipate a public opinion that had not yet been formed because the public was ignorant of the facts of the case, Baldwin displayed his political talents at their best. Here was Baldwin conspiring for morality, intriguing for justice, bringing the pressure of the social establishment of England to bear on the man who was its leader, eventually making him understand that the very tradition he represented must make him quit the post he desired to keep.

The facts of the abdication story can be recited briefly. As Prince of Wales, Edward had moved in fashionable London society as none of his predecessors, save only Edward VII and George IV, had done since the days of the glorious revolution. There had been comment upon the fact that when George V died on 20 January 1936, the new king at the age of 41, despite an obvious interest in women, was still a bachelor. However, he had by this time determined to marry Wallis Simpson, an American woman who had been previously married to an American naval officer and who now was married to a British citizen, Mr Ernest Simpson, a London stockbroker. Beyond the bare announcement by the court circular on two occasions of the Simpsons' attendance at Palace functions, on one evening in company with the Baldwins, British newspaper readers knew nothing of the king's friendship for Mrs Simpson, although by the late summer rumours in foreign papers were widespread. What Baldwin knew himself, or suspected, he did not reveal. Characteristically, he permitted the crisis to develop until circumstances forced him to act.

The critical chain of events began on 20 October, when Baldwin, having heard that Mrs Simpson was seeking divorce from her husband in court at Ipswich, asked the king about her and requested that the divorce suit be withdrawn. (By coincidence Ipswich was the birthplace of Thomas, Cardinal Wolsey, the minister most concerned with the only other royal divorce in British history. It possesses also the only Edward VIII post box in the United Kingdom.) Edward, apparently mistaking Baldwin's intent, did not realize the gravity of his situation. The divorce was not withdrawn, and a decree nisi, permitting Mrs Simpson to marry again in six months, was granted on 27 October. The case received no publicity in the British press. The king now was able, or soon would be, to marry Mrs Simpson, and Baldwin had to act. Within two weeks the lines of contest between the king and his first minister had hardened. Edward desired to be king, but he wished also to marry Mrs Simpson as quickly as possible. Baldwin was determined that, under these circumstances, he could not be king and must abdicate. He reminded Edward of the nonconformist conscience of Northern England and of the inextricability in the popular mind of the monarchy and the established Church. There is no question that he correctly described the sort of monarchy that Englishmen expected to have, no matter what standards of personal behaviour they set for themselves. Although there were demonstrations in his favour outside Buckingham Palace, frequently by extremists of the right or left, the king had virtually no support inside the world of politics except from a few individuals, Churchill, Beaverbrook and Rothermere being the most important. These men were motivated less by a conviction of the rectitude of the king's position than by a dislike of Baldwin.

Apparently the king briefly hoped to solve his problem through a morganatic marriage, one in which Mrs Simpson would be his wife but not queen. Baldwin continually insisted that such an arrangement, whether or not it was acceptable in the Austro-Hungarian Empire, was unknown in English law and refused to let the king put his case before the people by radio. Whatever chance there might have been for educating public opinion came to an end on 2 December when a chance remark by a provincial bishop about the king's need for grace, carried in the *Yorkshire Post*, ended the secrecy that had surrounded the crisis at the apex of the British government. Unless they had read continental or American newspapers while abroad (foreign papers coming into England were censored by their wholesalers), hitherto the average Englishman had known nothing of the crisis.

Between 2 and 6 December, when the king's final decision to abdicate was made, Baldwin was able to convince Edward that he had to choose between Mrs Simpson and the throne. No compromises were possible. On 10 December, the Speaker announced in the House of Commons that the king had determined to leave the throne and had signed an instrument of abdication. The next day an abdication bill passed through both houses and received the royal assent. That evening by radio the former king, now Prince Edward, introduced by the director of the BBC himself, Sir John Reith, said farewell to the British people in an admirable speech reportedly written by Winston Churchill. Nothing in Edward's short period on the throne, it has been said, so became him as his manner of leaving it.

The political results of the abdication crisis are too frequently overlooked. Because the impact on the monarchy itself was slight—the happy domesticity and attention to duty, particularly during the war, of George VI and Queen Elizabeth quickly healed any wounds—historians until most recently have looked on the affair simply as an aberration in a rather gloomy political period. This is far too simple an interpretation. The Hoare–Laval affair, the invasion of the Rhineland, the final Italian victory in Ethiopia in May, and the abandonment of sanctions in July, the last defeat being underlined by the disturbing eloquence of the diminutive Emperor of Ethiopia, served to emphasize the flabbiness and fecklessness of the Conservative government. During the summer of 1936, London was filled with rumours that Baldwin would soon resign. His old imperturbable self-confidence seemed to have deserted him and he sat hunched on the Treasury bench under fiercer and fiercer denunciations by Churchill and Lloyd George without the ability even to reply. The skilful handling of the abdication at once both rehabilitated Baldwin and diminished, for a time, the prestige of his enemies. The king disappeared as if by magic; a new one appeared leaving no visible scar. Churchill and a small group of his supporters, 'The King's Friends', seemed clumsy and outrageous by comparison. And so when Baldwin retired to the House of Lords on 28 May 1937, having remained in office only long enough to see George VI safely crowned, he departed on a wave of popularity, really of personal affection, that no Prime Minister of the twentieth century, not excepting Winston Churchill, has enjoyed upon leaving public life. The appalling revelations of British unpreparedness destroyed this when the war came, but for the moment his enemies were confounded, their voices stilled, their stature diminished. This was unfortunate in the years that lay ahead. For Britain and for the world Baldwin's triumph was a disaster.

CHAPTER FOUR

The Years of Muddle, 1937–40

APPEASEMENT

Neville Chamberlain kissed hands as Prime Minister on 28 May 1937. His succession had long since been taken for granted, both by himself and by the political world. 'There is no one else', he wrote that day, 'and perhaps . . . I have not made enemies by looking after myself rather than the common cause. . . .' In this he was right. He was by far the strongest man in the ministry. He was proud of his reputation for administrative expertise and, as he had noted in his diary, of his willingness to risk his political career for principle. He had done this in the budget of that very year with an innovation of his own, the National Defence Contribution, a tax on the rising profits of industries that were newly prosperous because of rearmament.

Yet even as Baldwin's chosen successor, Chamberlain certainly had no intention of permitting his administration to be simply a continuation of the previous one. He knew as well as anyone that Baldwin's cabinet had been dominated by older men whose tendency on any proposal, as the *Spectator* remarked in April when Baldwin had announced his retirement, had been to say either 'no', or 'wait and see'. This, thought the *Spectator*, accounted for the blight of the special areas and for the 'nerveless drift' in foreign policy.

Unquestionably the new Prime Minister intended to change this state of affairs. He looked upon himself as a man of action, a man with a programme. The essence of Baldwinism had been the absence of a programme and the continual adjustment to changing conditions. Particularly abroad Chamberlain would seize the initiative. Instead of responding in helpless agitation to the actions of the nations seeking to revise the Treaty of Versailles, he would put Britain in the lead actively seeking a compromise with Germany. He was confident of his powers of persuasion and of the logic of his position. Once the German trouble spots were cleared up, a general European settlement would be possible.

In pursuit of his policy of accommodation, Chamberlain met resistance not only in Parliament, but within his own Foreign Office. He was not comfortable with Foreign Office personnel, nor indeed with his Foreign Secretary, Anthony Eden, who had replaced the unfortunate Hoare, and whom he had inherited from Baldwin. Still less, however, did he like the Permanent Under-secretary at the Foreign Office, Sir Robert Vansittart, who urged resistance to Germany in long, stylized, literary memoranda that offended Chamberlain's terse and practical mind. At the end of 1937, Vansittart, although only 57 years old, was removed from his post in the civil service and given the meaningless title of Special Diplomatic Adviser to the Foreign Secretary.

So far as he depended on anyone for advice, the Prime Minister looked to Sir Horace Wilson, a man with very little diplomatic experience but with a personality similar to Chamberlain's own. Wilson's career had been chiefly in the Ministry of Labour, and Chamberlain had come to know him well at the Ottawa Conference in 1932 where he carried the title of Chief Industrial Adviser to the Government. Chamberlain used Wilson frequently in confidential assignments, particularly in connexion with the Munich Conference. In 1939, upon the retirement of Warren Fisher, the Prime Minister appointed Wilson Permanent Secretary of the Treasury and head of the civil service. Wilson shared Chamberlain's faith in the efficacy of personal conferences, in the ability of sensible men always to find a compromise, and he had, like the Prime Minister, a smug confidence in his own ability to master the facts of any situation. Unfortunately for Britain, and for the world, he shared, instead of compensating for, Chamberlain's weaknesses. Wilson, one historian of the period has remarked, 'from the best of motives was the worst of advisers in foreign affairs'.

Through most of his first year as Prime Minister, from the spring of 1937 to the spring of 1938, Chamberlain concentrated on finding an understanding with Mussolini. The outstanding problem in Europe was the civil war in Spain. Here Italian participation was becoming increasingly obvious. Italian submarines attacked supply ships sailing toward loyalist-held ports and Mussolini openly boasted of the number of regular army units employed fighting on the side of the rebels. Nevertheless, from Chamberlain's point of view and from the point of view of his advisers, a Fascist government in Spain was preferable in many ways to a Russian-oriented republican one. In any case, interference with Italian aid was certainly not worth the risk of driving Mussolini further into the German camp. On the other hand, the profits of a general agreement with Italy, aimed particularly at the maintenance of the *status quo* in the Mediterranean area, might be great. At the same time, but separately, there could be a search for a compromise with Germany over the danger spots in northern Europe.

In this policy Chamberlain was opposed by Anthony Eden, who argued that any general conference with the Italians should be preceded by an agreement on the conditions and the timetable for the withdrawal of Italian troops from Spain. So long as he was not tied by prior conditions Mussolini was more than willing to attend a conference. From his point of view it would be no trouble. The meetings could be prolonged indefinitely, and any promises made could be kept or not, as the situation required. While it was in progress, troops in Spain would move ahead toward winning the war. In the midst of the rising controversy with Eden on the terms of a conference with Italy, on 4 January 1938, Chamberlain received a confidential note from the American President Franklin Roosevelt, suggesting a general European meeting to consider ways of reducing tension. Only three months earlier, in a sensational speech calling upon peace-loving nations to band together to 'quarantine' aggressor nations, Roosevelt had tried, and had completely failed, to rouse American opinion about the growing danger abroad. His proposal to Chamberlain, Under-Secretary of State Sumner Welles explained, represented the only road to action left open. Chamberlain desired advice neither from his own Foreign Secretary nor from Franklin Roosevelt. He was confident of his ability to bring Mussolini to reason. He rebuffed, therefore, the first tentative steps toward American participation in European affairs and on 20 February accepted with some relief the resignations of his Foreign Secretary and the Under-Secretary, Lord Cranborne. Chamberlain appointed Viscount Halifax Foreign Secretary and now himself undertook the major explanations of foreign policy in the House of Commons.

Meanwhile began the series of events that within a month would lead to the annexation of Austria by Germany. On 12 February 1938, the Austrian Chancellor who had succeeded Dollfuss, Dr Kurt Schuschnigg, was summoned by Hitler to his Bavarian retreat at Berchtesgaden. Here he received a violent lecture from Hitler on the importance of the protection of Austrian Germans and a virtual ultimatum to take the leader of the Austrian Nazi party, Arthur von Seyss-Inquart, into his government as Minister of the Interior. Demands for unification of Germany and Austria were, of course, by no means new. Twice before since the war Austria had pleaded to be included in Germany and both times France had objected. More important in the present situation, on the very first page of his political testament, *Mein Kampf*, Hitler had mentioned as a matter of absolute importance the unification, or *Anschluss*, of Germany and Austria. But since the clumsy Nazi attempt at overthrow of the Austrian government in 1934 and the prompt Italian reaction, the danger of forcible unification seemed to have subsided and in 1936, among many other guarantees, the German Chancellor had included the integrity of Austria.

Nevertheless, by the autumn of 1937 Austria was clearly in danger. The cooperation of the totalitarian powers in the war in Spain, a triumphal visit by Mussolini to Germany in September of that year, Italy's adherence to the German-Japanese Anti-Comintern Pact on 6 November 1937, and her withdrawal from the League of Nations in December all suggested a growing spirit of cooperation among the two European Fascist powers that promised little hope for any future Italian protection of Austria. Even though Mussolini continued to lure Chamberlain with the hint that Italian military forces might protect Austria in return for British concessions in Spain and for British recognition of the Italian conquest of Ethiopia, postwar evidence shows he had long since decided that Germany's side was likely to be the winning one. (German diplomatic documents indicate that Mussolini told Göring as early as January 1937 that he would not forcibly intervene against an *Anschluss*.)

Chamberlain misread the signs of Italian-German collaboration. He sacrificed his Foreign Secretary and the possibility, unfortunately slight, of some American collaboration in Europe for the possibility of an Italian agreement. He accepted at face value Italian ambassador Dino Grandi's assurances that Italy and Germany had made no agreements concerning Austria. He further allowed himself to be convinced that it was only lack of Italian agreement with Britain that prevented Mussolini from moving troops into the Brenner Pass to support Austria. Grandi had implied that further conversations would encourage Mussolini, as Chamberlain noted contentedly in his diary, to take a 'more independent line' against Germany. Britain's attitude towards Austria's integrity, like her attitude toward Ethiopia's integrity, was thus determined by her policy toward Italy. But whereas in the earlier case she had hoped to buy Italy's friendship with the sacrifice of the African nation, in the present situation she hoped to buy Italy's protection of Austria with the offer of her own friendship. Unfortunately the premise of this policy, that Italy desired Britain's friendship enough to make concessions in order to get it, was unfounded.

Even though the Austrian crisis had been long developing, the final events of the *Anschluss* took the world by surprise. After his interview with Hitler on 12 February, Dr Schuschnigg appointed Seyss-Inquart Minister of the Interior as he had agreed to do. In the next few weeks German propaganda pressure built up. Unceasingly the German press and radio and Austrian Nazis expounded the overwhelming desire of the Austrian people to unite with Germany. Meanwhile, Schuschnigg received several encouraging messages from Mussolini reminding him of the Italian dictator's personal friendship for Austria. At the beginning of March, Schuschnigg prepared what he conceived would be a shrewd propaganda stroke, a plebiscite in Austria on the question of unification with Germany. On the 9th, he announced his intention to hold such a plebiscite four days later. This announcement brought on the German invasion. Hitler was determined that no such plebiscite should take place. Immediately riots by Austrian Nazis began in Vienna and on 11 March Schuschnigg received from his own Minister of the Interior an ultimatum demanding his resignation and the postponement of the plebiscite. At this juncture arrived a telegram from the Italian government saying that Italy could be of no help. Schuschnigg immediately resigned, and despite opposition from the Austrian President, Dr Wilhelm Miklas, Seyss-Inquart assumed the Chancellorship in a new cabinet and invited German troops into Austria 'to preserve order'. On 12 March Hitler arrived at Linz, his own birthplace, and on the 14th, preceded by such German armoured equipment as had survived breakdowns on the road, he entered Vienna. The day before, Austria had been absorbed formally into Greater Germany.

The occupation of Austria evoked almost no response in Great Britain. Friends of appeasement quickly turned out books and articles arguing that union with Germany accorded with the wish of the overwhelming majority of Austrians. This fact seemed to be confirmed by the plebiscite of 10 April, conducted under Nazi sponsorship, which showed that 99·7 per cent of the Austrian people approved of the union. Chamberlain, who was dining with the German ambassador Joachim von Ribbentrop when the news of the final ultimatum arrived, satisfied himself with a protest to Germany on the use of force against an independent state.

The most important effect of the German occupation of Austria, of concern to the British government even before 12 March, was the nearly defenceless position in which it put Czechoslovakia. The most populous and industrially important part of that nation was now surrounded by German territory. More dangerous, the Czech lands bordering Germany and Austria were inhabited almost exclusively by a discontented minority, the Sudeten Germans, who were well organized in a Nazi-style party under the leadership of Konrad Henlein. At their annual meeting at Karlsbad in April, only weeks after the *Anschluss*, the Sudeten German party announced a programme that demanded almost complete autonomy from Czechoslovakia for the Sudetenland. Echoing this programme, the German radio and German newspapers began to carry lurid and hysterical stories on the persecution of Sudeten Germans by the Czech government headed by Edward Benes. German pressure increased through the month of May when Czech national elections took place. Rumours of troop movements near the border circulated and the Germans ostentatiously began work on a huge line of fixed fortifications, the so-called Westwall, along the Franco-German frontier.

Since 1924 Czechoslovakia had been tied to France by a defensive alliance and after the Franco-Russian Treaty of 1936 she could technically count also the Soviet Union among her protectors. However, the Soviet Union's obligation to go to war came into effect only if France specifically invoked the treaty. This treaty, and the Russian connexion it represented, had never been popular in France and had grown increasingly less so since the late summer of 1936 with the beginnings of the Moscow purge trials and the outbreaks of Communist-inspired industrial violence in France that accompanied the establishment of the Popular Front government. These conditions made France's support of Czechoslovakia increasingly tenuous and unlikely even though the Daladier cabinet was at pains throughout the spring and summer of 1938 continually to reassure the Czechs of the firmness of French friendship. At bottom, France's support of Czechoslovakia had nothing to do with Russia, but would be determined solely by the strength of Britain's support of France. Without Britain, no alliance could have forced France into a war with Germany, but if Britain decided upon war France, albeit reluctantly, would follow. As Churchill well understood, the effect of the occupation of the Rhineland had been to place in London the responsibility for the direction of the foreign policy of both Western allies.

Chamberlain was determined to avoid war over the Czechoslovakian question. Nothing Britain or France could do would prevent the Germans overrunning Czechoslovakia. Yet in any resistance to a German attack the Czechs would certainly call upon French aid and Britain, he felt, inevitably would be drawn in. Still worse, Russia might go to the aid of Czechoslovakia, although Chamberlain was highly sceptical of Russian promises about this. But in any case it was questionable whether a Russian defeat leaving Germany dominant in Eastern Europe, or a Russian victory bringing Bolshevism to the banks of the Rhine, was more to be feared. The Czechs must be induced to pacify their German minority at all costs.

Chamberlain's solution was a personal emissary, Viscount Runciman, whom he sent to Czechoslovakia ostensibly to mediate between the government and the Sudeten Germans, but in fact to urge upon President Benes all possible concessions to the discontented alien minority. Runciman arrived in Prague on 3 August. By this time it was becoming clear that a grant of Sudeten autonomy along the lines of the Karlsbad demands would no longer satisfy either the Sudeten Germans or Adolf Hitler. Indeed, early in September, when President Benes proposed a settlement going even beyond the Sudeten German demands of the previous spring, it was contemptuously rejected.

It is now known that on 28 May 1938 Hitler had set 1 October as the final date for the solution of the Czech question and that he had determined from the beginning that one way or another Sudetenland should be incorporated into the Reich. For practical purposes he made these terms public in a speech of incredible violence at a Nazi party conference at Nuremberg on 12 September. Although he did not specifically demand here the cession of the Sudetenland, his screaming insults against Czechoslovakia and a neatly timed revolt by the Sudetenlanders themselves the next day made clear that the question of the German minorities would no longer be settled even by the most generous grant of local autonomy. Hitler's speech, the Sudeten rebellion, and a frantic note from the French cabinet, also on the 13th, saying that a German attack on Czechoslovakia must be prevented 'at all costs' convinced Chamberlain that negotiations between the Czechs and Henlein would no longer avoid war. He must see Hitler himself and discover in a personal conversation 'whether there was yet any hope of saving the peace'. Such conferences are commonplace today, but Chamberlain's journey, his first by air, at the age of 69, was a surprising innovation. The idea of a meeting, proposed to Hitler on the evening of 13 September, was characteristic of the Prime Minister. He was confident of his ability to arrive at an understanding with the German dictator. German demands, if harsh, were not unreasonable. Clearly the Sudetenland people did not wish to live in Czechoslovakia and did wish to live in Germany. Was there not here a basic question of self-determination? Behind it all lay the inescapable fact that Britain or France could not save Czechoslovakia. Threats were futile. There was no alternative to compromise.

The first of Neville Chamberlain's three visits to Germany occurred on 15 September. He visited Hitler at the German leader's mountain retreat at Berchtesgaden, where in the late afternoon of a grey autumn day Hitler told him that Germany would annex the Sudetenland by force if necessary, but that a peaceful transfer was possible if the principle of cession were accepted by England. Chamberlain replied that he personally had no objection to seeing the Sudetenlanders in the Reich, but that he would have to discuss the matter with his cabinet. He then flew back to London immediately without seeing Hitler a second time. (Runciman returned to England at the same time. With the delicacy of an experienced politician he altered his report to recommend the cession of the Sudetenland to Germany to coincide with the promise just made by his chief to Adolf Hitler.)

Immediately after his return to England Chamberlain met the new French Premier Edouard Daladier and his Foreign Minister, Georges Bonnet. At conferences in London on 19 September, the French agreed that the Czechs, in return for a guarantee of their country, should be forced to give up the Sudetenland. They would have to be told that any resistance to the Germans would lead to armed conflict in which Czechoslovakia would find herself alone. The Czechs were informed of this decision immediately and after initial objections reluctantly acquiesced. On 22 September Chamberlain returned again to Germany, meeting Hitler this time at Godesberg on the Rhine. At this conference, he assumed, the two leaders could discuss the areas to be ceded and the mechanics of the transfer.

At Godesberg, Chamberlain found, as was frequently the case in negotiations with Hitler, that he was faced by an entirely new set of circumstances. Suddenly there was a great need for speed. Hitler insisted he was being pushed along by events, even though the events

were of his own making. Delay was impossible. Hitler announced
that he was quite prepared to go to war; in fact the question of war
was immaterial. There was no time for negotiation over ways and
means. German-speaking areas must be occupied by German forces
immediately. On the second day of the Godesberg conference, Hitler
presented Chamberlain with a memorandum showing the areas Germany must have. German troops, stipulated the memorandum, would
begin occupation on the 26th, four days hence, and would be in complete control by the 29th. No Czech property whatever could be
removed. Hitler's sole concession, granted with a great show of
reluctance, was to extend his deadline to 1 October, which, in any
case, had been the original date for the solution of the Czech problem.

Chamberlain was deeply disturbed by the result of his second visit
to Germany. The Godesberg memorandum—Chamberlain pointed
out it was more of an ultimatum—had changed a carefully phased
transfer of certain territories that would be designated by plebiscite
into a demand for Czech acquiescence in an armed invasion of their
country. In Britain the memorandum seemed momentarily to stiffen
public opinion against appeasement and to increase the resistance of
British politicians to the dismemberment of Czechoslovakia. The
Czechs themselves immediately rejected the proposals and British
newspapers—including *The Times*, which on 7 September had suggested that the Czechs prepare for the partition of their land—now
began to support a stronger stand. In the next few days Britain made
ready for attack. Authorities distributed gas masks and men dug slit
trenches in city parks. London's pitiful supply of anti-aircraft guns,
44 in all, were prepared for use. War seemed very near.

Yet somehow no one was ready for war. The national determination
of 1940 had not yet solidified. The nation was dazed, not stubborn.
The rapid onset of the crisis and the almost hourly alternation of hope
and despair had prevented any preparation of the popular mind.
Chamberlain himself was still determined to avoid war. Secretly
he sent Horace Wilson to Germany to explore new avenues to
compromise and at the same time appealed to Mussolini for
mediation.

The means of escape suddenly appeared on 28 September, when
Chamberlain, in the midst of a speech in the House of Commons
gloomily recounting the events of the last few days, suddenly was
passed a note reporting that Mussolini had proposed and Hitler had
accepted a four-power meeting at Munich. On hearing this news,
the House broke into cheers, and most Englishmen in one way or

another manifested the same feeling of joy and relief. The next day Chamberlain flew again to Germany. There in a short meeting at Munich, attended only by himself, Hitler, Daladier and Mussolini, he agreed to a German occupation of the Sudetenland which would begin on 1 October and be completed on 10 October. The areas to be occupied were essentially those of the Godesberg memorandum. Hitler's only concession was to permit the creation of an international commission to supervise disputed questions. Britain and France took responsibility for seeing that Czech representatives, who had not been invited to the conference, accepted its decisions. The Czechs were given again the alternative of agreeing to the Munich settlement or of facing Germany alone. The eventual decision was made by President Benes, who acquiesced to the Munich terms and then resigned his post and went into exile.

Chamberlain saw Hitler again on the morning of the 30th, when the two men signed a separate document specifying that their countries would always use peaceful means in the settlement of differences. This paper Chamberlain fluttered in the air before the newsreel cameras at Heston airport when he returned to Great Britain. Privately he was gleeful. He had maintained the existence of Czechoslovakia. He had achieved, as he had hoped, the friendship of Hitler and had received from him a promise of 'peace in our time'. Most of all, he had avoided war. Hitler had promised that the Czech question was the last of his territorial claims in Europe and Chamberlain felt himself confirmed in the belief that reasonable men could always find a way to live together. The appeasement policy had been a success.

The Prime Minister viewed the peaceful partition of Czechoslovakia as a diplomatic triumph for Britain, and most Conservatives, as well as most influential newspapers headed by *The Times*, agreed. Chamberlain himself received a gratifying number of thankful letters praising him for avoiding war. Nevertheless, by the end of 1938, few Englishmen could take unalloyed pleasure from the fact that their government had been involved in the Munich settlement. The German occupation of the Sudetenland in the first days of October resembled in every way an invasion. The international commission that was intended to supervise boundary disputes and protect Czech interests was coldly pushed aside. The guarantee of the new Czech boundaries by Germany and Italy, stipulated to follow the Czech cession of small territories to Hungary and Poland, was never made. European war had indeed been avoided, but the anti-Axis forces were weaker by over 21 well-equipped Czech divisions, a force considerably larger than the British army, and the Reich was stronger by three million Sudeten Germans.

Czechoslovakia's final agony was not long delayed. The blow sustained at Munich began the dissolution of the nation. Latent Slovakian nationalism appeared, fanned by the loss of prestige of the Prague government and by Nazi encouragement. On 14 March 1939 the Czech President who had succeeded Benes, the aged Emil Hacha, was summoned to Berlin by Hitler, and there, early in the morning of 15 March, under a combination of threats and cajolery, was induced to place his state under the protection of Germany. Within hours, German troops already poised in the Sudetenland had crossed into what remained of Czechoslovakia. Hitler spent the night of 15 March in Prague and the next day announced that an independent Czechoslovakia had ceased to exist.

The destruction of Czechoslovakia ended the policy of appeasement. Chamberlain's personal reactions moved from disbelief to unconcern to anger. He appeared to regard Hitler's breach of confidence less as a tragedy for Czechoslovakia than an insult to himself. 'What has become of the declaration "no further territorial ambition"?' he asked in a speech at Birmingham on the 17th, the day before his seventieth birthday.

What has become of the assurance 'we don't want Czechs in the Reich'? What regard has been paid here to that principle of self-determination on which Herr Hitler argued so vehemently with me at Berchtesgaden when he was asking for the severance of the Sudetenland from Czecho-Slovakia and its inclusion in the German Reich?

Germany had destroyed what Chamberlain clearly believed was about to become a successful policy. Hitler had, Chamberlain continued, '. . . shattered the confidence which was just beginning to show its head and which, if it had been allowed to grow, might have made this year memorable for the return of all Europe to sanity and stability'.

Now, slowly and grudgingly, he began to prepare Britain for war. It did not follow he had given up all hope for peace and the Birmingham speech made no particular threats against Germany. Indeed the day after the Birmingham speech, on the advice of Sir John Simon, one of the most ardent appeasers in the cabinet, he declined to support a Russian proposal for an international conference of anti-Axis nations and so perhaps threw away the last possibility of cooperation with the Soviet Union. Nevertheless, before the end of March, Britain had made the commitments that would take her into the Second World War.

At almost the same time, the final crisis began. On 21 March the Polish Ambassador in Berlin received from von Ribbentrop, now German Foreign Minister, notice that Germany demanded the cession of the free city of Danzig, which had separated from Germany in 1919 to provide Poland with a seaport, and special rights for German minorities in the Polish Corridor. When these were given, Germany would make Poland a new guarantee of her frontiers. The following day, 22 March, after threat of invasion, Germany received from Lithuania the city of Memel, which lay immediately across the extreme north-east border of East Prussia. Polish Foreign Minister Joseph Beck rejected the German demands on 26 March. In the next few days, through a warning from a British journalist in Berlin and through communications from the Poles themselves, Britain learned of the growing threat to Poland. As a result, on 31 March in the House of Commons Chamberlain announced that in case of an attack on Poland, Great Britain would lend that nation 'all the support in her power'.

Chamberlain's guarantee of Polish territorial integrity, made almost solely on his own responsibility, was supplemented in the next week by a French renewal of her eighteen-year-old alliance with Poland. On 6 April Joseph Beck, in London, gave Britain a reciprocal guarantee of Polish assistance. These activities enraged Hitler. He had apparently hoped to avoid driving Poland towards the Western democracies. In any case, on 3 April he ordered his general staff to prepare plans for an attack across his eastern frontier that could begin any time after 1 September.

Britain's new policy of firmness against German aggression, which evolved in the last two weeks of March and the first week of April, made little sense in terms of diplomatic-military realities. Chamberlain's most rational defence of the Munich policy had been that no matter what obligations Britain or France assumed for the defence of Czechoslovakia they would be unable to keep the country secure in case of a European war. The strongest possible policy would not save Czechoslovakia, he insisted, and would simply involve Britain in a conflict with a nation with whom she herself had no quarrel. Czechoslovakia, therefore, was best advised to give up the part of her country inhabited by people who wished to become Germans anyway and save the rest. But now Chamberlain was giving unilateral guarantees of the most sweeping sort to a nation Britain was no more able to defend than Czechoslovakia. No single British soldier, indeed, as it turned out, would be available to fight the Germans in Poland.

Paradoxically the only nation able to render the Poles effective military aid, the nation whose proposals for a conference on mutual defence Chamberlain had already brushed aside, was the nation with whom the Poles absolutely refused to engage in an alliance—Russia. Although Chamberlain distrusted the Soviet Union, the blame for the extreme slowness of British negotiations for Russian assistance in the summer of 1939 and for the failure to arrive at an agreement must rest chiefly with Poland. Unfortunately, by his unconditional guarantee of that nation at the end of March, Chamberlain had thrown away nearly all possibility of forcing a change in this attitude by making the British-Polish agreement conditional upon a Polish-Russian agreement. The practical difficulties of furnishing any real military assistance to the Poles without some concert with Russia had been pointed out immediately and harshly in Parliament as soon as the guarantee of Poland was announced. At last, in the middle of April, under pressure from France, Chamberlain reluctantly proposed to the Soviet Union that she give a unilateral guarantee to Poland similar to that given by Britain. This the Russians declined to do, suggesting instead a multilateral mutual-assistance pact of Britain, France, Russia and the Baltic powers. Such a pact Poland would not sign, and essentially the attempts to bring the Soviet Union into a Western combination against Germany never proceeded beyond this point. Russia was unwilling to promise aid against Germany without the cooperation of Poland. Poland was unwilling to be aided by Russia.

Nevertheless, through the months of May, June, July, and the first half of August, negotiations with Russia for an agreement on military assistance proceeded, although at far too leisurely a pace. A British diplomatic mission in June, including no one of ministerial rank, was supplemented in August by a military mission whose members also were far from the highest level and were not empowered to sign an agreement. By this time, indeed as the British military mission was slowly making its way to Moscow, the Russians determined to bring the game to an end. On 12 August, the day after the British mission arrived, the Moscow government secretly notified the Germans that they were prepared for discussions. The Germans responded with enthusiasm. On 18 August a German-Soviet trade agreement was approved, and after a direct message from Hitler to Stalin on 20 August, Foreign Minister von Ribbentrop himself journeyed to Moscow, where on 23 August, to its amazement, the world learned that Germany and the Soviet Union had signed a non-aggression pact. Only the day before, the Franco-British military mission had received authority to sign a military agreement with the USSR. They had been put off by the senior Soviet negotiator, Klementi Voroshilov, with the excuse that he was going duck shooting.

The initiative for German-Soviet negotiations had consistently come from Berlin. The conclusion of the non-aggression pact effectively sealed Poland from her allies and made the conquest of that nation inevitable. During the next few days, Berlin was the scene of a series of false diplomatic negotiations aimed not at arriving at a peaceful agreement with Poland, but at attempting to convey to Britain and France that the German attack was the result solely of Poland's unwillingness to negotiate. To this end the British ambassador Neville Henderson had read to him in German a long and highly detailed set of compromises that Germany would have been willing to make had the Poles, who had not seen the document, accepted them. At the same time, Hitler attempted to lessen Britain's determination to go to war by offering guarantees of all British territory combined with a 'large comprehensive offer to settle all outstanding difficulties'. All the while, of course, military preparations, projected since the previous April, were going forward for the attack due on 1 September. At sunrise that day the Second World War began.

Britain and France declared war on Germany two days later. Hitler's interpreter, Paul Schmidt, recalls carrying the British declaration into the Führer's office in the Reichschancellery. Hitler, who had been promised by von Ribbentrop that the Western allies would not at last declare war upon Germany, received the news calmly. He turned to his Foreign Minister and said, 'What now?' 'I assume that the French will hand in a similar ultimatum within the hour', Ribbentrop replied. Schmidt recalls that as he left the office and walked through the anteroom he heard the Marshal of the German Air Force, Hermann Göring, remark, 'If we lose this war, then God have mercy on us!'

WAR—SITZKRIEG

Britain had been preparing actively for the conflict since the fall of Czechoslovakia the previous March. In the last weeks of that month, the various civilian ministries had received orders to plan for the security of their records and their personnel against air raids, an inventory of hospital beds and trial blackouts began, and a Ministry of Supply was created to look after the production of war materiel. The most startling sign of the determination of British preparations, however, was Chamberlain's announcement on 26 April that the government was preparing legislation to conscript men aged 20 and 21 for six months of military service. Surprisingly, this gesture, which would really add little to Britain's armed strength, was justified less on the basis of military preparedness than as a way of improving the physique of young men from the slums. As an evidence of Britain's lack of martial ardour, it was noted that among the first class of young men taken into the army, 17 out of every thousand claimed exemption on the basis of conscientious objection to war.

Despite the military activities of the summer of 1939, British opinion was singularly unprepared. Part of this may be accounted for by a deliberate attempt on the part of the national press not to alarm the public. The royal family's visit to North America was pacific and reassuring. The speed with which the final crisis had developed did not permit the national consciousness to focus on the grim events it portended. But more surprising, although Chamberlain's speech to the nation on 3 September was interrupted by an air-raid warning and the Cunard liner *Athenia* was sunk with heavy loss of life a few hours later, the mood of unreality continued after the declaration of war. Of the nearly one and a half million persons evacuated from large urban areas in the first days of the conflict, over one half had returned by the end of the year. Sandbags that had been hastily piled around shop fronts, and paper tape pasted in tasteful designs across large show windows to prevent flying glass quickly disappeared. Instead, doorways displayed the motto 'Business as Usual'. This mood was not dispelled by the quick defeat of Poland, whose resistance ended on 27 September with the surrender of Warsaw.

The reasons for this excessively casual attitude about the immense conflict in which the nation was engaged lay in the popular assumptions about the military position of Germany. There was a neat division of function between the French army and the British navy. France, it was taken for granted, was secure behind the great steel and concrete wall of the Maginot Line, which extended from Belfort on the Swiss border to the Ardennes Forest on the Belgian border. This line was manned by the French army, always designated as 'the best in Europe'. Should it be foolish enough to do so, the German army would batter itself to pieces against the French defences. Meanwhile, the overwhelmingly powerful British navy would sweep the Germans from the seas, blockade their coast, and eventually either starve the nation into submission or force it into a desperate gamble that would result in disaster. A static military defence and economic pressure would win the war. Britain's own military contribution was limited. She was committed to sending ten divisions to France by February 1940—four had been sent immediately—and, only by September 1941, an additional 22.

As a result the easy decision to do nothing became high policy. Military initiative was deliberately left to the enemy. Time was on the side of the Allies. Except for dropping propaganda pamphlets over Germany and watching for submarines, the Royal Air Force was inactive, and the first British soldier was not killed in action until 13 December. As the German conquest of Poland had been termed a '*blitzkrieg*', a lightning war, the new phase of the war that lasted from the end of September until the beginning of April was frequently designated a '*sitzkrieg*'.

On the sea there was more action. The Royal Navy had immediately established a sea blockade of Germany, and German submarines began activities in waters around the British Isles. On 18 September, the aircraft carrier *Courageous* was sunk by a submarine in the English Channel, and on 14 October a German submarine entered the great harbour at Scapa Flow and sank the anchored battleship *Royal Oak*.

Then on 13 December occurred one of the most dramatic, if not the most important, naval actions of the war. Two British cruisers and an Australian cruiser, although heavily outgunned, were able by sheer daring and seamanship to cause the German pocket battleship *Admiral Graf von Spee* to seek shelter in the estuary of the Plate River on the east coast of South America close to the Uruguayan port of Montevideo. Four days later, under orders to move, the *Graf Spee* was scuttled by her crew and her captain committed suicide.

Simultaneously with this rather gratifying naval action, the consciences of the Western powers were disturbed by the increasingly desperate plight of the tiny democracy of Finland. In a secret annex to the German–Soviet treaty of 23 August, the two powers had agreed that Finland, along with Estonia and Latvia, should be within the sphere of influence of Russia (the USSR eventually took Lithuania also). In the next two months, after invading Poland and partitioning that unhappy country between herself and Germany, the Soviet

Union obtained from Estonia, Latvia and Lithuania the right to establish military and naval bases on their territory to guard the southern approaches to the Gulf of Finland and Leningrad. At the same time, she began to bring pressure on Finland to gain control over the northern shore of the Gulf of Finland. The Finns agreed to some concessions, but refused to give the Russians the bases they demanded or to cede some portion of the Karelian Isthmus, which the Russians considered brought the Finnish border dangerously close to the city of Leningrad itself. As a result, on 30 November, Russian troops attacked Finland.

The Finnish war, and the brave Finnish resistance to the overwhelming Russian power, seriously disturbed public opinion in the West and caused the first widespread popular enthusiasm for military action. Unfortunately, Allied aid could not reach Finland without crossing the territories of Norway and Sweden and the necessary permission these powers steadfastly refused to give. Eventually, on 12 March 1940, Finland was obliged to surrender. The most important immediate effect of the Russo-Finnish war was the fall of the French government at the end of March and the replacement of Premier Daladier by Paul Reynaud, who at the last minute tried to inject some life into a dispirited French defence effort.

The Swedish and Norwegian refusals to permit the passage of aid to the Finns called to the world's attention the rather less than neutral position occupied by these two Scandinavian powers. The only conceivable route for Finnish aid would have been across the extreme north of the Scandinavian peninsula along the railroad running eastward from the Norwegian port of Narvik across the mountains into Sweden, where it connected with other railroads running south into Finland. This railroad normally was used for the transport of Swedish iron ore, which, particularly in winter, was carried to the Norwegian ice-free ports on the Atlantic. While the Norwegians and Swedes declined to permit this railroad to be used for military supplies for Finland, since the outbreak of the war the line had been consistently used for iron ore taken to Germany. The Swedish iron ore, put on ships at Narvik, was transported down the Norwegian coast through the fiords well inside Norwegian territorial waters so that it passed through the British blockade and fed the German war machine without out Allied interference. Winston Churchill, who had come into the government on 3 September as First Lord of the Admiralty, called attention to this leak in the blockade within weeks of his appointment and proposed bringing pressure on Norway to stop the flow of iron ore. The fact was, of course, that Norway was considerably more afraid of Germany than she was of Great Britain and so the Norwegians declined to interfere with this trade. Through the winter and early spring of 1939-40, Churchill continually urged on the cabinet the necessity of stopping this important traffic. Finally, on 3 April 1940, the cabinet agreed to permit mines to be laid in the Norwegian fiords. At the same time, because interfering with the flow of iron ore would inevitably provoke some German retaliation, the cabinet authorized the preparation of an expeditionary force to occupy the port of Narvik and several other Norwegian sea-coast towns further south. Early in the morning on 8 April, four British destroyers laid a minefield in the channel leading to the port of Narvik.

That night Norway was attacked by German air and naval forces and the next morning German troops occupied Copenhagen in Denmark, while by the afternoon of 9 April German forces were landing at several points in Norway. The German attack on Norway found the British and French completely unprepared. Although the Allies attempted landings at several points on the Norwegian coast, they were able to put troops ashore in force only at the northernmost city, Narvik. The Norwegians themselves resisted stoutly once they recovered from the initial shock of the invasion and overcame the confusion caused by the appearance of traitors in posts high in the government. But anti-German forces were hindered everywhere by German superiority in the air. German troops could be flown quickly up the 700 miles of coast to Narvik, while British supply ships came under continuous attack whenever they approached land. A lesson of Norway, important for the future, was that control of the surface of the ocean was of limited value without control of the air over it. Within a month of the original attack, when the invasion of the Lowlands began, the Germans held all of southern and central Norway and Allied troops were present in important strength only at Narvik, which was itself evacuated on 8 June.

The attack on Norway ended the *sitzkrieg* and opened the second phase of the war. The failures in Norway brought an end to the complacency that had marked Britain's attitude since September, and forced also the downfall of the Chamberlain government, which had contributed to that complacency. Understandably, a nation that had assumed for so many months that the war would be won without effort was disturbed at the sudden overwhelming evidence of a possibility that it might not be won at all and began to search for a scapegoat. Except for the appointment of Churchill at the Admiralty, the return of Anthony Eden to the cabinet at the Dominion Office, and the naming of Sir John Anderson, a civil servant, as Home Secretary, Chamberlain's cabinet during the first nine months of war resembled distressingly that of the unhappy last years of peace. He created, to be sure, a War Cabinet, but it was dominated by men— Simon, Halifax, Hoare, and Chamberlain himself—who represented peace and appeasement. (Churchill noted in an early memorandum to Chamberlain that the average age of six of them, including himself, was 64, only a year short of the old age pension.)

But now the months of illusion were over. On hearing the news of the attack on Norway, Chamberlain had boasted that Hitler had 'missed the bus'. The events of the past month suggested that this estimate, like others before, was mistaken. On 7 May after a motion by the Liberal and Labour opposition for a debate on the war situation, the attack on the Prime Minister in the House of Commons began. The debate lasted for three days, and before it had ended Neville Chamberlain's position as a leader of a nation at war had been destroyed. He was denounced not only by the opposition, but by Conservatives, particularly by the little group who had supported Churchill in his resistance to the appeasement policy. Churchill's own position was an embarrassing one. As First Lord of the Admiralty, he was as responsible as Chamberlain for the disasters in Norway. But it soon became clear that the House was less concerned with fixing responsibility for the failures in the Norwegian campaign than in debating whether Chamberlain should continue as Prime Minister. The question of Chamberlain's fitness was raised in many ways during the three days from 7 May to 9 May, but by no one more dramatically than by David Lloyd George in his last significant intervention in House of Commons Debate. The times called for sacrifice, said the former Prime Minister, and 'I say solemnly that the Prime Minister should give an example of sacrifice, because there is nothing which he can contribute more to victory in this war than that he should sacrifice the seals of office.'

When the House divided at eleven o'clock on 9 May, the government retained a majority of 81. However, 33 supporters of the government voted against Chamberlain and 65 Conservatives abstained. Chamberlain had hoped to see the formation of a national coalition over which he would preside, but early the next morning he learned that, although the Labour party would serve in a national government, it would not serve under him. This news showed Chamberlain that he must resign. He hoped now to pass the office of Prime Minister to Lord Halifax and might have done so but for Churchill, who declined to serve under the former Foreign Secretary.

In the midst of these negotiations, early in the morning of 10 May the German army, without warning and in tremendous force, invaded Belgium and the Netherlands. For a moment Chamberlain thought that the new emergency dictated that he should stay on. But he was told by his closest political friend and colleague from the Ministry of Health days, H. Kingsley Wood, and by a message from Clement Attlee that now more than ever he must resign. And so in the late afternoon of 10 May, as reports of heavy fighting in the Lowlands poured into London, Chamberlain visited the king, gave up his seals of office, and agreed that Winston Churchill become Prime Minister. Without Chamberlain's support Churchill could never have achieved or held the office of Prime Minister, and without Churchill the Second World War might well have ended in a British defeat.

CHAPTER FIVE

The War

THE YEARS OF DESPERATION, 1940–42

The Germans needed precisely six weeks to conquer the Netherlands, Belgium and France. Dutch and Belgian resistance lasted only a few days. By 22 June 1940 the Nazis had destroyed the French army and overwhelmed the French state. Within a month they destroyed as well, or at least rendered useless as a military organization, the British Expeditionary Force in France. Such a quick reversal of fortunes was almost without precedent. Until the spring of 1940, Germany had seemed isolated, doomed to expire miserably from starvation, or to batter herself to death against the iron ring composed of the British Navy and the Maginot Line. By mid-summer, Hitler bestrode Europe from the North Cape of Norway to the Pyrenees, while Britain, undaunted, but also virtually unarmed, stood alone.

The defeat of France was first of all a triumph of German military technology, and secondly the result of French weaknesses in materiel and determination. The Germans were able to organize their first blow in unbelievable strength. The Dutch army suffered 100,000 casualties, a quarter of its strength, in the first three days. By the end of the first day also the Belgians had surrendered their most powerful fort, Eben Emael, had evacuated their positions along the Albert Canal, and had retired to a line running roughly from Antwerp to Louvain. More serious, on 13 May Hitler's forces pushed through the supposedly impassable Ardennes Forest immediately to the north of the Maginot Line where French and Belgian fortifications had never been coordinated, crossed the Meuse River and opened a 50-mile breach in the French line between Namur and Sedan. Although it was not yet apparent, this action had disrupted the entire Allied defence plan.

In response to the attack upon Belgium, the French and British rushed the bulk of their mobile forces northward to support the smaller nation's defence. The French First Army and most of the British Expeditionary Force were soon in Belgium. But within seven days of the Sedan breakout, on 20 May, German armoured forces, not aiming at Paris as had been expected but moving straight down the Somme Valley, reached Abbeville on the Channel coast. Allied forces in Belgium were cut off.

Upon reaching the coast, without a moment's cessation, the German army turned and pushed to the north-east. On 23 May Boulogne was occupied, and on the 27th Calais came under attack. On the same day the Belgian king, Leopold, asked the Germans for an armistice and on the next day 400,000 weary Belgian troops surrendered unconditionally. The Allies in Belgium, nearly 400,000 men, were now in a desperate position. The only port available to them was Dunkirk. German army communiqués began to announce that the fate of the French and British armies was sealed.

In fact, the dramatic evacuation of the trapped Allied armies had already begun. As early as 14 May, the BBC, with its customary detachment, requested owners of self-propelled pleasure craft of 30–100 feet in length to 'send all particulars to the Admiralty within 14 days from today'. Between 26 May and 4 June, Operation Dynamo, the Dunkirk evacuation, took place. In all, 887 vessels, civilian and naval, participated. A total of 338,226 men, of whom about 200,000 were British and the rest French and Belgian, were brought out. The Germans claimed 40,000 prisoners. But worse, all the heavy equipment of the BEF, virtually all Britain possessed, was left on the beach.

The Dunkirk evacuation was successful partly because the Germans did not throw the entire weight of their armour against the port. German tanks, after three weeks of continuous operation, were badly in need of refitting. Moreover, Hitler had promised Marshal Göring that the final destruction of enemy forces at Dunkirk would be left to the German air forces. To these factors should be added the luck of bad weather that hindered German aerial observation. But these German mistakes detract nothing from the magnitude of the British accomplishment. Although little noticed at the time, the evacuation was possible because the Royal Air Force for the first time in the war was able to take control of the air from the German Luftwaffe. The heroism of the masters of the myriad small boats who navigated the choppy waters of the English Channel can be compared only to the stout determination of the troops they brought back. Dunkirk was indeed a miracle and its success most heartening after weeks of continuous bad news, but, as Churchill quickly reminded the nation, wars were not won by evacuations. More serious, the British army was now almost completely without modern equipment. The men were out, but they had little with which to fight.

The withdrawal from Dunkirk meant that Britain took little part in the last phase of the battle of France. During the first days of June the French worked frantically to establish a defence, christened the Weygand Line after their new commander. The Weygand Line ran approximately along the Somme and Aisne River valleys. The Germans, on the other hand, had no intention of permitting the French to prepare their defences in peace and on 5 June launched 100 divisions in a gigantic four-pronged attack that extended from Chemin des Dames to the sea. French resistance died quickly. On 10 June, Mussolini, exciting scorn and derision both in Britain and in the United States, declared war on France. The next day, with German columns already on the Marne, the French government declared Paris an open city and left for Tours. On the 14th the Germans entered Paris. On 16 June, overridden by his cabinet on the question of French surrender, Premier Reynaud resigned. Finally on the 17th the aged Marshal of France, Henri Pétain, who had assumed the post of Premier, announced to the French people on the radio that he had asked the Germans for an armistice. Five days later, on 22 June, in the old railroad dining car used for signing the armistice after the First World War, the French formally capitulated.

Churchill had attempted to prevent a complete French departure from the war. The legal arrangements between Great Britain and France were governed by a proclamation of the Supreme War Council made on 28 March 1940, in which the heads of the two governments jointly proclaimed that neither nation would negotiate 'nor conclude an armistice or treaty of peace except by mutual agreement'. Technically, therefore, France was obligated to continue the war against Germany with any means at her disposal even though the French army in France was defeated. Both Norway and the Netherlands were doing this and making substantial contributions to the Allied war effort. On 12 June, immediately after the government moved to Tours, Churchill flew to that city to confer with members of the French cabinet, to remind them of this promise and to persuade them to carry on the war from a base in the French Empire. Premier Reynaud was in favour of this course, and indeed resigned on this issue four days later, but the majority of the cabinet accepted the advice of General Weygand, who predicted that Britain shortly 'would have her neck wrung like a chicken's'.

Realizing that Premier Reynaud was almost the only member of the French government wholeheartedly in favour of continued resistance at any cost, Churchill sought to strengthen the French leader's position by some dramatic announcement that would underline British determination to fight on and give new heart to the French nation. To this end the Prime Minister proposed on 16 June a declaration of union between Great Britain and France which would provide for a common citizenship, common responsibility for making good the losses of war and, at the moment most important, for joint ownership and control of all weapons of land, sea and air. The proposal for union was transmitted to the French cabinet, now meeting at Bordeaux, which had a few hours previously asked to be released from the pledge of 28 March. It was disdainfully brushed aside. Marshal Pétain is reported to have remarked that the union represented 'fusion with a corpse' and later that day Reynaud resigned. The French government was not defeated. It gave up and left Britain alone.

An important factor in the calculations about the union with France was the control it would provide Britain over the French fleet. This was a substantial force, much of it modern, and Germany's acquisition of it would be a grave matter. The terms of the armistice had stipulated that the fleet was to concentrate 'in ports to be specified and there demobilized and disarmed under German or Italian control'. This could not be permitted to happen. Some units of the French fleet were in British ports. These were easily secured and many of their crews volunteered to join the British. But some important units of the French fleet were in the Mediterranean based on the Algerian port of Oran. Here, on 3 July, they were confronted by the overwhelming power of the British Mediterranean Fleet and after refusing an ultimatum either to proceed to a neutral port or to turn themselves over to the British, most of the heavy units, including three battleships, were put out of action by gunfire.

The result of this attack on Britain's former ally, which Churchill records as one of the most difficult decisions taken by the cabinet during the war, was a notable stiffening of morale at home. This could not be the action of a defeated people. No longer were there doubts about Britain's intention to fight on. The nation had shown a new resolution not displayed even during the evacuation of Dunkirk. This inner strength would be needed in the days that lay ahead.

The Battle of Britain designates the aerial attack launched by the Germans upon Great Britain which gradually intensified in the summer of 1940 after the French surrender and subsided as gradually the next spring, ending finally in May 1941. The Germans looked upon the air attack only as a preliminary to a cross-Channel invasion of the British Isles, although for some time a few optimists among them, notably Reichsmarshal Hermann Göring, hoped to force a British capitulation through bombing alone. Nevertheless, it is always important to recall, when contemplating the fortitude of the ordinary English civilian in the face of sustained aerial bombardment, that after the danger of sudden death from the air there lay the possibility of the overrunning of his peaceful land through military invasion. The providence which spared his family from the German bomb at night might have done so only to save them for the German paratrooper by day.

The German plans for the invasion of Great Britain, like much else in the first year of the war, were confused by the rapid collapse of France. In the early days of the war the German high command had surveyed the logistical requirements for an invasion of the British Isles. But according to the German naval staff war diary Hitler did not begin the serious contemplation of an invasion until 21 May, the day after the German army reached the sea at Abbeville and cut off the British and French forces in Belgium. Even so, during the next few weeks the German dictator assumed that the blow of the loss of France and the apparent hopelessness of Britain's position would induce her to sue for peace without an invasion. His illusions in this matter were reinforced by the clear difficulties of an opposed landing. Consequently throughout the month of June Hitler allowed his attention to be turned elsewhere, and only in July, nearly two weeks after the French surrender and after Britain's intention to fight on was unmistakable, did staff work for an invasion begin. At this time was chosen the code name 'Seelöwe' (Sea Lion), by which the operation became known. The July planning by the military and naval high commands revealed the conflicting difficulties that forced continual postponement and final abandonment of the proposed attack on Great Britain. The army's plans envisaged landing a total of 39 regular and two airborne divisions. To use fewer men would jeopardize the operation. The navy, on the other hand, insisted that an attack on such a scale was completely out of proportion to the naval facilities available. The situation was not comparable to Norway, the navy insisted. Strategic surprise could not be expected. The fleet could not even guarantee the security of the first waves of the attack, let alone the continued safety and materiel support of over 40 divisions.

As it turned out, this impasse was never resolved. The army could not guarantee success with fewer than 40 divisions. The navy could not guarantee the arrival of a force approaching that size. Nevertheless, Hitler insisted that planning go forward and that the collection of landing craft and other supplies be started. Meanwhile air attacks on the invasion beaches and on the Royal Air Force should begin. These raids, preliminary to an invasion the scope and timing of which the Germans had not themselves settled, became the Battle of Britain.

There is no clear beginning date for the battle. The first bombs on non-military targets fell on 10 May near Canterbury. The first serious civilian casualties were reported in mid-June at about the time France surrendered. Continuous heavy raids did not really begin until 10 July, the date normally assigned for the beginning of the battle.

The German attack falls easily into three main phases. The first, lasting from 10 July until 18 August, was the only phase specifically preparatory to a cross-Channel invasion. The others were themselves a response to the unexpectedly skilful and determined resistance put up by the Royal Air Force. In the beginning the Germans concentrated their attack upon shipping convoys in the Channel and on the Channel ports themselves. The first phase taught the Germans that conquest of the skies over Britain would be bought dearly. The week between 13 and 18 August saw some of the most closely fought air battles of the war. At this time the Germans mounted a maximum effort against the Channel and North Sea ports. They lost 236 aircraft, two and a half times the number lost by the Royal Air Force. By now Britain's strength in the air was clear and the Germans shifted their attack to the Royal Air Force itself.

In the last week of August and the first week of September the Germans came near to victory. They concentrated their bombing effort upon the fighter command sector stations and upon the airfields. Many forward airfields were rendered unfit for use, and, between 24 August and 6 September, 466 Spitfires and Hurricanes were destroyed or damaged, many on the ground. Most serious of all, 103 pilots were killed and 128 were seriously wounded, nearly one-quarter of the total fighter command pilot strength. The defence of Britain was at full strain. Machines could be replaced, and were, at the rate of 500 per month, but men could not. At last the German superiority in numbers was making itself felt. Then, unbelievably, the pressure on the fighter command lifted. The Germans, having nearly beaten the only obstacle to victory over Great Britain, allowed themselves to be diverted from the attack on the fighter command and on 7 September began the bombardment of London.

The Blitz represents the third phase of the Battle of Britain and constitutes one of Hitler's most serious mistakes of the war. The attack on London was the result of a series of British attacks on German towns that had begun on 25 August. These most ineffective night-time raids were themselves in retaliation for a German bomb on London dropped accidentally on 24 August. But the Blitz, however fearful and deadly, saved the fighter command, and probably Great Britain. Whereas in the week from 1 to 7 September the fighter command lost 144 planes in air combat, the highest total for any week of the entire battle, in the following week it lost only 67. It deliberately rested and regrouped, while permitting London to absorb the German fury.

Except for an extremely heavy daylight raid on 15 September, which may be taken as a culminating effort by the Germans, nearly all the attacks of the Blitz were in darkness. This was the result of the inability of German bombers to defend themselves against British fighters and of the short range of Germany's principal escort fighter, the Messerschmitt 109. Bombers alone were easy prey for British fighters in daylight and German fighters could carry only enough gasoline for about ten minutes' activity over London. Thus the approximately 200 planes that appeared over London each 24 hours from the beginning of September to the beginning of November dropped their bombs almost blindly. They paid for reduced losses with reduced effectiveness. The Blitz on London and the crippling attacks on other cities did not seriously hinder the British war effort even if they made wartime life hideously uncomfortable. The devastated residential streets of the East End, and the bombed schools and hospitals, were evidences of the Nazi taste for violence but not of German military efficiency. Moreover London's courage, and Southampton's, Plymouth's and Coventry's, which evoked the admiration of the world, had important consequences in modifying public opinion, particularly in the United States. Aid for Great Britain became politically feasible.

The nation paid with the lives of some 30,000 civilians during the Blitz, of whom somewhat more than half were killed in London. The panic and mass psychoses that had been feared as a result of large-scale bombing, and for which there was precedent from the minor bombings of London in the First World War, never developed. The three and a half million houses destroyed would add to the problems of austerity after the war. The difficulties caused by the dispersal of factories, by time lost due to disrupted transportation, and by inefficiency at work because of fatigue, cannot, of course, be measured. But on balance it must be said that the Blitz strengthened Britain's resistance rather than weakened it.

The Battle of Britain, as Churchill noted, was marked by the smallness of the numbers engaged on either side and by the tremendous stakes involved. For Britain it was a last-ditch stand. Victory did not ensure winning the war, but a loss would have meant her defeat. The Royal Navy's control of the sea approaches to Britain, as Norway had proved, were dependent on control of the air over the sea. Had the RAF been destroyed, the difficulties that so tormented the German navy about the transport of troops across the Channel would have been significantly lessened. Similarly, widespread panic and breakdown of morale as a result of the bombing of cities could have led to a British surrender, as Göring had expected it would do. Hitler's decision on 17 September to postpone active planning for the invasion until further notice had been predicated on Göring's promise that the Luftwaffe could defeat Britain without aid from the army and navy, in effect without an invasion. Hitler may not have believed this himself, but none of his advisers was enthusiastic about a cross-Channel effort. In any case, even though the Blitz continued for six more months, the danger of a cross-Channel attack was over for ever.

Britain won her struggle for survival first of all because the Germans were not prepared technically for the task they undertook. The Luftwaffe was designed for close cooperation with armed forces on the ground as it had brilliantly proved in Poland and in France, but not for massive long-range bombing. The inadequate armament of German bombers and the short range of German fighters were examples of this. Moreover it was badly commanded, by Göring who overestimated the capabilities of air power, and by Hitler who remained convinced far too long that Britain would surrender without an attack. Finally, at least as important, was the fact that morale among the German pilots and air crews carrying out the assault was by no means uniformly high. The commander of the German fighter forces, Adolf Galland, has written that the men under his command felt that the war effort had become a pyramid standing on its point. Letters from home, where rations were increased in the summer of

1940, indicated that the German civilian population regarded the war as over. Yet the men on lonely airfields in Normandy, Brittany, and on the Belgian coast, suffering serious losses in raids over England, knew better. They felt misunderstood and forgotten.

Conversely the equally small number of men of the Royal Air Force were among their own people defending, quite literally, their homes against attack. They were heroes to whom rightly every honour was paid. In case their aeroplanes were disabled, they could hope to land among a friendly population and return to fight again, while a German pilot was likely either to drown or be taken prisoner.

A second advantage for Britain, no less important than superiority of morale, was the technical excellence of RAF equipment and the easy flexibility and adaptability of its command. The critical importance of the development of Radar (radio detecting and ranging) is, of course, well known. It enabled the RAF to avoid the fuel waste and pilot fatigue of continuous high-level patrol, and made possible most efficient use of their limited resources of planes and pilots. (The German superiority in planes has frequently been overestimated. Comparable figures at the time of the Battle of Britain show Germany with a fighter strength of about 1,200 units to about 850 for the RAF. The Germans rarely sent more than 200 bombers in a raid.)

Another British technical advantage was the superiority of the British fighter over the poorly armed German bomber. There was little to choose between the German Messerschmitt fighter and the British Hurricane. (The more advanced Spitfire constituted only about one-quarter of Britain's fighter strength in August and September.) But the Messerschmitt had a short range and the bombers alone in daylight were almost defenceless against British fighters. However terrifying and deadly to the civilian population of crowded cities, the German resort to night bombing was a wasteful exploitation of military resources.

Finally, to all this should be added the genius of Air Marshal Sir Hugh Dowding himself. His flexibility of mind, willingness to accept innovation, and ability to force his opinions upon his superiors, eventually at the sacrifice of his professional career, stood in sharp contrast to the situation in the command structure in Germany. As has been pointed out, Germany was unsure about the best course to pursue in the invasion of Britain. The second and third phases of the Battle of Britain, the attacks on the Royal Air Force sector stations and the night bombing of London, were expedients at best. The Blitz itself was primarily a political, not a military, operation, begun out of pique and continued, at heavy cost to the Germans, long after any chance of invasion was gone, simply because no one could think of a better way to attack Britain. These decisions were not rational decisions. They were based upon self-deception, upon faulty intelligence, and upon Hitler's unwillingness to admit publicly that Germany had suffered her first military defeat.

While the Battle of Britain was at its height, in the first weeks of September, the Mediterranean became a theatre of war. Here, for the next four years, lay the principal zone of operations for the British army. Here also, against the Italians, Britain won her first important military victories on land. Italian forces in Africa in the summer of 1940 numbered nearly half a million men divided into armies of approximately equal size, based in Libya and in Italian East Africa (formerly Ethiopia). Early in August forces from Italian East Africa occupied British and French Somaliland, giving Italy substantial control of the Gulf of Aden and the entrance to the Red Sea, and making hazardous the supply route to the armies in Egypt. At the same time the Italians were preparing a thrust directly into Egypt from Libya with the goal of taking the Suez Canal. This attack began on 14 September 1940. To meet it the British had in Egypt, under General Sir Archibald Wavell, only 36,000 men, and another 27,000 in Palestine, to face an Italian army numbering about 250,000. Wavell's forces could do little, therefore, but retire. Within two weeks the Italians were 60 miles inside Egypt at Sidi Barrani. The British forces fell back to the village of Mersa Matruh, head of the railroad line leading to Alexandria.

As the invasion of Egypt went forward Mussolini prepared to expand his influence in the Balkans. He had secured a foothold there in the spring of 1939. Angered by Hitler's occupation of Prague in the middle of March, Mussolini, on 8 April, ordered troops into the tiny kingdom of Albania directly across the Adriatic from the heel of the Italian boot. While the occupation made little real difference in the status of Albania, which had been commercially and financially dominated by Italy for a decade, it enhanced slightly Mussolini's diminishing prestige.

Now in the autumn of 1940, further humiliated by Hitler's stunning victory over France, sensitive to Italy's declining position in the new order planned for Europe, and worried by Hitler's obvious interest in the Balkans (which was marked on 7 October by the German occupation of Rumania), Mussolini determined to expand to the south. On 28 October 1940, using Albania as a base, Italian troops invaded Greece. Britain immediately offered aid to that nation; the navy began to mine Greek harbours; a large loan was promised. But it soon became clear that Greece needed little help from the outside. By the middle of November, scarcely three weeks after the beginning of the war, the Greeks had taken the offensive and soon were invading Albania themselves.

A month later General Wavell counterattacked in Egypt and by the beginning of 1941 British, Australian and South African troops were deep in Libya. In January also a British force began the conquest of Italian East Africa, and by the middle of May 1941 the whole of the recently organized Italian empire in the horn of Africa had been surrendered. The first of the territories conquered by the Axis powers was redeemed.

However, by this time had begun a new series of British reverses. The Nazi occupation of Rumania was the prelude to increasing German pressure on other Balkan powers. Hitler was attempting to secure his southern flank in preparation for the invasion of Russia which was already being planned. In March 1941 Bulgaria succumbed to Nazi pressure by signing the Tripartite Pact, and Yugoslavia found it more and more difficult to resist becoming a Nazi satellite. (The Tripartite Pact was first signed on 27 September 1940 by Germany, Italy and Japan. The pact, in fact, contained little that was new. It reaffirmed the solidarity of the Axis powers and delineated the spheres of influence of each. It represented an attempt to institutionalize the new order in Europe and Asia. The signing of it by a small nation was taken to be the acceptance by that state of its place in the new order.)

Yugoslavia's failure to acquiesce in the German demands for a virtual protectorate over that country and the increasingly desperate Italian plight in the Greek war brought a German invasion of Yugoslavia and Greece that began on 6 April 1941. Within 12 days the Yugoslav army had surrendered and, despite the fact that Britain hurried some 60,000 men, whom Wavell could ill spare from the army in Africa, to support the Greek army, the Germans conquered nearly all the Aegean peninsula by the end of April. Britain was able to evacuate only about three-quarters of the force in Greece and, as at Dunkirk, much priceless heavy equipment was abandoned.

Of the 43,000 Britons, Australians and New Zealanders who had escaped from Greece, about 27,000 were evacuated to the island of Crete, lying approximately 60 miles from the mainland. Although the Royal Navy controlled the seas, and the commander in Crete,

General Freyberg, made some attempt to reinforce and re-equip his troops in the weeks following their arrival, the British found themselves unable to withstand the German assault on the island when it began on 20 May. The attack was almost solely by air, with paratroops and glider-borne infantry. By this means the Germans landed about 15,000 men and, although the Royal Navy was able to prevent for a time the transport of troops by sea, it suffered heavy losses doing so and within two weeks Nazi forces occupied most of the island. A second seaborne evacuation was necessary. Only about half the men on the island got away.

The Germans themselves suffered about 17,000 casualties, but from Crete they could protect Greece and threaten the Suez Canal. Also, the British diversion of troops to the Balkans so weakened General Wavell's army that it was unable to maintain the positions in Libya it had won the previous winter. On the other hand, perhaps most important, the Balkan invasion put off the German attack on Russia by five weeks so that neither Moscow nor Leningrad was taken when the Germans found themselves, unprepared, in the grip of the northern winter.

The Axis offensive that began in Africa on 3 April 1941, just three days before Hitler's attack on Yugoslavia and Greece, was far more dangerous than its predecessor of the previous autumn. Now the Italian forces in Africa were immeasurably strengthened by the addition of a number of German divisions and by the appointment of the German general, Erwin Rommel, as commander-in-chief. Within weeks after the beginning of the new offensive the imperial forces had been driven back into Egypt. But a strong garrison of Australians remained at Tobruk about 50 miles inside the Libyan border where they tied down a considerable number of Axis troops and served as a base for raids behind the enemy lines.

On 22 June 1941, 135 German divisions, supported by Finnish and Rumanian forces, attacked Russia. Despite the massive logistical preparations necessary for the operation and despite warnings of an impending attack forwarded to Stalin by American and British intelligence, the invasion came as a complete surprise to the Soviets. Churchill immediately announced British support for the Soviet Union. However, there was little Britain could do to help Russia in the early phases of her battle with Nazism. She herself was far from rearmed and the unfavourable course of the war in North Africa ensured that any diversion of arms from that theatre would be stoutly resisted by the fighting services.

The war in Africa remained throughout 1941 the chief anxiety for British strategists. An abortive offensive by Wavell in mid-June resulted in his replacement by Claude Auchinleck, who began an attack against the German–Italian forces on 18 November. But General Rommel had learned the lesson of desert fighting well. Endless square miles of desert could easily be given up to an enemy force in return for the security of one's army. Hence, by the end of the year Rommel had cheerfully retreated from Egypt and had evacuated most of the eastern portion of Libya. Yet, far from being defeated, as the year 1942 opened German forces were stronger, with shorter supply lines, than ever before.

By the end of 1941, on the other hand, it had become clear that Hitler's drive to take Moscow had failed. Then on 7 December the European war became a truly global conflict with the Japanese attack upon Pearl Harbor, the American military installation at Honolulu in the Hawaiian Islands.

The personal comradeship between Winston Churchill and Franklin Roosevelt, so important for the future of the English-speaking democracies in the Second World War, began on 11 September 1939 with a short note from the American President conveying congratulations upon Churchill's appointment as First Lord of the Admiralty. In the next nine months a substantial correspondence passed between the American President and Churchill, who signed himself at this stage 'Naval Person'.

Unhappily this easy rapport was not reflected in the official relations between the two nations. The strong isolationist sentiment of the interwar period in America had resulted in the passage of a series of acts, finally consolidated by the Neutrality Act of 1937, which made it illegal for Americans to sell arms, to loan money, to travel on the ships of belligerent nations, or indeed, at the discretion of the President, even to sell non-military equipment to a belligerent nation. In effect, every action that American public opinion felt had caused the nation's entry into the First World War was unlawful. President Roosevelt's failure to rouse American public opinion in 1937 after the Japanese invasion of China demonstrated this general feeling of Western Hemisphere isolation. His very tentative effort in February 1938 to engage America partially in European diplomacy had evoked no response from Chamberlain and had underlined American estrangement from European affairs. However, by the summer of 1939, with the clearly approaching war in Europe, the American Secretary of State, Cordell Hull, urged Congress to repeal the

Neutrality Act of 1937. The requested action was not taken immediately, but after the outbreak of war the President summoned a special session of Congress, which on 4 November 1939 amended the old embargo on all commercial intercourse with belligerent nations and permitted the sale of weapons to belligerent nations, provided that the weapons were paid for in cash and transported into the war zone in non-American ships.

The 'cash and carry law' was distinctly advantageous for the Allies. Both Britain and France held large liquid assets in the United States which could be used to purchase arms. Germany had none. In the following months the two western democracies established purchasing missions in the United States and placed large orders with American factories. These purchases gave the United States the double benefit of aiding nations that the majority of Americans hoped would win the war and of providing facilities at foreign expense that in the future could be used to produce arms for American military services. Hence much of the early cost of American rearmament was borne by Britain and France, both of whom sacrificed valuable assets in the United States for the purpose.

There was no question of American public support for the Allied cause in the war with Germany. Public opinion polls in October 1939 showed that less than one per cent of the population favoured Germany. But involvement in the war was another matter. The Allies seemed certain to win without American help. The assumptions made by the British population on the strength of the Royal Navy, the French army, and the Maginot Line were accepted at face value in the United States. (In October 1939, 71 per cent of the US population believed that Great Britain and France would win and only seven per cent expected a German victory.) As a consequence, the twin shocks of the Norwegian invasion and the seemingly irresistible drive into Belgium and France caused as much consternation in the United States as in Great Britain, and the quick surrender of France forced Americans to face the possibility that the Western Hemisphere might soon be alone on a planet otherwise completely dominated by aggressive, totalitarian Fascism. While this realization by no means ended all isolationism in the United States, it reduced isolationists to a small, if noisy, minority concentrated chiefly on the right wing of the Republican party. In the presidential election campaign of the autumn of 1940 the Republican candidate, Wendell Willkie, competed with President Roosevelt in protestations of support for the British cause.

Already America had given substantial secret aid to the United

Kingdom. Within hours after the completion of the evacuation at Dunkirk the Chief of Staff of the American army, General George C. Marshall, had ordered the disposal of about half a million rifles, 900 75-mm. field guns, and 80,000 machine guns with large supplies of ammunition for each. These were sold to an American corporation that turned them over immediately to Great Britain. This equipment, of First World War manufacture, partially made up for the tremendous losses suffered by the British Expeditionary Force in the defeat in Belgium.

Even before this, however, in his first communication to President Roosevelt after his appointment as Prime Minister, Churchill had outlined some more substantial needs for the future. Prominent among these, beside anti-aircraft guns, ammunition and aircraft, were 'the loan of 40 or 50 of your older destroyers to bridge the gap between what we have now and the large new construction we put in hand at the beginning of the war'. The need for these destroyers became more critical in the next few weeks after Italy entered the war, which Churchill had anticipated, and after France surrendered —which he had not anticipated. Churchill repeated his request at the end of July and through August anxiously pursued the possibility of the transfer of American destroyers. He was aware, as was Roosevelt, that the gift of destroyers was an unquestionably partisan act that would destroy any fiction of American neutrality and justify a German declaration of war upon the United States. He was aware also as an experienced politician that the military danger from abroad was matched, for Roosevelt, by the political danger of the act and the corresponding reduction in American defences. Roosevelt was in the midst of an election campaign. While sympathy for the British cause was hardly in question, the degree of American involvement in the European war most decidedly was under debate. On this account Roosevelt proposed and Churchill eventually granted, with a suspicion of reluctance, 99-year leases to the US on certain British North and South American areas that could become American naval and air bases. For reasons of his own the Prime Minister preferred to regard the transfer of the destroyers and the bases simply as reciprocal actions of goodwill and mutual solidarity, not as bargains, while Roosevelt in contrast presented them to the American people as a 'deal'. The destroyer–bases trade, finally announced on 3 September, aroused less opposition than Roosevelt had feared, even though it irrevocably involved the United States in the British cause. This easy public acceptance no doubt can be accounted for by the growing

American admiration for Britain that grew out of London's calmness and determination during the Blitz and by the wide personal popularity of Churchill.

The acquisition of the American destroyers emphasized a problem that was becoming grave by the autumn of 1940. This turned on the cash and carry requirement for the purchase of American arms. After the surrender of France, Britain had taken over all existing French contracts in the United States, even though at that time Churchill knew his nation no longer had enough foreign currency to pay for them. By November 1940, Britain had already spent in the United States about $4,500 million and was approaching the end of her resources.

President Roosevelt's solution to the dangerous problem of British financial exhaustion, first outlined in December 1940, was the 'Lend Lease Bill', formally entitled to make it palatable in America 'An Act Further to Promote the Defense of the United States'. The measure was introduced into Congress in January 1941 and finally passed on 11 March. Roosevelt signed it into law within half an hour after final congressional action and the next day asked for an initial appropriation of $7,000 million. Lend lease provided for the acquisition of military supplies or any other article deemed vital to the defence of the United States by the American government. This equipment would be lent to nations whose security had been designated by the President as vital to the defence of the United States. Presumably the article lent, or replacements, would be returned at the end of the war. In effect, the act placed the financial and manufacturing resources of the United States at the disposal of Great Britain.

The Lease Lend Act ended whatever pretence remained that America was a neutral country. The old policy of cash and carry had worked almost exclusively to the advantage of the Allies, but, technically at least, Germany also had the right to purchase arms in the United States. Lend lease, on the other hand, was selective in its application. The United States was choosing its friends and supporting them at its own expense. The act inaugurated a period of nine months of American semi-involvement in the European war during which German attacks on American merchant and naval ships became more and more frequent. The United States Navy retaliated with increasingly active pursuit of Axis submarines. Full-scale American involvement in the war in Europe seemed only a matter of time. Then suddenly attention turned to the Pacific area.

The Japanese attack on American naval and military installations in the Hawaiian Islands came as a shock to American public opinion and a surprise to the American administration. Roosevelt had felt from the beginning of the war that American interest lay with Britain. His personal envoy to Churchill, Harry Hopkins, had told the Prime Minister in January 1941 that the President was 'determined that we shall win the war together. Make no mistake about it.' Consequently the American administration was anxious not to provoke a crisis in the Far East that would interfere with American aid to Great Britain. It could reasonably be argued that the Japanese aggression into Indo-China following the fall of France did not seriously endanger American interests, and the war in China, although causing much indignation in the United States, seemed hardly closer to a Japanese victory at the end of 1941 than it had at the end of 1937. The American acts of July 1941 which finally drove the Japanese to war—the embargo on the sale of oil and the freezing of Japanese credits in the United States—came only as the result of extreme pressure from public and congressional opinion. Even after this breach of all but the most formal diplomatic relations, Roosevelt continued an extended series of negotiations that might have resulted in the Japanese withdrawal from Indo-China in return for American restoration of oil shipments, had it not been for pressure from powerful friends of China in American politics who refused to countenance any agreement with Japan that did not include a complete evacuation of the Asiatic mainland.

The breakdown of negotiations with Japan on 26 November caused the final Japanese decision for war. The fleet that attacked Pearl Harbor on 7 December had sailed from the island of Hokkaido on 25 November, although it could have been recalled by radio. The attack was a desperate gamble. It was successful far out of proportion to any reasonable estimate of the odds against it. United States naval intelligence had deciphered the Japanese diplomatic, although not the military, code and American commanders in Hawaii and the Philippines had been warned that negotiations with that government had broken down. Nevertheless, troops in the area that came under attack had not been put on a state of readiness, partly because the final warnings did not arrive until after the attacks began and more particularly because any reasonable assessment of Japanese intentions seemed to suggest that they would attack toward the south into the Netherlands East Indies. They would gain nothing, it was assumed, by deliberately antagonizing the United States. Their goal, after all, was oil.

At Pearl Harbor the United States navy sustained greater losses than it had suffered in the entire First World War. Eight battleships were damaged more or less severely, although within a year all except one were in action again. The significant Japanese mistake in the attack, altogether unnoticed at the time, was in their failure to find and destroy a single aircraft carrier. Fortunately all large carriers were at sea. But the American public was stunned. The Japanese had unified the nation. There was no question now whether the United States should enter the war. It was already at war, not only in the Pacific but, more important, in Europe as well. Paradoxically, the American defeat at Pearl Harbor, as Churchill well understood, had decisively shifted the balance of power in Europe against Germany.

While they were striking at the United States possessions in the Hawaiian and Philippine Islands, the Japanese attacked also the British holdings in the Far East. Fighting for Hong Kong and the Malay peninsula began almost simultaneously with the blow against Pearl Harbor. Hong Kong fell on Christmas Day. By that time British forces in the Malay peninsula were under severe pressure, being thrust continually southward toward the great naval base at Singapore. On 30 January 1942 the peninsula was evacuated altogether and on 15 February the island and the base at Singapore, with a British force of some 70,000 men, were surrendered to the Japanese.

The fall of Singapore was only one of the more serious in a chain of disasters. On 10 December, just three days after the attack on Pearl Harbor, Japanese torpedo bombers sank the British battleships *Repulse* and *Prince of Wales*, which were seeking to intercept a Japanese convoy off the coast of Malaya. The lesson of Norway, that surface ships without air escort were highly vulnerable to aerial attack, particularly by large, land-based aeroplanes, had to be learned again. The destruction of these two ships, coupled with the heavy American losses at Pearl Harbor, meant that in the western Pacific Great Britain and the United States faced conditions neither nation had known for more than a century—fighting without control of the sea. Dominating the ocean from the Macassar Straits between Sumatra and Malaya in the west, to Wake Island over 4,500 miles to the east, the Japanese were able to move troops and supplies with virtual immunity from Allied attack. On 6 May the last organized American force in the Philippines, operating on the Bataan peninsula guarding the north entrance to Manila Bay, surrendered. By this time the Japanese had already invaded Burma. Rangoon fell on 9 March, and Mandalay on 1 May. With the loss of this area went also the last effective route for sending aid to General Chiang Kai-shek's forces in China. At the same time, the Japanese struck southward. They overran the Netherlands East Indies early in March and by the end of the month were established on the north coast of New Guinea and in the Solomon and Gilbert archipelagos to the east. Now they could threaten the sea routes to Australia and indeed the continent itself. The lines of communication within their great diamond-shaped perimeter were longer from north to south and east to west than the distance from London to Bombay. All of Europe and Russia east of the Urals together with Asia Minor could easily have fitted inside it.

Japan's expansion came to an end almost as suddenly as it had begun. Two naval battles in early May and in early June turned the tide of the war in the Pacific. The first of these was the Battle of the Coral Sea on 7 and 8 May when a strong Japanese naval force, rounding the eastern tip of New Guinea and heading either for the Australian coast or for the chief New Guinean city of Port Moresby, was turned back with considerable losses by an American carrier force. The American victory here was by no means decisive, but the Battle of the Coral Sea showed that Allied forces at least had ceased to retreat.

Far more important, less than a month later, was the Battle of Midway Island when a serious Japanese attempt to extend their perimeter eastward toward the Hawaiian Islands in preparation for an attack on that archipelago resulted in a defeat with heavy losses. This battle, although technically a naval battle, was fought entirely by aeroplanes. The two fleets never came within sight of each other. Its consequences for Japan were most serious. At Midway she lost four aircraft carriers and, most important, a large percentage of her experienced air crews, the men who had attacked Pearl Harbor and whom she did not have the facilities to replace. The necessity of using only partly trained aviation personnel would, after Midway, make Japanese aviation progressively more inefficient and would decrease therefore the efficiency of her army and navy. Her shortages in replacement crews were principally the result of a lack of aviation fuel that would become more and more critical in Japan as the American submarine blockade of her islands cut the flow of oil from the Netherlands East Indies to the home islands. The nation's growing weakness in the air made more difficult the protection of the supply routes of the vast empire she was attempting to defend and also, in the long run, made impossible even the aerial defence of the home islands themselves. The shortage was not of aircraft; serious bombing of aircraft factories in Japan itself did not begin until late in 1944. The problem was that there were too few experienced men to fly them.

On land also, in the summer of 1942, the Allies were able to seize the initiative, although here Japanese tenacity and the innumerable advantages that jungle warfare gives to the defence ensured that any victories would be far less dramatic and clear-cut than had been the Battle of Midway Island. On 7 August 1942 a force of American marines taking the Japanese by surprise were able to land on the island of Guadalcanal in the Solomon archipelago and so to begin the long and bloody process of island hopping that would carry the Allied forces to the shores of Japan itself. Nineteen days later, on 26 August, Australians turned back a Japanese amphibious attack on Milne Bay at the south-eastern tip of New Guinea and so, bringing an end to Japanese expansion toward the south, relieved the threat to Australia. The Japanese were by no means defeated in the summer of 1942, but they were contained. They had no longer any chance of victory. Australia, New Zealand and for practical purposes, India were safe. The war in the Pacific could safely be given a second place to Europe and the bulk of Allied strength moved to the other theatre. The decision to do this Franklin Roosevelt and Winston Churchill had already made.

Britain declared war on Japan on 8 December 1941 and because, unlike the United States, the government could act without a vote of Parliament the British action anticipated by a few hours the American declaration of war which occurred the same day. On that day also Churchill determined to visit the United States immediately. There was some fear in the cabinet that the Japanese attack might cause a sudden concentration of American attention in the Far East and thus lessen, rather than increase, American participation in the struggle against Germany. Churchill hoped from the beginning to concert with the United States government a division of activity that would avoid any lessening of pressure against Hitler.

The Prime Minister arrived in the United States on 22 December after a slow crossing of the Atlantic by battleship. He spent Christmas at the White House with President Roosevelt and on 26 December spoke to a joint session of the American Congress. In these days was born the easy working partnership which, with the addition of Russia, the Prime Minister would term the Grand Alliance in recollection of the combination of British, Dutch and Imperial forces who fought the French in the War of the Spanish Succession. Finally, and most important, Churchill secured the commitment he had hoped for: that the European theatre of war would receive priority over the Pacific. The extension of the war to Japan would cause no slackening of the war upon Germany. Churchill specifically urged at this time that the western democracies prepare a descent upon Africa which would clear the southern coast of the Mediterranean of Axis forces. This was eventually agreed to by President Roosevelt and the invasion, 'Operation Torch', took place in November 1942.

On the evening of the day of his speech to Congress, 26 December, Churchill suffered a slight heart attack. This event, kept from him at the time, did not prevent a journey to Ottawa three days later and a second, highly successful, speech to the Canadian Parliament. However, most of the first week of January 1942 the Prime Minister spent resting in Florida. He did not return to Great Britain until 17 January.

The first months of 1942 were in some ways worse for Britain than any preceding period. They lacked the exaltation of the grim, back-to-the-wall struggle of 1940 when the nation stood alone under the attacks of the Luftwaffe. The momentary excitement of American participation quickly slipped away with the disasters in the Pacific and with the hideous shipping losses along the East Coast of the United States which marked the climax of the Battle of the Atlantic. German resistance in North Africa, beginning in mid-January 1942, ended the British drive of the previous November that had taken Allied forces nearly to the middle of Libya. The bad news from Africa was compounded by the reversals in the Far East where the surrender of Singapore on 15 February brought, for Churchill at least, the gloomiest day of the war. Nevertheless, in Europe and in the Pacific the last six months of 1942 would see the beginning of Allied offensives which marked the turn in the course of the war.

THE DEFEAT OF GERMANY

Discussions of the war in Africa had occupied much of the time during Churchill's visit to Washington at the end of 1941. Despite some American interest in immediate preparations for a cross-Channel invasion into France, Churchill convinced President Roosevelt that Allied energy in 1942 should be directed toward clearing the southern shore of the Mediterranean. At the time of the White House meetings Churchill had assumed that General Auchinleck would soon win a decisive victory in western Libya. Therefore he urged an Anglo-American invasion of French North Africa within the next six months that might bring the large numbers of French troops there over to the Allied side and would be a prelude to a quick Axis defeat in that continent.

Unfortunately Auchinleck's advance into Libya stopped on 18 January 1942 without having destroyed the Axis armies. In desert war, where the destruction of enemy forces is far more important than the mere acquisition of territory, this failure was decisive. As a consequence the plans for an Anglo-American descent upon French North Africa had to be pushed back for many months. Auchinleck deceived himself about the amount of damage he had done to the Axis forces under General Rommel. By the end of January he had been forced to withdraw from the area of his most extreme penetration in central Libya and to retire to a position just west of Tobruk and not far inside the Libyan border. Here on 26 May he was attacked by General Rommel in a powerful drive which recaptured Tobruk on 21 June and drove the imperial forces back deep into Egypt where at the beginning of July they took up a position only 70 miles west of Alexandria at El Alamein. The entire Allied position in the Middle East was threatened.

However, Rommel had far over-extended his lines of communication; his troops were weary, his equipment depleted. The German spearhead in Egypt was as exposed and vulnerable as had been Auchinleck's in Libya six months before. The British Eighth Army, now under the command of General Bernard Montgomery, who had replaced Auchinleck, was receiving an increasing flow of supplies from the relatively safe, but long, route around the Cape of Good Hope and through the Red Sea. The line at El Alamein, compressed between the impassable Qatar Depression and the sea, withstood a series of German attacks while Montgomery patiently built up his forces until his power far exceeded that of his opponents. Finally, on 23 October 1942, in overwhelming force and achieving almost complete surprise, he attacked General Rommel's army. Within three weeks, by 12 November, the last enemy troops had been expelled from Egypt.

Four days before, on 8 November, began Operation Torch. An Anglo-American invasion force commanded by General Dwight Eisenhower landed on the French North African territory in Morocco and Algeria. Within the next few days, after some French resistance, most of the important towns were taken. The German forces now were trapped in Libya and Tunisia, between the Eighth Army pushing west out of Egypt and the forces of Operation Torch driving eastward from Algeria. By the end of January 1943, British forces had expelled the last German and Italian troops from Libya.

In these last days in an attempt to hold at least a portion of Tunisia Hitler gave General Rommel the men and supplies he previously had denied the German forces in Africa. Now, however, it was too late. The men and machines that might have enabled Rommel to capture all Egypt six months before in the summer of 1942 were insufficient to do more than slow the American and British forces pushing in from the east and the west. On 7 May 1943 the main body of Rommel's army, although without Rommel himself, surrendered.

Even before the German surrender in Africa, between 14 and 23 January, Churchill and Roosevelt met at Casablanca to plan the next phase of the war. The Casablanca conference ranks perhaps as the most important meeting between the two leaders of the western democracies. By and large the decisions taken there followed the lines proposed by Great Britain and were a tribute to the careful and detailed preliminary work of the British military and naval staffs. For the immediate future, Roosevelt agreed, after strong protests from the American Chief of Staff, George C. Marshall, to forgo any landing in France in 1943 and to continue the clearance of the Mediterranean by an invasion of Italy through Sicily. This would have the multiple advantages of relieving German pressure on the Russian front and hopefully of bringing Turkey into the war as an active ally. But there would be no further major military operations in the Mediterranean, no attack in Greece or elsewhere in the Balkans, and, with all possible speed, an invasion force would be built up in the British Isles to prepare for a cross-Channel attack into the centre of Hitler's empire. Until that time pressure on Hitler could be maintained through intensified aerial attacks on Germany itself, and at Casablanca a table of priorities for bombing targets, beginning with ball-bearing factories and synthetic gasoline plants, was worked out. The Soviet Union would be supported with the largest possible volume of supplies. This maximum effort in Europe inevitably meant a reduction in the effort in the Pacific, and Roosevelt agreed to this over the strenuous objections of the American admiral Ernest J. King.

A final decision to come from the Casablanca conference, made public by President Roosevelt at a press conference, was the determination by the Allies to insist upon the unconditional surrender of Germany, Italy and Japan. The words 'unconditional surrender' had never been agreed to by Churchill, and Roosevelt later admitted that the use of this term was accidental. Many historians have argued that by barring any negotiated peace the demand for complete submission probably lengthened the war and cost many Allied lives. On the other hand, one may question whether a person of the frame of mind of Adolf Hitler, or of the Japanese generals who had begun the war in the Pacific, would have acted differently had the stipulation never been made. The only way that Germany ever would have come to the negotiating table would have been through the removal of Hitler. When an attempt to accomplish this failed, German resistance to the end was inevitable even without the Allied demand for an unconditional surrender.

The invasion of Italy, the most immediately important decision made at Casablanca, began quickly after the German surrender in Africa. British, United States and Canadian forces landed in Sicily on 10 July 1943, and in little more than a month had forced the surrender of all Axis troops on that island. Meanwhile, on 25 July Benito Mussolini had been removed as Italian leader. On 3 September the new Italian regime under Marshal Pietro Badoglio surrendered to Allied forces.

The surrender of the Italian government did not end the fighting in Italy. The Germans had anticipated such a contingency since the previous May and quickly occupied all of the northern three-quarters of the peninsula which included most of the principal Italian cities. The Allies, who had only invaded the Italian mainland on 3 September, the day the armistice was signed, were in no position to contest the Germans' control and so lost much of the fruit of the Italian surrender. Probably the blame for the Allied delay in this case should lie with the chief of American intelligence, Allen Dulles, and with his faulty liaison with Allied military leaders. As a consequence Italy remained a theatre of war where fighting of the bitterest kind continued until the German surrender in May 1945.

By the summer of 1943 the tide had turned decisively in Russia. The vast German offensive of the last six months of 1941 stalled before Moscow and Leningrad at almost precisely the time that the Japanese attacks began in the Pacific. The next spring, holding their line in the north, the Germans began a huge new offensive in the Ukraine directed toward the rich natural resources in the area between the Caspian and the Black Sea to the north of the Caucasus Mountains. By the end of August German troops had reached the Volga at the city of Stalingrad where the Russians began a desperate resistance to prevent the Germans from crossing the river. In November the Soviet armies launched a great counter-offensive to the north and south of Stalingrad so that by the beginning of December 22 Nazi divisions in that city were cut off. The winter of 1942–43 saw a fierce battle during which the German perimeter around the city gradually diminished. With her surrender of Stalingrad on 3 February 1943, Germany lost the initiative in Russia as she had lost it the previous August in Africa.

Meanwhile, in Great Britain preparations went forward for the invasion of the Continent. A concentration of ground forces and a beginning of a day and night bomber offensive inaugurated formally in June 1943 warned Germany of violence to come. (The aerial attacks on Germany represented the most important part of the preparations for the invasion. Allied planners assumed the large repeated raids over German industrial centres would destroy enemy productive capability and significantly lower civilian morale. Investigation since the war has shown that the damage done by the raids was small in proportion to the Allied resources devoted to them.)

The long-awaited invasion of Europe occurred on 6 June 1944. On that day, 156,000 troops, of whom about half were British and Canadian, stormed ashore on the beaches of Normandy. (Until the first days of July British and American troops were in France in approximately equal strength, between 15 and 16 divisions. But after that time began the tremendous American build-up so that by the end of August about three-fifths of the two million men in France were American.) Although the Germans inflicted 10,274 casualties on the first day, the invasion was a success. Britain and the US profited by the sort of luck that for so many years previously had seemed to reside with the Axis. The Allies achieved tactical surprise. The German commander in France, Erwin Rommel from Africa, was away on leave. Hitler was asleep when the invasion began and his aides dared not wake him. Thus critical German armoured reserves under his personal control were held back until too late. When committed, the Germans frequently had to use their armoured forces as weapons of defence for which they were never designed. They were able to delay the British Second Army briefly from the capture of Caen until 18 July. But by this time the American army had taken Cherbourg and although the Germans thoroughly destroyed the port its loss meant nevertheless that the first phase of the invasion had come to an end.

But there was still much hard fighting to be done in Normandy which was not finally secure until the middle of August. On 15 August American and French troops invaded France from the south, landing on the coastline just to the east of Toulon. The bulk of this force, which had been intended to make the Germans withdraw troops from the north but which arrived too late to accomplish this, drove straight north up the Rhône Valley, being aided along the way by large numbers of French guerrilla forces. By this time German troops in the interior of France were withdrawing rapidly toward the Rhine lest they be cut off by the onrushing Allies. On 25 August 1944, Paris surrendered. By the end of the month British and Canadian forces had cleared most of France north of the Seine River and early in September were attacking the Channel ports in Belgium.

At the beginning of September it appeared that the war would end very soon. Two million troops and 3,500,000 tons of supplies were ashore. Thousands and thousands of German prisoners had already been captured in France and even where they continued resistance, as in Bordeaux, St Nazaire, and Lorient, German forces were cut off and desperate, receiving only uncertain supplies by plane and submarine. The last remaining obstacle to a drive directly into the heart of Germany was the Westwall, the great line of fixed fortifications thrown up by Hitler in 1938. But this line did not extend along the entire western border of Germany. It had never been continued along the Dutch frontier where the delta of the Rhine River made crossing difficult. If the Allies could seize the beachhead on the German side of the Rhine they could outflank the Westwall, avoid many bloody battles involved in piercing the German fortifications, and speed the end of the war.

The plan evolved was extremely simple. American parachute forces would seize the bridges at Nijmegen and Eindhoven across the Waal and Maas Rivers in southern Holland where the delta of the Rhine began to form and a strong British force would land at Arnhem on the northern bank of the Lower Rhine. Once these bridgeheads were seized, no further obstacles remained to a sweep over the north German plain. The British Second Army could then drive into Germany. On 17 September began the largest airborne operation of the war. Although the bridge at Nijmegen was taken, the landing of 8,000 men of the First British Airborne Division, who had the most difficult assignment of all, became a disaster. They were unable to effect a juncture with the forces from the south and the Germans, who had the good luck to seize a complete set of the plans for the operation, reacted furiously. The Red Devils, as they were called, held out for nine days. Finally, after heroic resistance, with their supplies gone, about 2,000 men were evacuated by air.

The failure to turn the flank of the Westwall made necessary a direct attack on the fortifications along Germany's western border and a major winter offensive was in fact in the final planning stages when on 16 December 1944 the Germans counter-attacked in force. They attempted to drive straight west through the Ardennes Forest, which they had penetrated with such ease in the spring of 1940, and continue to the English Channel at the port of Antwerp. Their hope was to divide the troops in the north from those in the south and to restore, as Hitler put it, the war of movement. Before the end of the year the Battle of the Bulge had ended in costly German defeat. But the Allied offensive into Germany was set back six weeks and by the time British and American forces had smashed the Westwall and reached the left bank of the Rhine, in the first days of March, Soviet troops, which had crossed the old German-Polish frontier nearly a month earlier, were within 30 miles of Berlin. The Allied difficulties in the West in the last months of 1944 would have important consequences for the future of Germany and of Europe.

The battle of Germany was nearly over. On 25 April, Allied and Russian forces met at Torgau on the Elbe; on the 30th Hitler committed suicide in the Führerbunker under the Reichschancellery and on 2 May Berlin fell to the Russians. On the same day the Nazi forces in Italy surrendered and on the 7th, all German forces gave up in their own country. The official victory in Europe was finally proclaimed on 8 May.

BRITAIN IN TOTAL WAR

The Second World War affected the people of the British Isles more intimately and immediately than any previous conflict in modern times. The air raids of 1940 and 1941 killed about 30,000 civilians and over three and a half million houses were destroyed. Food rationing, the continuous and ever-widening shortages of all necessities of life, the flying bombs and rockets which began on 13 June 1944, seven days after the invasion of France and which in nine months killed nearly 9,000 more civilians, all made a reality of the term total war.

Yet mobilization at home, like mobilization of the military force, proceeded at a leisurely pace in the Second World War. Although the government had taken the precaution on 24 August 1939 to arm itself with virtually dictatorial powers over all activities of British subjects, it used these powers slowly. The air of unreality, the expectation of a cheap victory that had been behind the civilian lassitude during the 'phony war', made politicians hesitant to impose strict rationing or industrial controls. The call-up of men for the armed forces went forward only slowly and indeed in June 1940, after the surrender of France, as the Battle of Britain was beginning, 434,000 men and over 200,000 women still drew unemployment insurance benefits. Too frequently there was a tendency to continue an easy and expensive expedient—to subsidize the cost of food rather than to enforce rigorously the control of prices, to give in to wage demands of labour rather than to use the ample powers available for the prevention of strikes. As a result, in the early months of the Second World War, both prices and wages rose rapidly, more rapidly than in the same period of the First World War.

The atmosphere of undisciplined inertia, of 'business as usual', began to disappear with the formation of the wartime coalition and Churchill's assumption of the premiership. But at the same time it is almost impossible to say what part of the new vigour and direction that came to British domestic affairs was the result of Churchill's personal drive—although he had been a consistent critic of the government's earlier lack of purpose even while he was himself a member of the ministry—and what part was the result of the increasing desperation of Britain's position.

A most sensitive indicator of British difficulties, one that immediately affected conditions in the British Isles, was the monthly total of losses of merchant shipping. The loss of Norway in April and May infinitely extended the coastline available for bases for German submarines and indeed for a time made it almost impossible to control the passage of German submarines in and out of port. Between May and June of 1940, tonnage of British merchant shipping lost to enemy action tripled from 82,000 to 283,000 tons. In the last six months of 1940 and the first six months of 1941, with the entrance of Italy into the war, the extension of the zone of conflict to Africa, and the loss of the French Biscayan and Mediterranean ports, British shipping losses averaged nearly 200,000 tons a month. After a short respite in the autumn of 1941, losses for 1942 increased sharply again so that through the whole of 1942 the rate of sinking averaged nearly 300,000 tons per month and for October and November of that year totalled 879,000 tons, the highest figure of the entire war. Particularly cruel during the long hours of summer daylight were the sinkings among convoys attempting to carry aid around the North Cape of Norway to the Soviet Union.

The losses of shipping that became critical in 1942 might have been disastrous had not the government by this time evolved the planning techniques that would make possible the efficient allocation of the limited resources available in total war. The year 1941, in the words of the official historian, was a 'watershed in the conduct of the war'. John Maynard Keynes's appointment as adviser to the Treasury at the end of 1940, Kingsley Wood's budget of April 1941, and Horace Wilson's retirement as permanent secretary of the Treasury in 1942, each in different ways marked steps in the transition. In those days the British civil service began to learn, and British politicians to accept, the techniques of control of the national economic plant. They began to understand the meaning of the interchangeability of resources: that labour used to produce a given commodity at home might under certain circumstances be better employed producing ships to bring it from abroad, that sometimes in a period of critical stringency of foreign exchange it was more economical to buy food from far-away dominions in sterling and waste the shipping necessary to bring it to Europe than to buy the same food in North America and waste the dollars. Political leaders began to see the national economic plant as a whole and to think of income and expenditure in national terms. The first of the annual statements on income and expenditure dates from 1941. As Britain in the First World War had learned that government intervention and planning in social and economic affairs could be useful in time of crisis, in the second the nation learned to accept it as a normal and desirable area of state action.

Social planning for peace went on even during the darkest days of the war. Indeed it is likely that the very universality of the British war effort itself, the widespread demand for the fullest measure of sacrifice from all sections of the community, ensured that some sort of social revolution would come with the peace. The extent of social participation in a war effort, many scholars have argued, is directly proportionate to the extent of social reform that will be demanded afterwards.

The government was never faced during the Second World War with the widespread war weariness, the exhaustion and despair, that made it necessary for Lloyd George in the First World War to saddle himself with extravagant promises of a land fit for heroes. Rather the problem was the reverse. It was generally accepted that Britain would be a poorer nation after the second war. Therefore the responsibility for the distribution of resources and for the maintenance of institutions of human welfare would have to fall more heavily than ever upon society as a whole. The support of hospitals, for instance, could no longer be left to private charity. Schools would have to be more generously endowed, especially as Britain's relatively declining place in a competitive economic world made more necessary than ever the fullest possible training of her people. The vast expenditures of capital for the prosecution of the war and the immense damage done to domestic housing by bombing ensured even greater government activity in house building than during the interwar years. Contrasted with her attitude during the first war, when the nation had expected that by some miracle a defeated and vengeful Germany would build a better Britain at no cost to its inhabitants, in the second war the nation looked forward grimly to making the best use of its own efforts, directed closely by the government, to ensure that all citizens enjoyed at least a fair share of whatever benefits peace had to offer.

From the ordinary citizen's point of view postwar planning began on 1 December 1942 with the publication of the Report on Social Insurance and Allied Services, the so-called 'Beveridge Report'. The Beveridge Report receives praise or blame for many social institutions with which it was unconcerned. It did not found the National Health Service, nor did it provide against mass unemployment, as one recent historian has stated. Indeed its author specifically assumed the establishment of a comprehensive health service and of some policy for the maintenance of full employment, as well as a system of children's allowances. (Children's allowances were enacted by the coalition in the spring of 1945.) Generally the Beveridge departures lay not in coverage or in new plans of insurance; his innovations were philosophical. Beveridge institutionalized the ideal of the national minimum, that each citizen of a modern society had a right to a basic decent standard of life not because he was a worker, nor because he was old, nor because he had been injured in an industrial accident, but simply because he was a human being. He proposed social security in the true sense.

The Beveridge Report achieved tremendous public notice and laid down the lines upon which social thinking would progress. By handling the report badly, leaving the nation with the feeling that it was frightened of any discussion of postwar plans and that it distrusted the idea of social insurance, Conservative leaders in the coalition gave Labour the opportunity to attack Toryism in the abstract without attacking Churchill and allowed the party to frighten the electorate with the prospect of the return of the economic grimness of the interwar years. The voters in 1945 cast their ballots against Baldwinism, the means test and unemployment. They were urged not to trust the Tories. Churchill, a war leader, was irrelevant in peace.

The popular expectations raised by Beveridge forced the coalition government into some serious efforts at social planning for peace. Specifically Churchill wished the coalition he headed to show some accomplishment in education and health. In education the results were significant. The Education Act of 1944 provided for raising the school-leaving age, instituted the well-known eleven-plus examination, and established a tripartite division of secondary schools into grammar, technical, and modern.

In health the coalition was less successful. A plan published by the Ministry of Health (health, like education, was always kept safely under Conservative ministers) in February 1944 outlined a comprehensive tax-supported national health service, without, however, nationalization of hospitals. Nevertheless, it met strenuous opposition from the medical profession. Negotiations with the doctors dragged on through the rest of 1944 and into 1945 when they were cut short by the German surrender. Thus the Conservatives had only a set of 18-month-old proposals, now considerably diluted, to offer as a programme of health reform in the election of July 1945.

Churchill called the election that drove him from office with reluctance. Although he had promised in 1944 to dissolve Parliament once Germany was defeated, within a week after the German surrender he proposed to the Labour and Liberal leaders, Clement Attlee and Sir Archibald Sinclair, that the coalition should continue until the defeat of Japan, which he then estimated would take 18 months. Neither of the opposition leaders was anxious for a general election. Everyone assumed that any party or group led by Churchill would win, even though since June of 1943 public opinion polls had shown an increasingly strong popular preference for Labour. (The Labour preference over the Conservatives grew from seven per cent of the electorate in June 1943 to 16 per cent of the electorate in April 1945 and stood at the end of June 1945, on the eve of the election, at 47 per cent Labour and 41 per cent Conservative and Liberal National.)

Upon receiving the opposition's refusal to continue the coalition Churchill resigned on 23 May and formed a caretaker government made up exclusively of Conservatives. Three weeks later, on 15 June, he dissolved Parliament. The campaign which followed was notably acrimonious and offended many people. The ability of British political opponents to put aside partisanship in time of emergency somehow made the return of partisanship conspicuously disagreeable. Churchill's violent, frequently tasteless, attacks on his former colleagues were widely resented, as was the fact that the Conservatives appeared to be running the Prime Minister in every constituency. Although to the historian the outcome seems a foregone conclusion, the overwhelming Labour victory on 26 July (the final announcement was delayed by the necessity of waiting for returns from the military forces overseas) was a great surprise to Churchill and to the world at large. Labour elected 393 Members of Parliament against 213 for the Conservatives. The Liberals, who had counted on William Beveridge much as the Conservatives had counted on Churchill, were reduced to 12. Churchill, who was at Potsdam negotiating with Joseph Stalin and the new American President, Harry Truman, over the disposition of Germany and Eastern Europe, resigned immediately. Although fighting continued in the Far East until 19 August, for Britain the conflict was over. Once more, within a generation, the nation faced the problem of reconstruction from war.

CHAPTER SIX

The Welfare State

THE LABOUR INHERITANCE

The new Labour Prime Minister, Clement Attlee, brought to his office far more experience in cabinet administration than had been possessed by Ramsay MacDonald. Attlee had been leader of the Parliamentary Labour Party since the resignation of George Lansbury in 1935, had been in Churchill's War Cabinet from its formation in May of 1940, and since February 1942 had held the title of Deputy Prime Minister. In personality he was the antithesis of the flamboyant MacDonald and the masterful Churchill. He was reserved, seeming almost shy, and during the war this apparent insignificance beside the monumental figure of the Prime Minister had been the subject of many jokes. Yet Attlee proved to be a strong leader, giving the King's government the stability and sound common sense it needed. He was not an originator of policy, but Labour did not need such a man. The supply of policies was most adequate. The government needed a head who could harmonize conflicting interests, one who could mediate within the cabinet between trade union leaders and university intellectuals and who could balance the demands for the immediate extinction of capitalism against the desperate national need for economic reconstruction and expansion.

The Second World War had been far more costly than the first. To be sure, fewer men had been killed. Battle deaths amounted to slightly fewer than 250,000 as opposed to 750,000 before. But of all instruments of war, men are perhaps the cheapest. They need little maintenance; they do not become obsolete; they do not need to be manufactured. However, the Second World War, a war of machines, imposed a far greater strain on Britain's economic and productive resources than had the first. In simplest terms, the national debt increased by about £14,800 million or almost exactly twice the increase incurred in the previous conflict, although this comparison means little, for prices were much higher in 1940 than in 1914. But, more significantly, as in the First World War, annual government expenditures far exceeded the total national income of any prewar year. British national income in 1938 had been £4,671 million. In each of the seven fiscal years, from the year ending 31 March 1940 to 31 March 1946, the government spent an average of £4,734 million, reaching a peak of slightly over £6,000 million in the year 1944–45. Even these figures would have been higher had it not been for the slow start made during the easy optimism of the Chamberlain administration when until the end of March 1940 the government succeeded in spending only slightly more than £1,400 million. Put another way, between 1940 and 1945 the total yearly consumption of goods and services in Great Britain, both personal and governmental, exceeded the total production each year by an average of 13 per cent. In effect, for each £100 of goods and services in these years, British citizens and their government used £113. During this period the war took slightly less than half of all the goods and services created, although in 1943, the peak year, military demands almost precisely equalled all other personal and governmental consumption. The strain on capital resources would have been worse had the government not been able to control, far more efficiently than in the first war, personal civilian expenditure. Throughout the war this was cut to about 80 per cent of normal. Yet because of efficient rationing, the scientific supervision of civilian diets (particularly children's diets), and because of more adequate distribution of medical and hospital services through the emergency medical scheme, British vital statistics show that the nation emerged from a period of considerable deprivation far healthier than it had been at the beginning of the conflict, in marked contrast to the First World War.

An important factor in the maintenance of the British war effort was the proportion of both civilian and military resources obtained from the United States through lend lease. Lend lease put off also, for the period of the war, the chronic problem of the maintenance of a balance of trade. By the end of the war Britain had spent abroad about £16,900 million and earned in the period between September 1939 and December 1945 only about £6,900 million, or about 40 per cent of its imports. The rest had been financed by the sale of £1,200 million of capital abroad, a new indebtedness of £3,300 million (the sterling credits) and by grants and lend lease from the United States and Canada, to the amount of £5,400 million. (Sterling credits were earnings for sales to Britain by foreign nations, chiefly, but not exclusively, within the Commonwealth. These nations agreed to deposit them in London in pounds rather than insisting upon their conversion into their own currencies. These balances earned interest and represented a British indebtedness that presumably would be paid off at the end of the war. The exports necessary to redeem the sterling balances, because they only liquidated past indebtedness and earned no new income, were the so-called 'unrequited exports' which after the war made the maintenance of Britain's balance of payments all the more difficult.)

Britain's absolute dependence upon American lend lease suddenly became clear on 21 August 1945, scarcely a week after the end of the war in the Pacific, when, as he was required to do by law, the American President Harry S. Truman abruptly terminated lend lease aid. This action precipitated a financial crisis in the United Kingdom. Lord Keynes was immediately sent to Washington, where in the winter he was able to obtain a loan to begin in July 1946 of $3,750 million from the United States and another $1,250 million from Canada. Attached, however, were the hard conditions that imperial trade preferences should be ended and that the pound should become freely convertible to the dollar for current transactions in July 1947. This last requirement would help to make 1947, like 1931, a year of crisis.

REFORM AND AUSTERITY

The administration of Clement Attlee falls easily into two distinct phases. The first covers the 18 months from the summer of 1945 to the beginning of 1947. This was the 'glad confident morning'. The party was dominated by hope, eagerness to be at work, and by an almost evangelical enthusiasm. Labour seemed at last to have arrived at the place where it could establish true social democracy in Great Britain. Economic problems, to be sure, were present but they could be pushed to the back of men's minds and in any case a breathing spell had come with the United States and Canadian loans. The second phase, beginning in 1947 and lasting until October 1951 when Attlee resigned, was overshadowed by the struggle to keep Britain afloat economically. During this time there was no single year, with the possible exception of 1948, in which the nation's leaders were not harassed by the deficit in the dollar account, by the need to support sterling, by price inflation, or usually by all three.

In the first 18 months of its tenure Labour compiled a record in social and economic legislation that probably never has been equalled in so short a period either in importance or in sheer bulk. By the end of 1946 Parliament's energy was exhausted and several members of the government were dangerously weakened in health. Labour's first important bill, introduced only weeks after the new Parliament assembled, receiving its second reading on 29 October 1945, provided for nationalization of the Bank of England. Under this measure the government purchased the equity of the approximately 17,000 stock-holders of the Bank who received government bonds, and took the power to appoint a governor, deputy governor and the 16 directors of the Bank. Historically, the Bank of England Act was a significant measure. In a way it was Labour's revenge for the crisis of 1931, for the return to gold, and generally for the deflationary policy promoted by the Bank in the years after the First World War. Financially, in terms of asserting Treasury control over the Bank's policies and through it over the British money market, nationalization probably was far less important. It did indeed give the Treasury power to give the Bank such directions as were 'necessary in the public interest' and the right to supervise in a general way the Bank's relations with the financial community. However, as it turned out, the Bank, although nominally the servant of the crown, appeared to have nearly as much independent influence over government financial policy as ever. The solid expertise of its officials all too frequently was not matched by the men at the Treasury, and so the advice of the servants frequently became the command of the master.

The bill for the nationalization of the Bank of England received the royal assent on 1 March 1946. By this time the Coal Industry Nationalization Bill had been introduced. This measure, finally enacted in July 1946, transferred to public ownership 1,634 coal pits in the United Kingdom and a large number of ancillary facilities—coke ovens, brick works, together with 250,000 acres of farm land, 141,000 houses, and other living and recreational amenities for miners. Altogether, more than 800 private companies with assets of nearly £154 million were taken over.

Neither the bill nationalizing the Bank of England nor the coal industry was seriously opposed by the Conservatives. In fact, during the election Churchill's party had advocated such widespread re-organization and government direction of the coal industry that the question of ownership would have been almost academic. Viewed historically, both measures had their origin in attempts to solve problems of the 1918–39 period. For the Bank this had meant the enforcement of public responsibility over a large amount of financial power. For the coal mines, nationalization was the only possible way to modernize a vital but hopelessly antiquated British industry.

A third great measure of nationalization, comparable in many ways to the nationalization of the mines in that it dealt with an ancient, huge, essential and impoverished industry, was the Inland Transport Act, which was introduced in November 1946 and took effect on 1 January 1948. This bill dealt not only with the railroads but with all other forms of inland transport: road transport and canals, as well as dock and harbour facilities. It brought into government employ even more men—nearly a million—than had been affected by the nationalization of the coal mines. The act created a central British Transport Commission under the general supervision of the Ministry of Transport as the National Coal Board was under the authority of the Ministry of Fuel and Power. The day-to-day administration of the various services was to be handled by six executive boards under the transport commission: for docks and inland waterways, railway hotels, railways, London transport, road haulage, and road passenger transport. The number was reduced to five in 1953 when road haulage was denationalized.

In addition to these three basic nationalization acts passed in the early period of the Labour government, a number of other measures provided for government ownership in industries already partly within the public domain. The Civil Aviation Act of 1946 brought into existence under the Ministry of Civil Aviation two corporations, British European Airways and British South American Airways, to join the British Overseas Airways Corporation which had existed since 1939. The Cable and Wireless Act of 1946 created a public corporation for overseas communication responsible to the Postmaster General, and the Electricity Act of 1947 brought under a single national authority the generation and distribution of electric power. In this case, the Central Electricity Board had been in existence since 1926 and many electrical generating stations were already publicly owned.

Besides these large steps toward public ownership of the instruments of production—by 1948 about 20 per cent of the nation's workers were on the government payroll or the payroll of a public corporation—Clement Attlee's government took steps also to regulate in the public interest the use, development and exploitation of the British land. There were a series of measures on agriculture, subsidizing farm income and restricting agricultural imports, aimed generally at improving farming as an industry and diminishing the heavy expense in foreign currencies of imported foodstuffs. Taken together, these measures rapidly increased the profitability of British husbandry and increased also the price of British agricultural land. Both trends, of course, were warmly approved by the Conservatives, who qualified as a party as friends of agriculture and as individuals, in many cases, as farmers.

The opposition, however, was less uniformly enthusiastic about legislation that aimed at redesigning and relocating British cities and at rehousing a large proportion of the British population. Perhaps no single effect of the war caused so much hardship as the shortage of housing. Britain's housing situation had been far from ideal in 1939, although nearly one-third of the nation had been rehoused since the First World War. Nevertheless, in 1945 about three million houses, or about one-third of the total, were over 80 years old. Moreover, German bombing had destroyed or damaged nearly one-third of English homes, with a net loss of half a million units, and in the six years of war the population of the United Kingdom had increased by nearly two million people. These shortages of living accommodations ended for a time much thought of slum clearance, which had been the principal intent of subsidized housing programmes in the thirties. In many ways the housing problems of 1945–50 were similar to those of 1918: a shortage of building materials, disorganization of the building industry, enormous relocations of population, and rising prices. The Minister of Health, Aneurin Bevan, was responsible for two major housing acts, of 1946 and of 1949, during his tenure. Essentially he revived the housing policy of the 1920s, giving local authorities responsibility for meeting housing needs for all classes of their area, not only in slum clearance but also in the construction of new housing estates. In order to protect critical supplies of building materials, Bevan's measures went further than any previous legislation had done in permitting local authorities to license and restrict all but the most critical private building. (Deliberately postponed, among other things, was the construction of new hospitals, which helped to add to the difficulties of administration under the National Health Service.) At the same time, landlords were offered large financial inducements to modernize and reconstruct unnecessarily spacious flats and apartment buildings. Bevan's heroic efforts, although falling short of the planned goal by some 200,000 units, by 1949 had provided, nevertheless, by repair, reconstruction, or new building, about a million new homes.

Besides housing and nationalization, Labour's domestic programme had promised above all the extension and reform of Britain's welfare institutions. The core of these, the bases of the welfare state, were the National Health Service Act of 1946, the National Insurance Act of 1946, the National Insurance (Industrial Injuries) Act of 1946, and the National Assistance Act of 1948. When taken together with the Family Allowances Act of 1945, these measures provided the so-called 'cradle to the grave' security that had been the goal of British social reformers since the First World War. At the time Labour came to power, plans for National Insurance were further advanced than those for the National Health Service, the latter having been the subject of continuous, and rather acrimonious, discussions with the medical profession since the first coalition plans on the subject were published early in 1944. The new insurance proposals were specifically the outcome of the Beveridge plan. They provided for the unification of the separate unemployment, pensions, and sickness insurance reserves into a unified fund which would receive a single contribution from each worker and from which all benefits would be taken. Parallel to the national insurance scheme was a second plan providing for compulsory insurance against disablement as a result of industrial accident. The National Insurance (Industrial Injuries) Act provided for a state-run insurance fund that would supersede the multitude of widely varying provisions for employers' liability that had been the rule in Great Britain since the turn of the century.

Underlying the contributory insurance plans, making a reality of the implied guarantee of a decent minimum standard of living for everyone, was public assistance. The National Assistance Act of 1948 finally superseded the ancient Poor Law which in varying forms had existed since the reign of the Tudors. With public assistance the national government took from the local authorities the ultimate responsibility for care of the poor and for establishing a comprehensive backstop which would make good any shortcomings in the insurance programmes. Because of rapidly rising prices since the war, National Assistance—now 'Supplementary Benefit'—has had to supplement payments under national insurance, particularly old age pensions, where the amount due the recipient is too small to live on.

Most controversial of all Labour welfare programmes was the National Health Service. Here Labour inherited from the coalition only a skeleton plan first published in the White Paper of 1944, and Aneurin Bevan, responsible for health as well as housing, soon made clear that the new government considered itself in no way bound by the concessions previously made by the coalition Minister of Health in the many months of negotiations with the British Medical Association. In effect, Bevan took upon himself the sole responsibility for the creation of the new health service.

The National Health Service Bill resulted in the most serious party contention of all early Labour measures. Bevan departed from the coalition's health service plan by nationalizing all British hospitals, municipal and voluntary, and by forbidding the sale of medical practices. He justified these modifications, in the first case on the basis that only through large infusions of government money could hospital facilities be made adequate to provide modern medical service and in the latter case because the continued purchase and sale of medical practices would make impossible the redistribution of physicians throughout the United Kingdom.

The nationalization of hospitals was seriously resisted by Conservatives within the House of Commons, while the abolition of the sale of practices—even though the government eventually agreed to compensate doctors for the lost value of their patients' goodwill to the extent of some £60 million—caused widespread unrest in the medical profession. Professional discontent nearly approached proportions of a medical strike in the early months of 1948. Fortunately at the last moment cooler heads averted what might have been a dangerous act of professional irresponsibility.

The National Health Service, as well as national insurance and public assistance, came into effect together on 5 July 1948. By this time the most productive period of Clement Attlee's ministry was over, and the previous year had seen a financial and economic crisis which for a time seemed to threaten not only the Labour government, but also the stability of the British economic system itself. The disasters of 1947 began on 7 February with the astonishing announcement by Emanuel Shinwell, Minister of Fuel and Power, that due to a shortage in the production of coal and the most severe winter since 1880–1, electric power would have to be cut off to a large number of industrial establishments and seriously rationed even to domestic consumers. This announcement took Parliament and the public by surprise. It was a heavy blow to the confidence and prestige of the government, particularly since the official nationalization of coal had occurred only a little more than a month before on the first day of the year. Still worse, it caused heavy unemployment. The numbers out of work rose within two weeks from the almost irreducible minimum of 350,000 to 2,300,000—15·5 per cent of the work force.

The closure of industries, which lasted three weeks, was also a heavy blow to the export drive, costing an estimated £200 million in lost exports.

The fuel crisis was only the beginning of the year of agony. Far more serious, because it seemed to be permanent, was the chronic deficit in British trade with dollar areas. British imports from dollar areas were about three times her exports to them. British exports to the United States were little more than enough to cover the cost of tobacco bought there, about 80 per cent of all tobacco used in the United Kingdom. The loan of July 1946 had given the United Kingdom only a breathing space and much of the benefit that should have accrued from it was erased by a rapid rise in American prices in the years immediately after the war. (By 1947 prices of imports from the United States were up 40 per cent over those prevailing in December 1945.) This change in the terms of trade against the United Kingdom added £329 million to the import bill. Combined with the cost of the fuel shortage, the result was that in the nine months from July 1946 to April 1947 the United Kingdom drew $1,300 million of the total credit of $3,750 million. By the second quarter of 1947 the average drain on Britain's dollar reserves amounted to $75 million per week. This was more serious because, according to the terms of the American loan, the United Kingdom was obligated, beginning on 15 July 1947, to make the pound freely convertible into dollars for current transactions. This requirement was strenuously opposed by the British government, particularly by the Chancellor of the Exchequer, Hugh Dalton. The unfavourable export figures of the previous spring, the fuel crisis, and the rapid drawing on the American loan had all undermined international confidence in British currency. Inevitably, any creditor of Great Britain would demand dollars rather than pounds for his payment if he could get them. As had been feared, the announcement of convertibility of the pound on 15 July began a flight from British currency. British losses of dollars immediately leaped up from $75 million to $115 million per week and in the last full week before dollar convertibility was suspended on 20 August, Britain lost $237 million. By 1 September only $400 million remained undrawn on the original loan of $3,750 million. It was 'like watching your child bleed to death', Hugh Dalton remarked.

Even before the suspension of dollar convertibility, on 6 August 1947, the government took steps to avert the approaching bankruptcy. The series of measures now enacted made a reality of the word 'austerity'. Food rations, particularly butter and meat, were cut (bread had been rationed since July 1946), imports from dollar areas were seriously controlled, tourist spending outside the sterling area was reduced, and in October stopped altogether, while new goals and incentives were provided for British industry. Taken together, the new measures, the 'siege economy', made even more stringent demands upon the British citizen than had been the case during the war. They reduced the momentum and confidence of the Labour administration. There never again could be, as there had been in 1945, talk of the 'glad confident morning' of socialism. The morale of the party declined and in the summer there was a brief attempt led by Dalton, Herbert Morrison, and Sir Stafford Cripps, who succeeded Dalton at the Exchequer in November 1947, to replace Attlee as Prime Minister with Ernest Bevin.

While the economic crisis of 1947 was at its worst, the means for its solution appeared. This was in the proposal made at Harvard University in June 1947 by the American Secretary of State, George C. Marshall, for American economic aid to Europe, the so-called Marshall Plan. Marshall envisioned a general European economic recovery programme in which Britain would participate, the general easing of tariff barriers and financial restrictions of all kinds. He proposed from the first that the initiative for economic planning should come from Europe. Foreign Secretary Ernest Bevin quickly seized upon the possibilities offered by Marshall and made Britain from the beginning a leader in European economic planning. In April 1948 the American Congress passed the Economic Cooperation Act and of the $4,875 million that became available for the first year, 1948–9, Britain received $980 million. Generally 1948 seemed a year of hope as 1947 had been a year of despair. Domestic production and exports rose. The huge deficit of trade with dollar countries was strikingly reduced; imports from the sterling areas increased; Britain achieved for the first time since 1935 a small credit balance in current international payments.

Unfortunately the respite of 1948 did not last. A slight economic depression in the United States reduced the demand for British products and increased the competition of American exports in world markets. Unfavourable trade reports brought again in the spring of 1949 a sustained attack upon the pound. Britain's defences against foreign speculation now were even weaker than in 1931. In the years immediately after the war her gold and dollar holdings of approximately $2,000 million were minute in terms of the total trade of the sterling area for which this sum was the reserve. Her ability to pay for imports, therefore, was dependent directly upon her ability to export. A relatively small decline in the market for British goods had to be met immediately with a corresponding decline in British purchases. There was virtually no reserve of debts due Great Britain to tide the nation over until she could pay her way again. (The Treasury now maintains a portfolio of foreign interest-bearing securities.) And the very fact that the traders of the world knew that practically no reserve of gold and foreign currency existed made all the more insistent the demands for the exchange of pounds into foreign currencies when a trade drop occurred. Britain's weakness compounded her weakness. The situation in 1949 was in some ways comparable to that of 1931, but whereas in the former year the government's concern had been chiefly to guard the gold convertibility of its currency, in effect to maintain the credit of the British nation, in 1949 the problem was essentially to save enough foreign assets simply to buy the goods the British people needed to live. By July gold and dollar reserves had dropped below the $2,000 million considered to be a safe minimum, and the government halted all purchases from dollar areas. Nevertheless, the attack on sterling continued and finally in September, with reserves approaching the $1,000 million mark, the Chancellor of the Exchequer, now Sir Stafford Cripps, announced the devaluation of the pound from $4·03 to $2·80.

As in 1931 the recovery, once the bitter initial step was taken, seemed miraculous. Nevertheless, it can be argued that the devaluation itself did little good and the sudden growth in Britain's exports was less the result of lower prices for British goods than of the economic recovery abroad, particularly the expansion of the American market that began with the outbreak of the Korean War on 25 June 1950. It has been argued that a devaluation of 30 per cent was larger than necessary and that Britain's failure to export was less the result of high British prices than of a sheer inability to produce. In any case, much of the advantage that might have accrued to British exporters from lower prices of their products evaporated quickly as a result of devaluations in other countries and as a consequence of a nearly 25 per cent inflation in British prices within the next four years that resulted from Britain's own rearmament programme in 1951. The sacrifices of the late forties did not solve Britain's basic imbalance of low productivity and high consumption. Through the fifties and into the sixties the nation's prosperity would continue to be dependent on world economic conditions beyond its control. The rising standards of living throughout the Western world, European recovery, and the immense prosperity of the United States allayed the symptoms of British economic weakness, but the disease remained.

Before beginning a discussion of British external affairs, two major pieces of legislation of the second phase of the Attlee administration should be mentioned. The first of these, the Independence of India Act passed in July 1947, will be discussed in another section. The other, the Iron and Steel Act of 1949, which nationalized 90 per cent of the British steel industry, became a major issue in the general election of 23 February 1950. As has been noted, iron and steel was one industry that had substantially reorganized itself in the decade of the thirties and, unlike the coal mines and railroads, had a consistent record of profitability. Labour, nevertheless, had included steel in its manifestos before the 1945 election as one of the industries to be nationalized. But during the first four years of office the government showed clear reluctance to take action on this promise. The disappointing record of the coal industry in both profitability and production and the vast expense of the reconstruction of British railroads—even though it could be argued that the condition of both these industries was simply the result of years of capitalist neglect—made the principle of nationalization appear less attractive than it once had been. What *were* the aims of nationalization, it was asked. Was it not possible that the demand for government ownership proceeded simply from the fact that steel, unlike other nationalized industries, was likely to be profitable? But then, was government ownership to be thought of simply as a way of ministering to sick but vital industries, an economic poor law, while profitable industries were left in private hands? Many Labour spokesmen argued that nationalization was an essential part of social democracy itself, necessary in simple political terms because of the danger accruing to popular government when too much wealth was concentrated in the hands of a few self-appointed and irresponsible individuals. On the other hand, less radical Labourites expressed fears about the impact of steel nationalization in the United States at a time when Britain's economy was dependent upon Marshall aid.

Unsure of its position, the Labour government hesitated until 1948 before introducing a bill for steel nationalization. Before long it was clear that the Lords might well use their suspensive veto to delay the bill for two years. This would have placed the date of steel nationalization beyond the five-year statutory life of the Parliament elected in 1945. As a consequence, in 1949, Labour introduced a bill to reduce from two years to one the Lords' power to hold up

House of Commons action. After a bitter debate this measure passed. Nevertheless, it was apparent that even with the second chamber's power thus reduced, the immensely complicated business of government assumption of ownership of the British steel industry could hardly be completed before 1950. At a conference of the two parties, therefore, it was agreed that while the Lords would pass the Iron and Steel Bill in 1949, the date for the transfer of the industry should be put back to January 1951, that is, after the general election scheduled for the previous year. Even with this agreement the Conservatives promised during the election that they would denationalize the industry if they came to power, and other large industries which considered themselves candidates for nationalization, cement and sugar prominently, began concerted advertising campaigns attacking the Labour government. (The Iron and Steel Act came into effect in November 1949 and the vesting date was set at 1 January 1951. Although the Labour government formally nationalized the industry the Conservatives sold all the companies but one, Richard Thomas & Baldwin, back to their stockholders after they returned to power in October.)

The election of 23 February 1950 was held on registers that had been newly revised under the Representation of the People Act of 1948. This measure abolished university representation and plural voting for electors who held business premises as well as residences, thus hurting the Conservatives. But at the same time it redistributed seats according to the large and impermanent relocation of British citizens which had occurred during the war. The centres of many large cities, Labour strongholds, had been evacuated during the bombing. Country districts, tending to be Conservative, received extra seats. Thus when the election came, although the government's share of the total vote dropped only from 47·8 per cent in 1945 to 46·1 per cent, in 1950 it elected only 315 candidates as opposed to 393 previously. The Conservatives returned 298 Members, the Liberals nine. Labour's working majority had disappeared.

The last 20 months of Labour administration, from the election of February 1950 until the government's resignation after the election of 25 October 1951, were a time of frustration and unhappiness. Clement Attlee's government suffered severely from internal divisions between those of its members of traditional trade union background and the substantial group of men, frequently, but by no means exclusively, of middle-class background with connexions in the universities and the Labour party constituency associations. The trade unionists, and the ordinary Labour politician from an industrial town, generally reduced political questions to terms of personal or trade-union economics and supported socialism because it seemed to constitute the best way for a working man to protect himself from the vagaries of capitalist society. The intellectuals, on the other hand, tended to be militant socialist ideologists who were impatient with the more modest working-class objectives of social insurance and nationalization of industry and who hoped to use the power of the government to remodel British society. Frequently they were convinced pacifists and sought for an accommodation with the Soviet Union while distrusting the United States. Generally they thought in political and doctrinal rather than economic terms. Within the cabinet the socialist purists were led by Aneurin Bevan. They resented their more pragmatic colleagues whose leaders were Herbert Morrison and the Chancellor of the Exchequer who had succeeded Cripps in October 1950, Hugh Gaitskell. Particularly they were impatient with Gaitskell's budget of the spring of 1951, which proposed the spending of £4,700 million on rearmament in the next three years and the introduction of charges for dentures and spectacles under the National Health Service. Attlee, who was ill, was unable to play his customary role as a mediator and on 24 April 1951 Bevan and the President of the Board of Trade, Harold Wilson, resigned. Bevan's loss was a serious blow to the government and was compounded by the fact that his resignation coincided with the departure of Ernest Bevin, who left the government solely on the grounds of health, but who nevertheless deprived the Treasury bench of its strongest figure. (Bevin had resigned the Foreign Office early in March, to be succeeded by Herbert Morrison, and had held briefly the office of Lord Privy Seal. He died on 14 April 1951.)

Out of the government, Bevan and his followers were in a position to attack directly the moderate members of the cabinet and the leadership of the trade unions. They denounced rearmament, the introduction of charges for the health service, and the apparent unwillingness of the party leadership to proceed with a pure Socialist programme. The Labour Party went into the general election of 25 October 1951 seriously divided, the situation being made worse by the rapid deterioration of Britain's financial condition. The decline of party spirit, the loss of forward drive, and the angry mutual recrimination between the left wing of the Parliamentary party and the trade union leadership tended to obscure the very great accomplishments of the first two years of the third Labour administration.

All things considered, it is surprising that Labour did not lose more heavily in the election of 1951. The party received nearly 700,000 more votes than it had in 1950 and actually polled over 200,000 more votes than the Conservatives. But the Conservatives returned 321 Members of Parliament to Labour's 295. Labour continued to waste votes, as it had in the twenties and thirties, in the overwhelming socialist constituencies of the North of England and Wales, while the redistribution of 1948 broke up the huge constituencies in the South and gave the Conservatives new seats in the suburbs of London and in the large towns of the Midlands. Moreover, the pendulum was swinging against austerity. In 1951 Britain voted for the affluent society that seemed to be promised in the Conservative slogan 'Set Britain Free'.

FOREIGN AND IMPERIAL AFFAIRS

In 1945 Britain possessed on paper greater armed strength than she had ever controlled before. But her international position was weaker than her massive efforts during the war should have made her. Her ability to maintain the large military forces she possessed at the end of the war would in the long run be determined, like much else in her postwar history, by conditions of international trade. Probably it is impossible to overstate the importance of the national economic position in the assessment of foreign policy. Repeatedly in the years between 1945 and 1951 Britain found decisions of international politics becoming dependent upon conditions of domestic finance. The support of the large occupying force in Germany and the necessity of feeding the civilian population were important contributing factors to the crisis of 1947. The financial cost of the maintenance of British forces in Palestine, and above all the support of Greece, would be important determinants of policy in the eastern Mediterranean. Yet despite repeated warnings the real precariousness of Britain's financial position, the almost absolute dependence of the nation upon international conditions, did not finally come home to the population at large, or indeed to the government, until the disastrous Suez Canal invasion of 1956.

When Clement Attlee succeeded to the office of Prime Minister in 1945, leaders from Britain, the United States and Russia were meeting at Potsdam in an attempt to chart the political future of Eastern Europe. Soviet military successes in 1944 and 1945 had enabled Russia to occupy Latvia, Estonia and Lithuania, Poland and East Germany, as well as the succession states of the old Austro-Hungarian

Empire and all of the Balkans, excluding Yugoslavia and Greece. In effect, except for the failure to hold the Straits of Dardanelles, the aims of Russian foreign policy since the days of Peter the Great had been achieved. Russia was now a truly European power with hegemony both in the Mediterranean and in the Baltic. Although the problem was old—Castlereagh had faced the same threat in the Polish-Saxon question in 1814—Britain's resources to meet it were relatively far less than they had been at the time of the Congress of Vienna. Britain found herself in the years immediately after the Second World War unable to play her traditional role as the leader of the Western democratic forces, maintainer of the balance of power, and policeman of the world's sea lanes. To a considerable extent the history of her external affairs in the postwar decade is the story of her gradual abandonment of old responsibilities in Europe, in the Mediterranean and in the Far East.

The first of the three central facts of British foreign policy as it evolved after the war was the great division between the Communist and Western worlds that appeared almost immediately after the elimination of the German threat, designated by Winston Churchill in March 1946 as the Iron Curtain. This division would affect British policy, not only diplomatic but imperial, at every turn. Even in areas unconcerned with the struggle between the collectivist and capitalist economic systems, in emergent colonial areas and in such old spheres of British domination as Egypt and India, the ability of uncommitted national leaders to play off the two great power blocs one against another gave exceptional importance to the diplomatic position of otherwise minor nations.

Second was the fact of Britain's poverty. The resources to maintain a navy larger than that of any potential enemy simply no longer existed, nor did the ability to absorb the far greater expenses necessary to enter the technological race toward the development of greater and more fearsome nuclear weapons and delivery systems. The basis of Britain's power in the nineteenth century had been her separation from all foreign enemies by water dominated by her own navy and her own consequent invulnerability to foreign attack. The assumption of this strength survived the First World War and, justifiably or not, dominated popular attitudes toward Europe and the rest of the world in the 1920s and 1930s. But now this strength was gone. Britain's isolation was at an end and a drastic reorientation of her military relations with Europe became inevitable.

The third factor of British foreign policy, intimately connected, yet in some ways contradictory, to the second, was Britain's 'special relationship' with the United States. This relationship had been a product of the cooperation between the two great English-speaking democracies during the war. After the conflict it assumed a character, like the Entente with France before 1914, easy to recognize but difficult to define. For the US in the years immediately after the war, Britain was the one stable and powerful democracy in Europe, the one nation upon which the United States could depend to assume a diplomatic attitude similar to its own. From Britain's point of view, in the beginning at least, the special relationship had the advantage of providing United States cooperation in the task of policing the world, in effect of giving help in accomplishing those things Britain was no longer able to do alone. On the other hand, with the liquidation of Britain's empire, her interest in policing the world declined and as the importance of closer ties with Europe became more apparent the usefulness of the special relationship began to diminish. Indeed by the sixties the unique friendship with the United States began positively to hinder the formation of closer ties with Europe.

Consciousness of her altered position in the world, as well as of the political disorganization of Europe, prompted a significant departure in British foreign policy in May 1948 with Britain's adherence to the Brussels Treaty, in which she associated herself with France, Belgium, the Netherlands and Luxembourg (the so-called Benelux States) in a 50-year military alliance. The Brussels Treaty soon became, as had been anticipated at the time of its signing, the core of a larger group which formed into the sixties the essential element of Britain's defence posture, the North Atlantic Treaty Organization. NATO, as it was called, had at the beginning the Brussels nations plus the United States and Canada, but included also Italy, as well as Norway, Denmark, Iceland and Portugal. Introducing it to the House of Commons in March 1949, Ernest Bevin called the attention of the Members to the fact that it provided for the first time in history American participation in the maintenance of the stability of Europe. The treaty, finally approved by the American Senate in October 1949, was given particular significance by the first Soviet explosion of an atomic bomb the month before.

Britain's interest in the maintenance of a European military front against Communism was symbolized by her continued willingness, at heavy cost to herself, to maintain a strong troop commitment in Germany and by her agreement after the outbreak of the Korean War to begin a large, and exceedingly expensive, rearmament programme.

But her interest in European military cooperation did not extend to participation in European economic integration. The almost universal poverty of the continental powers after the Second World War dissolved to some extent the barriers of nationalism and prompted the continental states to think in terms of some type of cooperation for the long, and surely painful, process of rebuilding. This cooperation was immeasurably hastened by, indeed made a precondition of, Marshall Plan aid. The leading proponent of European economic union was the French businessman and economist Jean Monnet, who, working through his nation's Foreign Minister, Robert Schuman, proposed the integration of coal and steel production of France, Germany, Italy and the Benelux nations. This association of European productive facilities, which became formally known as the European Coal and Steel Community, and informally as the Schuman Plan, was the result of discussions in Paris in June 1950. The plan came into effect under a treaty signed on 18 April 1951. Britain, although invited to participate in the Paris discussions, declined to do so. An important consideration in this decision, so far as Labour was concerned, was the fact that the British steel industry at this point was in the process of nationalization, while coal had already been nationalized. The Conservatives supported this position, although for the reason that the economic integration of Europe would mean a loosening of ties with the Commonwealth. The decision taken in 1950 largely determined Britain's attitude toward the formation of the European Common Market in 1957. Participation in European defence arrangements did not imply any willingness to subordinate British economic institutions to a supra-national body.

Even though she was heavily committed both militarily and diplomatically in Europe, the day-to-day concentration of British external affairs tended to be less concerned with the Continent, where the United States took the lead in planning cold war strategy, than with the more traditional areas of British interest, the Mediterranean and the areas to the east of Suez. Here in many cases Britain had to proceed alone, although in one critical activity, the support of Greece and Turkey, nations which had looked to Britain as a protector for well over a century, she was able to turn to the United States for help. The British announcement, in March 1947, that she would no longer be able to give her customary financial and military aid to Greece, evoked a quick announcement from the American government that the United States would continue the aid Britain was no longer able to give. This announcement, the so-called Truman Doctrine, marked the beginning of direct American intervention in Europe and stands in many ways as a precursor of the Marshall Plan. But in essence British and American actions in the Near East, even when they were mutually advantageous, sprang from different motivations. Britain was interested in the maintenance of political stability and ensuring her access to oil supplies. America sought primarily the containment of Communism. As a consequence, on some occasions—as in Palestine in 1948 and in Egypt in 1956—where the Russian menace was not apparent, American and British policies were sharply divergent, with consequent serious difficulties for Great Britain.

Perhaps the key action in external affairs during the period of the Labour government, affecting British policy both in the Mediterranean and beyond, was the freeing of India on 15 August 1947. The modern Indian drive toward independence began during the First World War. From the beginning of British rule in India until the end of the second decade of the twentieth century, Indians had no voice whatever in their government. Political power lay either with the British Viceroy or, in the princely states, in the hands of autocratic royal rulers who were themselves subject to considerable British control. India's entrance into the first war against Germany had been taken for granted by Britain, but well before the conflict came to an end it was clear that Indians would expect some degree of self-government by way of compensation for their sacrifices. Britain attempted to meet these demands with the Government of India Act of 1919, which provided a limited degree of provincial self-government in the hands of Indians, while reserving certain powers for the British central authority. Unfortunately, in the spring of 1919, before the act came into operation, disorders broke out which culminated in the so-called Amritsar Massacre in which nearly 400 civilians were killed and 1200 others wounded. As a result the chief nationalist organization, the Indian National Congress, condemned these first attempts at native self-government and thus destroyed whatever likelihood there had been that Indians could be satisfied with such a limited amount of domestic control over their affairs.

Emerging at this time as the leading spokesman for India and the leader of the Indian National Congress was a middle-class lawyer named Mohandas Gandhi. Gandhi's character was saintly and his personal tastes ascetic in the extreme, but he proved to be a shrewd negotiator and an adversary able to confound all the power that the British Empire could bring against him. His weapon, in contrast to the violence of previous decades, was passive resistance, the refusal by unarmed Indian civilians to obey the law, an invitation to martyr-dom. His willingness to risk and suffer imprisonment inspired India's millions and made British rule seem crude and despotic by contrast.

The act of 1919 had envisioned further instalments of Indian independence in the future and after the accession of Labour in 1929 the government began a series of conferences with Indian leaders. Indian self-government was a matter of serious contention among the opposition and was resisted by several important figures, most important Winston Churchill, who in 1931 resigned from the shadow cabinet of the Conservative party. On the other hand, the Government of India Act, which in 1935 established a new constitution giving legislative control of Indian affairs to Indian lawmakers in all departments except defence, foreign relations and religious affairs, did not satisfy the leaders of the Indian National Congress, who looked forward to complete independence.

Under the pressure of the Second World War, London, in 1942, offered India dominion status after the war. This proposal, however, was rejected both by the Congress and by the Moslem League, which claimed to represent India's Moslem minority of some 70 million people. The growing hostility between the two chief religious sects in the Indian subcontinent complicated Britain's problems. There was fear, well justified as it turned out, that once Britain's power was withdrawn, enmity between the two sects would break into violence. The Moslem League was by now demanding complete separation from India and the establishment of an all-Moslem state, Pakistan. After the war the fear of civil war in India was the chief hindrance to the grant of complete independence. Britain did not desire to be an accessory before the fact to violence, yet neither could she hold on until Hindu and Moslem leaders came to an agreement among themselves. Outbreaks in Calcutta and the clear unwillingness of Hindu and Moslem leadership to compromise with each other caused the Labour cabinet to conclude that the Indians could be forced to take responsibility for their own future only by a clear time limit when British rule in the subcontinent would end. On 20 February 1947 the government announced that British authority would cease not later than June 1948. The next month Lord Louis Mountbatten was sent to India as the new Viceroy charged specifically with effecting the transfer of power.

The bill granting Indian independence went through Parliament quickly. It established two independent nations, Pakistan and India, and specified that the princely states were required to join one or the other. Although the independence day of 15 August 1947 passed with general expressions of goodwill both from Karachi and New Delhi, the autumn of the year saw mass migrations of Hindus and Moslems accompanied by looting and massacre, especially in Punjab. Gandhi, who sought to quell the violence, was assassinated on 30 January 1948. Both Pakistan and India elected to remain in the Commonwealth, although India became a republic in 1950 and Pakistan in 1956.

Indian statehood was followed within six months by the independence of Burma and Ceylon. Burma received her sovereignty on 4 January 1948 and Ceylon on 4 February. However, while Ceylon chose to remain a dominion, Burma unequivocally broke all ties with the Commonwealth.

Britain's grants of complete self-government to over 500 million people over whom she had ruled for a century or more, retaining at the same time these people's friendship for herself if not for each other, must stand as one of the great achievements of recent political history. A number of members of the Labour party have declared that these actions represent the greatest accomplishment of the Attlee government and have argued that if Churchill, whose record of support for Indian independence was more than conditional, had been Prime Minister the consequences for Britain as well as for India might have been disastrous. Attlee's ability to recognize that Britain's immediate departure from the Far East was vital, and his courage to take the steps that were necessary, saved three nations of the four for the Commonwealth and earned Britain the goodwill of the world.

Unfortunately in another area, Palestine, British success was much less complete. For Britain, the traditional importance of the Middle East derived from the necessity of protecting the Suez Canal, which represented the lifeline to India. But with the loss of India and her surrounding territories this factor diminished in significance. On the other hand, the continuing discovery of new oilfields in the Arabian peninsula and in the Persian Gulf, and the rapid increase of the European use of oil after the Marshall Plan, made more necessary than ever the maintenance of British power in the area, even after the Indian independence.

The break-up of the Ottoman Empire, which had occurred during the First World War, had released innumerable conflicting nationalist forces among the Arabs. Between 1914 and 1918 Britain had encouraged this nationalism as a military measure. But after the Armistice she found herself opposed by Arab leaders who resented the continued British presence in her area no less than they had resented Turkish power. Arab unhappiness was compounded because in 1917, again as a war measure, Britain had promised to create a 'national home' for Jews in Palestine. (The Balfour Declaration specifically avoided the use of the words 'national state' or 'nation'.) Britain received Palestine as a mandated area from the League of Nations and in the twenties and thirties permitted Jewish immigration into the country. Although the number of Jews coming to Palestine varied from year to year and dropped practically to nothing at the end of the twenties, after 1933 with the Jewish persecution in Nazi Germany it leaped up and was a continual source of friction between Britain and the Arabs. As ruler of the territory, Britain was in the unhappy position of receiving blame from the Arabs for permitting Jewish immigration and from the Jews, not only in Palestine but in the rest of the world, for failing to prevent Arab violence against the Jews. The situation was further complicated by the fact that Britain maintained as a client state the desert kingdom of Trans-Jordan (now Jordan), whose government she supported with subsidies and whose army was commanded and to some extent trained by Englishmen. At the same time she attempted to remain on good terms with Iraq and Iran and with the various desert sheikdoms, all of whom controlled lands rich in oil. Successive governments of the interwar period hence were caught in the dilemma of the political necessity of placating Jewish opinion within the United Kingdom, Western Europe and America, and of the economic necessity of placating Arab opinion in the Near East.

With the approach of the Second World War the danger of Arab hostility became paramount. There was no question that world Jewry would support the Allies, but there was considerable question about which side the Arabs would take. As a result, in May 1939, after failing to force agreement between Jews and Arabs and seeking to counter Nazi influence in the Arab world, Britain issued a white paper restricting further Jewish immigration into Palestine to 100,000 individuals. At the end of the war in 1945 this policy was still in effect and Arab nations, upon whom Britain depended more than ever for oil, now that imports from dollar areas were restricted, were insisting upon its implementation. On the other hand, the horrors of the Nazi extermination of Jews in Europe and the plight of the hundreds of thousands of Jewish refugees made its continued enforcement politically almost impossible. Moreover, since the war the Jews in Palestine had acquired arms and were determined to force the British to leave the mandate, certain that they were now powerful enough to protect themselves from the surrounding Arab states.

Official British policy, and perhaps the personal inclinations of Foreign Secretary Ernest Bevin, lay in the direction of continued enforcement of the immigration restrictions. On the other hand the United States, where Zionism was strong and where large blocs of Jewish votes were important factors in Democratic political calculations, continually put pressure upon Attlee's government to disregard Arab protests and to open Palestine to further immigration. Between these opposing pressures British administration was further distracted by a campaign of terrorism launched by the Palestinian Jews themselves against the British occupation forces. This reached a climax on 22 July 1946 when one of the Jewish nationalist organizations succeeded in blowing up the British Headquarters in the King David Hotel in Jerusalem, killing about 90 people.

Affected by the world unpopularity the nation was incurring and the heavy economic burden imposed by the maintenance of a large military force in Palestine, British public opinion at this time began to favour withdrawal from Palestine and resignation of the responsibility there. Within the government there was a good deal of irritation at the United States, which seemed content to give advice, but no tangible help, toward the solution of the Arab-Jew dispute. Consequently in 1947 the government announced that it would give up the Palestine mandate and turn the administration of the area over to the United Nations. In the autumn of 1947 the United Nations voted to try to partition the country between Jewish and Arab sectors with an internationalized Jerusalem and sent a group of experts to the country to try to draw a partition line that would separate two independent states, one Jewish and one Arab. The partition plan pleased the Jews, who were supported by both the United States and the Soviet Union, but displeased the Arabs, who fought it in the United Nations. While the United Nations was debating the future status of Palestine, Britain announced that, regardless of the future of the country, her mandate would come to an end at midnight on 14 May 1948 and that her troops would be withdrawn immediately. Although the United Nations moved reluctantly to assume the administration of Palestine, when the British forces were withdrawn the Jews in the area itself chose the date of the ending of the British mandate to proclaim independence and announce the formation of the state of Israel. The new nation was promptly recognized by both the United States and Russia and was promptly attacked by its Arab neighbours led by Egypt. The Jews defended themselves with vigour and, although unable to preserve intact all the former territory of Palestine, by June of 1949, when a United Nations supervised truce came into effect, had established the substantial military security of their nation. Arab states, on the other hand, unanimously refused to recognize the existence of independent Israel. The chronic bad feelings between the new nation and its neighbours would complicate British policy in the Eastern Mediterranean in the next decade.

CHAPTER SEVEN

The Fifties and Sixties: The Affluent Society?

THE WORLD AND DOMESTIC POLITICS

Britain's foreign policy suffered two defeats during the Conservative tenure that defined clearly the nation's diminished world position. Taken together, they constitute a turning point perhaps more significant than any other in the period covered by this book. Occurring at the end of October 1956 and at the end of January 1963, they were the failure of the attack upon Egypt and French President De Gaulle's veto of British attempts to enter the European Common Market. Beside marking departures in foreign affairs, both of these failures had domestic political and economic repercussions. Each significantly weakened the government and the international position of the pound, and each, in different ways, affected Britain's relationship with the United States.

As discussed in the previous chapter, during the forties Britain's interest in European economic, as opposed to military, cooperation had been slight. When the Churchill government returned to office in October 1951, plans for closer military and economic ties among continental nations were still under consideration and Britain herself was attempting to evolve a policy toward them. Any British movement toward Europe was warmly supported by the United States as a means of bolstering Western Europe's ability to defend itself.

After the first Soviet nuclear explosion in October 1949, and particularly after the outbreak of the Korean War in June 1950, the need for the further strengthening of Western European defences was apparent. Inevitably this meant that, one way or another, Western Germany, still potentially the strongest non-Communist European power, would come into European defensive arrangements. But how this could be accomplished without reviving the danger with which Europe was by now all too familiar posed a difficult question. The solution strongly supported by the Churchill government, and by Churchill personally, was the European Defence Community. This organization would be patterned on the Coal and Steel Community. Each member would furnish components for a supra-national military force which, under a combined command, could at once provide a large and effective armed force without giving any individual state control of a balanced military unit.

Promotion of the EDC became a major project of British foreign policy almost from the beginning of the Churchill administration until 30 August 1954 when the French National Assembly rejected the proposed treaty. French hostility to giving up control over her armed forces did not, however, destroy the more important project of the revival of Germany as a military power. Largely through the work of the Conservative Foreign Minister, Anthony Eden, the French were induced to consent to the rearmament of Germany and to her incorporation into the North Atlantic Treaty Organization. Germany was readmitted to the family of European nations on terms of virtual equality. The occupation of that country technically ended and French, British and American troops east of the Rhine remained there under authority granted by Germany.

In supporting the reinstatement of Germany as a full member of the Western European community in the face of hostility from a politically divided and suspicious France, Anthony Eden had shown himself once again to be an astute, hard-working, professional diplomat. So far as there could be training for Prime Ministers, he seemed in every way suited to the task that finally fell to him on 6 October 1955, when Winston Churchill, now 80 years old, resigned the Premiership and designated the Foreign Secretary as his successor. Even though he led the Conservatives on 26 May through a successful general election in which they more than doubled their parliamentary majority to 58—for which they had prepared a few weeks previously by a budget dropping some 2,400,000 people from the income tax rolls—Eden's short tenure was dominated by a single overpowering mistake in his own chosen field, foreign affairs.

The story of Britain's eclipse from the Eastern Mediterranean, which began with the withdrawal from Palestine and ended with the Suez Canal disaster, entered its final phase in the last month of the Labour tenure before the general election of October 1951. In the summer of that year Iran, under the leadership of its eccentric Prime Minister, Dr Mohammed Mossadegh, expelled British technicians and nationalized the installations of the Anglo-Iranian Oil Company at Abadan. Encouraged by the profound British humiliation, the Egyptian government of King Farouk, under pressure from its own population for its failures against Israel, unilaterally denounced the treaty of 1936 under which British troops were stationed in the Suez Canal Zone. This action, however, was insufficient to restore Farouk's prestige with the Egyptian people. He was accused, incorrectly, of being a tool of Great Britain, and, correctly, of being corrupt, weak and inefficient. In January 1952 began anti-foreign riots which climaxed on 26 July with the overthrow of Egypt's royal government. Farouk was replaced by a military clique under a figurehead general, Mohammed Neguib, who was himself the servant of a younger army colonel, Gamel Abdel Nasser.

The new republican government took as its first goal the elimination of British power from Egypt. Britain herself had intended after the war to transfer her main base for the protection of Suez from the Canal Zone to Palestine. But the change of policy on Palestine and the Jewish declaration of independence prevented this. Therefore, the 80,000 British troops in Suez remained crowded into a narrow strip on either side of the Canal. Almost immediately after taking power the new Egyptian government called upon its citizens to force, by any means short of open conflict, the British evacuation of the Canal Zone. To this end the Egyptians had many weapons available —the withholding of labour, interference with water supply, sabotage and economic pressure. By the end of 1953, life for British troops in the Suez had become nearly intolerable. Moreover, Eden had an alternative to the base in the Canal Zone. He had begun to work on a defence agreement based upon Turkey and Iraq, which in 1955 would become the Baghdad Pact. It was no longer necessary to deploy large numbers of expensive British troops in hostile Egypt to protect a lifeline to an empire that no longer existed. The one obstacle to a full settlement with Egypt was the future status of the Sudan, which Egyptian nationalists had long claimed. However, this was removed by a treaty signed on 12 February 1953, in which the Egyptians agreed to permit the Sudanese to determine their own future. Thus in July 1954 Britain announced what was at the time regarded as the greatest change in her Eastern policy since the gift of independence to India: the evacuation of the Suez Canal Zone.

At the end of 1954, it appeared that Britain's hardheaded realization of the limitations of both her needs and her resources would result in a new period of genuine accommodation with Arab nationalism. But this was not to be. The evacuation of Suez was undone by the Baghdad Pact, by British involvement in the new 'northern tier' of Middle Eastern states. In fact, Nasser, now the acknowledged dictator of Egypt, disliked the Baghdad Pact nearly as much as the occupation of Suez. Moreover, he had discovered, like the leaders of many other uncommitted powers, the value of playing off the Communist bloc against the West. By the spring of 1955 he was purchasing arms both from Britain and from Czechoslovakia and, far more important, was negotiating both with Russia on the one hand and with Britain, the United States and the World Bank on the other, for loans for the construction of a high dam across the Nile at Aswan that would greatly increase the amount of arable land in Egypt, but which was far beyond Egypt's resources even to consider building alone. Yet while soliciting loans from the West for a dam that would cost perhaps a thousand million dollars, he was unable to refrain from attacking Western economic and military penetration of other Arab countries. The enormous prestige he had derived from the British withdrawal in Suez made him popular with the masses in nations whose governments were officially unfriendly to Egypt. (His influence with the population of Jordan was great enough to cause the government of that country, which otherwise had no love for Egypt, to dismiss in March 1956 Major General Sir John Glubb as commander of the Arab Legion and so to deprive Britain of the last friendly military force in the southern Arab states.)

The decision not to grant the Aswan Dam loan to Egypt, beginning a chain of events that would make 1956 a year of foreign disaster and humiliation for Britain comparable only to 1936, is a matter more of American than of British history. Nasser did not understand the American Secretary of State, John Foster Dulles, nor the significance of the coming American presidential election, nor the power of the pro-Zionist and anti-Egyptian forces in American politics, nor indeed (in common with many other neutralist nations) the simplicity with which American public opinion viewed foreign aid: one rewards friends but one punishes enemies. Hence Secretary Dulles's abrupt withdrawal of the American offer for the Aswan Dam loan on 19 July 1956, precisely one month after the last British troops left the Suez Canal Zone, came as a shock to Nasser and a serious blow to his prestige. There could be no question that he would, indeed would be required to, react vigorously. His counter-stroke came just a week later, on 26 July, the fourth anniversary of his revolution, when he announced nationalization of the Suez Canal. The Suez Canal Company was an Egyptian corporation and Nasser's right to nationalize it was technically as good as Britain's right to nationalize her railways and canals. But its ownership had always been foreign—about two-fifths of the shares belonging to the British government—its management almost exclusively French, and its operation, particularly the highly paid and skilled pilots who guided ships through the Canal, entirely in the hands of Europeans. (Egyptians had been excluded from gaining knowledge of the operation of the Canal—thought of as a safeguard against nationalization—by the requirement that Canal pilots have at least ten years high seas experience.)

Although American diplomacy began to press for some form of internationalization of the Suez Canal in the days following Egypt's seizure of the waterway—a 'Suez Canal Users' Association'—Eden, now Prime Minister, perhaps without any clear idea of precisely what he intended to do, prepared for military action. Through August, September and October, in concert with the French, troops concentrated on Malta and Cyprus. Eden always denied knowledge that Israel, with French support, was also preparing an attack, although certainly other members of the government were aware of this fact by the middle of October. But in any case the Israeli attack upon Egypt through the Sinai Desert on 29 October owed less to Western encouragement than to Israeli fear of a similar attack upon itself by Arab neighbours and was probably helped along by the diversion offered by the Russian attack upon Hungary a few days before.

Whether or not Britain and France had evolved a timetable for the reoccupation of the Suez Canal Zone, their plans were disrupted by the Israeli action. Announcing to the world that their only aim was to separate the Jewish and Arab combatants, the two European powers now began aerial attacks upon Egypt. Unfortunately air bombardment and the dropping of a few paratroopers were all that could be accomplished. Here lay the great mistake of the entire Suez operation. A British landing force had to steam six days from Malta. The only substantial, pro-Western military force available, the Israeli army, Britain had deliberately ordered out of action. By the time British and French troops could arrive in force—indeed unnecessarily overwhelming force considering Egypt's military weakness—Nasser had taken the only step possible for him but the one that would be decisive. He had blocked the Suez Canal. At the same time world opinion, not only American and Russian but even Australian, turned against Britain. A disastrous run on the pound began, caused by the combined fears of the expense of the military operation, the interruption of trade caused by the blocking of the Canal, and by Russian Premier Bulganin's speech on 5 November threatening a rocket bombardment of London. On 6 November Eden ordered British troops, most of whom had arrived only the previous day, to cease fire.

Like the Munich crisis or the Lloyd George government's treatment of Ireland, the Suez invasion left an imprint on the collective political mind of Britain which lasted long after the formal diplomatic and parliamentary repercussions of the event had faded away. Half the nation had opposed the attack. The other half opposed the cease fire and the subsequent evacuation. Particularly in the Conservative party, the Suez adventure caused a breach which into the sixties had not healed and which would cause continued resentment among right-wing Tories toward the United States and the United Nations as well as toward those among their own colleagues who acquiesced in the withdrawal. (One prominent member of Eden's cabinet, Duncan Sandys, remarked recently that the mistake of his political career he most regretted was his failure to resign after the decision to call off the invasion.) This bitterness would be reflected again and again in Conservative government policy between 1956 and 1964, in Britain's unwillingness to cooperate in the pacification of the Congo, in pressure for the maintenance of an independent nuclear deterrent and delivery system, in general unhappiness over Britain's growing economic and military dependence upon the United States, and at home in ensuring that R. A. Butler, who supported the withdrawal, would not become Prime Minister when Eden resigned on 10 January 1957.

The blow sustained at Suez rocked British politics to the foundations. By any rules the disaster should have been followed shortly by the overthrow of the Conservative government. This, however, did not occur. Eden was succeeded by his Chancellor of the Exchequer, Harold Macmillan, who had made a reputation between 1951 and 1954 as minister in charge of the highly successful Conservative housing programme. Manifesting a political expertise seldom equalled, Macmillan rebuilt the confidence and morale of the party, and with the aid of general world prosperity, a fall in international commodity prices, and by skilfully timed reductions in the bank rate, he was able to overcome the economic effects of Suez. Finally, by the elimination of restrictions on hire purchase (instalment plan buying) and in December 1958 by the announcement of unrestricted convertibility for sterling, he restored the illusion, if not the substance, of British prosperity.

Nevertheless, by this time also, Macmillan had allowed to slip from him perhaps the best opportunity Britain had had since the war to re-establish genuine economic viability and to bring to an end the agonizing triennial exchange crises that symptomized the unhealthy state of the British productive plant. The lost opportunity was Britain's determination—one can hardly call it a decision—not to enter the European Common Market at the time of its formation in 1957. The penance for this mistake came in January 1963 after Macmillan's government, quite literally hat in hand, applied to join the Market and was rejected in a curt and humiliating fashion by the French President, Charles de Gaulle. The impact of this rejection, both on Britain's prestige in Europe and upon her self-confidence at home, was far more pervasive and important than the result of the dramatic failure at Suez.

Proposals for a European Common Market were in many ways the product of the success of the Coal and Steel Community of the early fifties, as that institution had itself grown from the Organization for European Economic Cooperation which had been set up to administer Marshall Plan aid. The men behind its formation, Jean Monnet of France, Paul Henri Spaak of Belgium and Ludwig Erhard of Germany, hoped to widen the areas of continental economic collaboration by providing for mutual development of nuclear power and more importantly for the establishment of a single consuming and productive area of the six most important European industrial nations—the Benelux states plus Germany, France and Italy. They envisaged an economic union that would be protected against the outside by a uniform tariff and which would contain a free market equal in size to that of the United States, thus enabling the newly revived industries of Europe to make the fullest use of the mass productive efficiencies of modern technology. Discussions for the union began early in 1956 based upon a plan drawn up by Spaak, at that time President of the Coal and Steel Community.

Britain's attitude toward the proposed Common Market was ambivalent. On one hand, perhaps most important, she was convinced that the plan could not succeed without her cooperation. On the other, she had no wish to see it fail—prosperity in Europe was important for her own prosperity. Yet for a quarter of a century her trading patterns, particularly in agriculture, had been designed to build economic links with the Commonwealth and in this direction lay ties of loyalty and sentiment that, although not perhaps dependent upon economic ties, nevertheless were reinforced by them. In addition there were party objections. Many, perhaps over-enthusiastic, supporters of the Common Market hoped to see economic union followed by political union. This was an idea viewed with suspicion by many patriotic Englishmen, particularly Lord Beaverbrook, who pointed out that even without formal political union the requirement of a uniform tariff would mean Britain's forfeiture of sovereign control over this area of government activity. The left wing of the Labour party led by Aneurin Bevan, in uncomfortable alliance with right-wing Tories, feared the economic dislocations and unemployment that would result if Britain's carefully-organized and well-protected labour market were thrown open to underpaid foreign workers and if Britain's productive plant, loaded with the costs of an expensive social welfare system, were forced to compete on equal terms with foreign industry without these costs. A 'return to the law of the jungle', Bevan described it.

As an alternative Britain suggested surrounding the Common Market with a Free Trade Association which would include herself, the Scandinavian countries, and other Western European industrial powers who cared to join. Between the Common Market and the Free Trade Association there would be no tariff barriers. But while the members of the Common Market would be protected against the part of the world not included in either association by a common external tariff, each member of the Free Trade Association would set its own tariffs against the rest of the world and agricultural products would be excluded from agreements between the Common Market and the Free Trade Association. Thus Britain would be free to discriminate against continental agricultural products in favour of Commonwealth agricultural products, but her industrial products would have free access to Common Market countries on equal terms with other members of that organization. This alternative, the *Economist* remarked, was 'too ingenious. It neatly reconciled every British need but forgot other people's.' Several continental countries, the journal continued, were not willing to open their markets to British industrial goods unless their farmers received equal access to the British food market. Consequently the plan for linking a European Free Trade Association and a European Common Market died. On 25 March 1957 the six European countries signed the Treaty of Rome setting up a European Economic Community and a European Atomic Energy Community (EURATOM). (The critical date for the Common Market, however, was the ratification of the treaty by the French Assembly in July.)

Britain, nevertheless, proceeded with the formation of the European Free Trade Association, designated the 'outer seven'—Britain, Norway, Denmark, Sweden, Austria, Switzerland and Portugal—in contrast to the 'inner six'. It came into existence in 1959. The failure of her proposals for the Common Market caused little worry. The last half of 1957 as well as 1958 and 1959 were prosperous years. The British working man, as Prime Minister Macmillan reminded the nation at the end of 1957, had 'never had it so good'. Britain appeared to assume that the Common Market could not succeed without herself and the Scandinavian countries and that eventually she would be invited to join on her own terms. She assumed, also mistakenly, that the leading political force in the Common Market would be Germany, whose links with the United States were intimate. Finally, as the Beaverbrook press never tired of reiterating, British exports to the six were increasing dramatically, over 50 per cent. Hence Britain did not need the Common Market. The fact that this was in itself a manifestation of general world prosperity and indeed of the success of the Common Market was forgotten.

The years between 1957 and 1961 saw large changes in the relative importance of the Commonwealth, Europe, and in Britain's special relationship with the United States. Europe prospered, and France, under Charles de Gaulle, emerged as a leading spokesman of a newly revived continent proclaiming its independence both from the Communist bloc and from America. At the same time the importance of the Commonwealth seemed to decline, a fact symbolized by South Africa's withdrawal in 1961. Finally, there could be no mistaking the fact that Britain's economic growth, however rapid, lagged behind that of nearly every other industrial country, that the terms of trade, beyond her control, were turning against her, and that her highly protected, almost encapsulated, economy made fewer demands of imagination and efficiency upon both managers and workers than did the economies of the more competitive European countries. As a consequence, on 31 July 1961, Macmillan announced a government decision to apply for membership in the Common Market and appointed the Lord Privy Seal, Edward Heath, former Conservative chief whip, to negotiate the terms of Britain's entrance. The first meetings began in October and continued through the year 1962 until the end of January 1963. Then, on 29 January 1963, Charles de Gaulle announced that France would veto the British application for entrance.

The last 20 months of the Conservative tenure of office, from the rejection of their application to join the Common Market until their defeat in the general election of 15 October 1964, were as sterile and feckless as the last 20 months of Clement Attlee's administration at the beginning of the decade of the fifties. Government thinking had been directed toward preparations for a reorientation of the British economic system more profound than the adoption of free trade in the middle of the nineteenth century. Departmental plans, the work of many months, suddenly were useless. Having taken the courageous decision to lead Britain into the modern economic world, the government had found that the world did not want Britain and had prepared no alternatives. No legislation was in the pipeline. While forcing itself to meet the problems of entering the Common Market, it gave no thought to the problems of staying out. Moreover, the blow to Britain's prestige was enormous. For a decade and a half it had rejected association with Europe and now found itself rejected. The value of Britain's friendship seemed uncomfortably small. This feeling was compounded because only a month before the end of the Common Market negotiations, in December 1962, President Kennedy of the United States told Prime Minister Macmillan, with scarcely more ceremony than De Gaulle would use, that the United States had determined to end development of the Skybolt missile upon which Britain had planned to depend for nuclear striking capability. Britain, Kennedy said, could spend large sums to develop the missile herself or she could accept as a substitute an American missile, the Polaris. On the surface this was perhaps a reasonable bargain, but it implied a dependence not only upon American weapons but upon American decisions that was widely resented within the United Kingdom.

On 18 October 1963, Macmillan, who had been in hospital undergoing a major operation, resigned as Prime Minister to be succeeded by Sir Alexander Douglas Home. Home, who had recently vacated his seat in the House of Lords, was a surprising choice to lead a party already suffering from a decline of political vigour and a shortage of new ideas. Although he had made a good record as Foreign Secretary in the last years of Macmillan's cabinet, his acquaintance with the Conservative party machinery that would soon have to fight an election was slight and his knowledge of economics and of the grave economic difficulties into which Britain was already sliding was nonexistent. His selection appears to have been dictated by the fact that he offered the only possible alternative to R. A. Butler, who was not acceptable to an influential segment of the party.

Given the new Prime Minister's lack of experience as a party leader, his willingness to delay a general election to the autumn of 1964, within a month of the statutory five year period, was probably wise. On the other hand Home's year in office was insufficient to provide him with the aura of permanence that a party leader in Britain must have. There existed always some sense that his regime was temporary, that he held his position because although he was few people's first choice he had been everyone's second choice. In spite of his reputation as 'the best Foreign Secretary since Bevin', he seemed unsure of himself in the more public post of Prime Minister.

Considering the Conversatives' difficulties in office, the disarray of the party's electoral machinery, which meant that Labour for once ran a more efficient campaign than the Tories, the normal swing against any party in power for 13 years, and the unexciting leadership offered by Home, it is surprising that Labour did not win by a larger margin in the general election of 15 October 1964. In fact, even in winning, Labour received a smaller vote than in any of the three previous elections, all of which it had lost. Its victory was provided by a massive drop of 1,750,000 in the Conservative vote, of which about two-thirds appears to have defected to the Liberals, who themselves nearly doubled their total vote. The results, 317 Labour, 304 Conservatives and their allies, and 9 Liberals, reflected the uncertainty of the nation. The Conservatives had clearly lost the election, but it was not clear that Labour had won it.

HAROLD WILSON AND LABOUR, 1964–66

The new Prime Minister, James Harold Wilson, was younger at 48 than any man to assume that office since Rosebery and was the first, as was remarked at the time, to have been born in the twentieth century. He had held the party leadership for only a little more than a year and was the beneficiary of the fact that most of the better known leaders of the interwar political generation and of Attlee's government had died during the party's long period in opposition. Wilson had been the only former Cabinet member among the contenders for the party leadership after Gaitskell's death and was one of only three former cabinet members in the government he announced on 17 October.

Basically Wilson was, and remains, an enigma. As has been noted he had resigned from the Board of Trade in 1951 in sympathy with Aneurin Bevan's protest against health service charges. Moreover he had been identified with the Bevanite wing of the party during the ideological struggles of the 1950s. His elevation was extravagantly applauded by the Labour left. Yet there was always an ambiguity about his socialist purity which would become more pronounced during his prime ministership. The gulf between declaration and performance was wide. Like Lloyd George he was a polished actor before the press and Parliament and possessed a similar quickness of mind and tongue that enabled him to explain away to men less gifted than himself awkward past promises and decisions. He was secretive, withholding his plans from the cabinet as Ramsay MacDonald had done, and sometimes in a crisis he seemed unwilling to force a decision. At bottom he was a closet pragmatist parading as a left wing idealist who wanted very badly to lead his party. This, in politics, is not crime, nor is it a condemnation of a politician to say he is unable to deliver all that he has promised. But Wilson in the next 12 years, during which, in office or out, he was the dominating and certainly the most visible figure in British politics, developed a reputation for shiftiness that tended to obscure his very real talents.

The Labour party, particularly Wilson, fought the 1964 election on a platform which, without being specific, promised modernization, technology, planning, efficiency, and generally an end to the hit or miss government of the past, 'the 13 wasted years'. Pursuing this theme in office, the Prime Minister created two new cabinet departments, a Ministry of Technology, and more important a Department of Economic Affairs. The latter was supposed to be of equivalent rank to the Treasury and was charged with the preparation of a comprehensive plan for economic growth. The National Plan was published with great fanfare in September 1965. It proposed to increase the gross domestic product by 25 per cent between 1964 and 1970 and promised a 3.4 per cent annual increase in productivity with a 5.5 per cent increase in exports.

Unfortunately the National Plan was obsolete by the time it appeared. The story of the next five years was not of continued growth but of efforts to fight off devaluation, of wage and price controls, of restraints on imports and of higher excise taxes. In effect government policy moved in entirely the opposite direction from that postulated by the National Plan. Wilson had hoped for export-led economic expansion but refused to permit devaluation of the pound, the one thing that would have made that expansion possible. The difficulties were not, to be sure, entirely of his making.

The Labour government inherited in 1964 a current account international payments deficit of £374 million (down from a surplus of £96 million the previous year) most of which was the product of a horrifying £553 million deficit in visible trade. As a result in November, 1964, after Labour had been in office only a month, the Bank of England was forced to obtain a £3,000 million credit from 11 foreign and intergovernmental banks while the government itself, contradicting international commitments, imposed an emergency 15 per cent surcharge on all imports except food, fuel and raw materials. The rapid mobilization of what seemed at the time to be a mammoth international load was more than a demonstration of the Bank of England's unquestioned skill in money management. It was also testimony to the faith in Britain's underlying fiscal health still retained by the leading financial powers of the world. Nevertheless the crisis of the fall of 1964 constitutes the beginning of the chronic financial desperation in Britain's external finance which has made, into the late seventies, the balance of payments, productivity, maintenance of employment, and trade union pressure, the controlling, almost the exclusive, political problems of government. Meanwhile Britain has moved from a position of approximate equality in standards of living among the other Western European nations to one of the lowest.

Paradoxically, the trade crisis of 1964 derived precisely from the Macmillan affluence of the previous ten years. The critical figure in the imbalance of trade was a surge of imports of finished manufactured goods—foreign machinery, indeed ships, but also automobile and household appliances—articles that Britons ought to have made for themselves. Imports of these commodities had quadrupled since 1955 while total imports had not doubled and while the import of basic raw materials, excluding fuel, had in fact declined. (The increase in cost of imported finished manufactures between 1963 and 1964 alone was £183 million or 28 per cent.) Exports had risen to be sure, although at a lower rate than imports. But most disturbing was Britain's relatively slow economic growth in the past ten years which, when combined with a somewhat higher inflation rate than that of its industrial competitors, suggested problems for the future.

The pattern of the 1964 crisis would be repeated in the next decade and a half. Prosperity at home always meant increased imports and an unfavourable trade balance. To counter this the government was forced to take steps to suppress demand in Britain by imposing price and wage controls, punitive interest rates and heavier taxes. When domestic consumption was sufficiently reduced and a payments surplus restored, controls relaxed in the hopes of stimulating economic growth. But as growth came it was always overtaken by inflation compounded by the arrears of demand built up in the previous period of restrained consumption. As a result imports would leap up, a disastrous trade deficit would appear, and the cycle would begin again.

All of this meant that Wilson's first period of five years and eight months as Prime Minister was dominated by the intractable problem of Britain's increasing economic uncompetitiveness. This affected the government's foreign, commonwealth, and defence policies, its relations with the Common Market, and with Wales and Scotland. It affected tax policy and economic regulation. But above all, Labour's attempts to modernize Britain economically brought the government into collision with the trade unions, a process that culminated in a modest, but fiercely resisted, government attempt to establish some legal restrictions on union authority.

At its simplest the Labour government's problem with organized working men lay in the fact that the steps needed to raise production, to reduce inflation, and to increase exports, to do everything necessary to put Britain back into economic health so that the periodic raids upon sterling would end, represented acts which the trade unions instinctively opposed. The fact was that salaries and wages in Britain in the middle-sixties were lower than similar costs among Britain's industrial competitors. But overmanning, restrictive trade union practices, out of date machinery and plants, and inept management caused Britain's manufactured products to suffer in comparison with similar products in the world market. (In 1964-65 the steel industry in Britain, by no means the most backward enterprise in the nation, produced 81.6 tons of crude steel for each employee. For the same period the figure in Germany was 104.1 tons.) For Wilson, the easy way, and probably the most sensible way, to begin would have been with a devaluation of the pound making Britain's goods more competitive abroad while raising the cost of imports. Ensuing overseas demand, ideally, would have increased profits in export industries, caused new investment, and forced the expansion of British industry. Almost from the moment Labour came into office, the government's economic advisors seriously urged devaluation. But Wilson refused even to discuss such a course. It might have been good economics, he was supposed to have said, but bad politics. (However in his memoirs of the 1964-70 administration he asserts it was bad economics and good politics.)

Through its first year the Labour administration was kept in office, as the members of the cabinet themselves believed, only by the ineptitude of the Tory opposition and by the tactical skill and persuasiveness of the Prime Minister. The government produced a stream of reports, white papers, projects, and plans, culminating in the September, 1965 National Plan. It dropped charges for the National Health Service, provided rates rebates for poor tenants, and announced plans to force local educational authorities to end tripartite division of British secondary schools—grammar, technical, and secondary-modern—in favour of the more democratic and classless comprehensive schools. Wilson himself began a series of well-publicized initiatives aimed at settling outstanding foreign and commonwealth problems in Rhodesia, Vietnam and elsewhere. All of this frantic activity kept the Labour party before the voters and directed attention away from the serious difficulty of Britain's economic position. Nevertheless the busy comings and goings were not meaningless. Wilson and many of his cabinet understood that British industrial enterprise could not be rebuilt by a party with an effective House of Commons majority of fewer than five votes and they were well aware that economic hardship for the voter, inflicted both by the vagaries of the world market and by government programs of retrenchment, was likely to grow worse rather than better in the months to come. Accordingly, even though after a year in office the best that could be said was that the Labour party was probably less unpopular than the opposition, Wilson began to consider a second general election. On 22 February 1966 he announced that Parliament would be dissolved on 10 March and that polling would take place on 31 March.

The 1966 electoral contest illustrates the personalization of British politics that had been growing since the war. Party manifestoes were little changed from 1964—revitalization of the economy, modernization, 'the white heat of the technological revolution,' increased growth, and the nationalization of steel, with the significant addition, in a speech by Wilson, that if the terms were right Britain would seek to enter the Common Market. But in fact the electorate seems to have been indifferent to party programmes. When asked by the British Institute of Public Opinion during the campaign whether the Labour party had kept its previous election promises, the division was 44 per cent yes to 43 per cent no. In reality the Labour programme was Harold Wilson. Of the electorate, 54 per cent saw

Wilson as a 'strong forceful leader' as opposed to 28 per cent for the new Conservative leader, Edward Heath, and 30 per cent thought of him as 'warm and friendly' as opposed to 20 per cent for Heath. (Interestingly, half again as many, 15 per cent versus 10 per cent thought Wilson rather than Heath was 'not to be trusted'.) And when it was all over, Wilson, with virtually no record to stand on, had given his party a significant victory. Labour captured 364 seats to provide a safe House of Commons majority of 97.

There would be in the future many complaints about Wilson's indecisive leadership, his political expediency, his companions, even the level of his personal taste in dress and food, but these were unimportant. 'A lot of politics is presentation', he has been quoted as saying, 'and what isn't presentation is timing.' In this area Wilson was a master. He was, and would remain until his elegantly timed retirement, the best electoral asset the Labour party possessed. ('Wilson as the party leader' was the explanation given most frequently by people after the election to the B.I.P.O. for voting Labour.)

Except for the electoral victory, 1966 was a grim year for Labour. Six weeks after the election, on 16 May, for the first time in half a century, the seamen went out on strike. Because of the nature of the seaman's articles, ships at sea carrying imports continued to sail while ships in home ports, loading exports, immediately went out of service. On 23 May the government declared a state of emergency. The balance of trade quickly tipped against Britain. June's trade figures were terrible and a new run against the pound began. Even though the seamen conceded defeat at the end of June and went back to work, the pressure on the pound continued. In mid-July a movement of rebellion against the Prime Minister began in the cabinet with the demand that as the price for an agreement on a drastic programme of deflation there be a commitment to end the Bank of England's support for the pound. In the end the Prime Minister defeated a nearly united cabinet. 'Take the package and be damned' was the way Richard Crossman felt it was put to himself and his colleagues. On 20 July Wilson announced a programme of economic cuts: increases in excise and income taxes, a reduction in foreign travel allowances, and above all a freeze on wages, prices and dividends, but no devaluation.

So the July crisis concluded with another exercise of authoritarian prime ministership, and Britain lived, until the end of the decade, with a combination of increasingly stringent exchange and purchasing controls instituted in the first instance to defend the pound at $2.80

and then after the inevitable devaluation in 1967, to dampen home demand and prevent inflation so that the nation could receive the export benefits of a cheaper pound.

Of course the answer to Britain's problems, the only avenue to ending the cycle of payments crisis, emergency deflation, relaxations of restrictions, rising production, and a new wave of imports, and finally a new payments crisis, was through a reallocation of resources within the domestic productive plant. This had been Labour's platform in 1964 and 1966 and it represented Wilson's own view of how government, under his leadership, should pull Britain out of the selfish, consumer-oriented amateurism into which the Tories had allowed her to fall. Britain must be forced to pay its way in the world. To this end the Prime Minister and the Chancellor of the Exchequer, James Callaghan, with the help of Nicholas Kaldor, the Cambridge economist from whom the idea came, put together in the spring of 1966 between the election and the presentation of the budget a plan for a special tax of 25 shillings for each male employee (12 shillings 6 pence for women and young persons) to be levied on employers and paid through the National Insurance stamps. The unusual feature of the so-called Selective Employment Tax was that sums raised were to be returned to selected manufacturing employers, in some cases with a premium. Essentially the aim of the tax was to make more expensive their hiring of labour in service industries and to encourage manufacturers with export potential to expand operations. This fairly crude attempt at national economic engineering through fiscal policy had been unmentioned in the budget preview Callaghan had given the House of Commons before the election. Moreover it caused some anger in the cabinet who themselves had heard of it only the day before it was announced in the budget statement of 3 May.

The SET became a part of a general package of deflationary measures hastily thrown together in the anxious days of the late summer, 1966. As it would take over £315 million from consumer demand in the current fiscal year, and as payments to manufacturing industries would not begin until the next year, the tax could be defended, as Callaghan did in his budget speech, almost entirely as a step toward cooling the economy. Whether in the long term it served to divert labour to the manufacture of products that would help the balance of payments is unclear, although the topic has been the subject of considerable study. In 1967 the SET was modified to provide premium payments only to industries in development areas, in a sense a contradiction of its original intent because by definition they already suffered high unemployment. In 1968, following devaluation, it was increased by 50 per cent. Finally, it was killed, unlamented, by the Heath government in 1972. Nevertheless for the student of social and economic policy, SET is intensely interesting as the most ambitious attempt as structural engineering of the economy undertaken in Britain perhaps since the repeal of the Corn Laws.

The furious activity of the July 1966 crisis did not solve the export problem. Britain's share of world markets continued to fall regularly, as indeed it had done since the late forties, at a rate of slightly less than 1 per cent a year apparently unaffected by anything the government did. At the same time the rising numbers and affluence of the home population insured ever-increasing demand for foreign imports. With underlying trading patterns thus unfavourable, the stability of the pound depended far too much on the ability of Britain to attract capital, which ability itself was a reflection of the opinion of speculators and money managers about political events within the country and of their estimate of the governments' determination to continue to require the Bank of England to buy all pounds offered at a fixed rate. (It should be noted in this connection that the fixed exchange rate made speculation against the pound riskless. Pounds sold in anticipation of a profit in case of a possible devaluation could always be repurchased at virtually the same price if the devaluation did not occur.) Hence Britain's domestic economy tied to measures to defend the pound was exposed to the vagaries of the international movement of risk capital, and vulnerable to pressures both internal and external over which the government had no control. (In his memoirs, the Prime Minister displays an almost pathological hatred of currency 'speculators' whom he blames, along with hostile newspapers and the BBC, for most of his government's troubles.)

All the effort of 1966 was nevertheless in vain. A new run on the pound began with bad trade figures in April 1967 which was exacerbated by the Israeli attack on Egypt on 6 June, the so called 'six day war'. This led to the closing for the second time of the Suez Canal and to an Arab oil embargo. Pressure increased in September with the outbreak of a dockers strike in London and Liverpool. Through the first weeks of November there were hurried negotiations with the central banks in France and the United States and with the International Monetary Fund as the Prime Minister attempted to avoid the inevitable. In the end the necessary loans were refused or attached to such stringent deflationary requirements that they would have been politically impossible. Devaluation of the pound from $2.80 to $2.40 was announced on Saturday, 18 November.

THE SEASON OF DISCONTENT

Devaluation was the first of four serious defeats suffered by Labour, and by Harold Wilson particularly, between the end of 1967 and the summer of 1969. The second came nine days after devaluation, on 27 November 1967 when French President Charles DeGaulle announced almost casually at a press conference that Britain was not yet ready for membership of the Common Market.

Wilson had first announced that Britain would seek to join the European Economic Community during the 1966 election campaign. In the succeeding year, despite warnings from France that DeGaulle would never permit her entry, ample evidence at home that such an act would put even more pressure on a much overvalued pound, and that entry would split the Labour party, not to mention the cabinet, the government pushed forward with preparations. Like the maintenance of the pound, the Common Market was a personal project of the Labour Prime Minister. Even after DeGaulle's unfriendly remarks he continued negotiations only to meet the inevitable formal veto of Britain's membership three weeks later on 19 December 1967.

Coming as it did in the midst of continued speculation against the now devalued pound, the rejection by France was a severe blow. Since the devaluation the government had, to be sure, the backstop of a new loan from the International Monetary Fund, but this had been obtained with the promise of further restraints on consumer demand which accordingly had depressed the government's popularity. Nevertheless it was at this time that the Prime Minister chose to begin a battle with the trade unions.

A part of everyone's plan for the revitalization of British industry and the promotion of exports was the establishment of some kind of rule and order in organized labour. Poor workmanship, uncertain delivery dates and irregular part supply hindered British entrance into foreign markets as much as high prices. (But in addition between 1958 and 1966 British export prices had increased more than those of any manufacturing country except Switzerland.) Much of the responsibility for this had to be laid upon the trade unions. Wage rates, when Labour came to power, it should be remembered, were not high when compared with other northern European nations, yet

British exports gained little advantage from this fact because of worker irresponsibility and misbehaviour. (The British automobile industry was the only one among the industries of the ten automobile manufacturing nations to produce fewer cars in absolute terms between 1964 and 1969. On the average the ten major automobile manufacturing nations increased their production by about 30 per cent and by the end of the decade British automobile manufacturers were in fact losing their share of the market within Great Britain itself.) The trade unions had always defended themselves by arguing that the number of days work lost by striking workers in Britain was smaller than among any of her European competitors and far less, scarcely one quarter, of the days lost in the United States. This was quite true. The British problem was not in massive strikes of an entire industry which escalate statistics, but of innumerable small strikes, organized on the shop floor, not sanctioned by the parent union, of perhaps tool room workers, power or transport workers, or component fabricators. These involved few men and caused few man days lost but nevertheless often shut down an entire industry either because non-striking workers refused to cross picket lines or because the dispute deprived an industry of a vital part or service. Of these unofficial strikes there were a great many, twice as many stoppages per one thousand workers per year in Britain as among her major competitors, and the number was growing. Of all strikes, 95 per cent it was estimated, were unofficial, as frequently over industrial grievances, the maintenance of employment, the introduction of new technology or union jurisdiction, as over wages. Moreover the settlement of wage claims themselves had become a disorganized patchwork affair conducted at the shop floor level and divorced frequently from central union authority, involving personal competition among union leaders and among individual crafts within a firm. The result often was the erosion of traditional differentials among various trades so that any settlement would be followed by new strikes as individuals saw their accustomed margins of superiority narrowed.

In a sense the British labour problem in the last half of the twentieth century was not that Britain's national trade unions were too strong but that they were too weak. The terms 'fellowship' and 'solidarity', incantations of labour history, applied chiefly at the shop floor level, not to members of the union nationally and emphatically not to the working class in general. Nationally union leaders might be admired, indeed revered, but they were not obeyed. The national leaders themselves always regarded their function as the preservation of the labour movement's peculiar immunities in the political arena rather than its control and discipline. Since 1906 the unions, although they could make contracts and sue, could not themselves be sued in any matter dealing with industrial relations. Moreover, British labour leaders had always maintained that government regulation of any sort had no place in collective bargaining no matter how crucial the agreements were to the national welfare. The most that the government ought to do was to bring pressure on employers, as Frank Cousins proposed before his resignation over the Prices and Incomes Bill, to induce them to resist more firmly. The result was that workers, secure in the knowledge that neither their union funds nor their leaders could suffer in action through the courts, saw no reason to obey orders from higher union officials. Hence any individual grievance could quickly escalate into a strike which, however meaningless or harmful in terms of the general industrial condition, was beyond the power either of the employer, the national union, or a desperate government to end.

In the past 15 years, the central importance of the struggle between the government and organized labour cannot be overestimated. Control of union militancy would be a significant issue in all four general elections in the decade of the seventies and was the determing factor in the defeat of the Conservatives in 1974 and the defeat of Labour in 1979. In addition labour's insistence on the maintenance of employment through resistance to new technology or to the abandonment of obsolete plants or machinery had become, in the late seventies, the principal, although certainly not the only, obstacle to the revival of the productive efficiency which was the stated goal of both political parties.

For a Labour government, an attack upon the ancient and well-entrenched privileges of the trade unions was an act of audacity, or recklessness, as Wilson certainly must have known. That a government under his control should undertake such a project illustrates the importance he attached to the matter. (The Amalgamated Engineering Union's book of rules, he is supposed to have remarked, was so out of date it belonged in an industrial museum.) In any case he proceeded slowly. In April 1965 the government appointed a Royal Commission on Trade Unions and Employers' Associations, whose memberships included both union members and employers, under the chairmanship of an eminent judge, Lord Donovan, to examine the entire question of labour organization. As a source of information on Britain's troubled unions, the Donovan Commission

Report, published on 13 June 1968, was of great value. But its proposals for solving labour problems were meagre. It admitted it had no answer to the question of unofficial strikes while agreeing nevertheless that a state of 'indecision and anarchy' existed in employer-union and interunion relations. Obviously this unsatisfactory document could not become the basis of government action and so immediately Barbara Castle, former chairman of the Labour party, a member of its National Executive Committee since 1950, and a woman of great influence within the left wing of the party, who since April had been minister of the new Department of Employment and Productivity, set to work on a plan for legislation that went well beyond the Donovan Report. (As if to illustrate the dimensions of the problem of union jurisdictional disputes, on 11 November 22 engineers began an unofficial strike at the Girling Brake Works in Bromborough, Cheshire which eventually shut down a substantial part of British automobile production.)

Although Mrs Castle consulted fully with the unions during the preparation of her paper and, to the anger of the Cabinet, showed the completed White Paper, entitled *In Place of Strife* when it was published on 17 January 1969, to the general council of the Trades Union Congress before submitting it to the government, the legislation that it proposed caused consternation in organized labour. With the full backing of Wilson, Mrs Castle, among other things, undertook to control by statute unofficial strikes, particularly when they were the result of union jurisdictional disputes. As a final sanction the Industrial Relations Board, envisaged in the recommendations, could impose settlements between disputing unions to be enforced by fines.

These so called 'penal clauses' were denounced by the unions—although some union leaders admitted privately to Mrs Castle that they recognized the need for regulation—by many members of the Labour party, and by some members of the Cabinet. The Home Secretary, James Callaghan, indeed voted against the White Paper when it came before the National Executive Committee of the Labour party even though it presumably represented the policy of the government to which he belonged. In bitter negotiations during May and June, 1969 Wilson offered to drop the penal clauses if the Trades Union Congress would change its own rules to allow disciplining of unions engaged in unconstitutional strikes. (There are suggestions in Barbara Castle's diary that the penal clauses were inserted to frighten the trade unions into the strengthening of their own control over industrial action.) However, the TUC refused either to sanction the proposed Industrial Relations Bill or to take steps to amend its own procedure so that the bill would be unnecessary. In the end Wilson, faced by a revolt not only of the unions but of Labour's National Executive Committee and of part of the back bench of the parliamentary party, agreed to drop the penal clauses without any reciprocal concessions except a 'solemn and binding' promise, proposed evidently by Hugh Scanlon, from the Trades Union Congress (immediately christened 'Mr Solomon Binding') to try to avert unofficial strikes.

Wilson and the Labour government had been defeated and humiliated by the trade union movement. The measure which the Prime Minister had declared as late as April 1969 to be essential for Britain's economic recovery was vetoed by union power that in effect denied the right of Parliament to legislate in the field of industrial relations. (This is not an inference from events. Hugh Scanlon and Jack Jones stated this position in exactly these terms to Wilson and Mrs Castle at a private meeting at Chequers on 1 June.) Even though he apparently had believed that unless he found a way to control shop floor militancy he would lose the next election, the Prime Minister clearly decided at this time never to challenge organized labour again. When he returned to office in 1974 he quickly repealed the Conservative Industrial Relations Act and took no other action in the domestic economic field without union consent. The 'Social Contract' of the second Wilson administration was the Son of Solomon Binding.

THE HOUSE OF LORDS AND RHODESIA

The Industrial Relations Bill was not the only measure stifled by back-bench revolt during the last years of Wilson's government. In its anger at what seemed to be an unwarranted usurpation of authority by the House of Lords, the Labour back bench also brought to an end what might have been the most important accomplishment of the Wilson administration, the reconstruction of parliamentary rules and practices, and so caused Wilson's fourth defeat. Because all of this involved in addition the tortured question of Rhodesia and generally British relations with the black Commonwealth, it deserves some attention.

Soon after the 1966 election the cabinet had begun to discuss methods of reforming the House of Lords as part of a general reform of procedures in both chambers of Parliament, possibly including also a remodelling of Westminster Palace. In 1966 the powers of the House of Lords were as they had been left by the Parliament Act of 1911 (except that the power to delay non-money bills had been reduced from two years to one in 1949) but the peers still had the right permanently to reject delegated legislation, that is Statutory Orders, which had the force of law unless one house or the other took negative action. Although the peers had never used it, this power, not understood by the general public nor for that matter by many scholars, had been untouched in 1911 and 1949. But it could have been particularly devastating in complex modern legislation where many matters were left to be dealt with by administrative decision.

In October 1966 an all party conference under the chairmanship of the Lord Chancellor began to discuss plans for reforming the upper house. Generally the Tories hoped to strengthen the Lords by limiting its size and changing its membership so as to conform more nearly to the party alignment in the House of Commons. The Labour left, on the other hand, opposed any change in the composition of the upper house that would reinvigorate it and bring it closer to the mainstream of modern politics, insisting instead that it simply be stripped of its remaining powers. In May, 1968, the committee finally agreed on a compromise that would have both strengthened the personnel of the House of Lords and reduced its power. But little more than a month later, on 18 June, the Tory peers for the first time used their majority to destroy a Statutory Order approved by the House of Commons the day before, which applied economic sanctions to Ian Smith's newly independent state of Rhodesia. In doing so the peers insured that the left wing of Labour would be content with nothing less than root and branch destruction of the power of their chamber and would filibuster, as they did the next year, any reform of the archaic composition of the Lords.

Because, like the American war in Vietnam, it divided both the party and the country, the Rhodesian situation, and Wilson's attempts to solve the problem it presented, are of some importance. Since the early fifties the orderly movement towards independence among Britain's black African colonies had turned into a stampede. On the whole Labour remained sympathetic to this evolution but upon assuming office was presented with the difficulty of a small but prosperous white minority (in what had been since 1911, Southern

Rhodesia) who had controlled, since 1923, the government of an enormous territory largely populated by unrepresented blacks. The Churchill government in 1953 had sponsored the formation of the Central African Federation of Northern and Southern Rhodesia and Nyasaland on the assumption that within a decade the entire federation would become independent. But neither Northern Rhodesia nor Nyasaland wished to retain the connection with Southern Rhodesia and so the federation died on 21 December 1963. And just as Labour came to power in 1964 the two black dominated colonies proclaimed their independence as the republics of Zambia and Malawi respectively. Thus Labour inherited in Southern Rhodesia the problem of a white minority government under Prime Minister Ian Smith, exercising political control over a black population more than 20 times as large. Under these circumstances Wilson did not feel ready to grant independence. Between November 1964 and November 1965 he carried on continued negotiations with the Rhodesians. These came to an end on 11 November 1965 when Smith, with practically unanimous support from the Rhodesian white electorate, fortified by the knowledge that his cause commanded much sympathy among British Conservatives both in and out of the House of Commons, and sure of the help of South Africa, announced a unilateral declaration of independence for Rhodesia. (Always referred to as UDI.)

Wilson spent more time on Rhodesia in the next five years than on any other issue. He wished of course to induce by negotiation the Smith government to find some political accommodation for the black majority. At the same time he had to prove Britain's concern for the cause of racial equality to the black nations of the Commonwealth. In December 1965 with much publicity, he announced an oil embargo against Rhodesia. The embargo, he assured the nation, would quickly force the Smith government's capitulation. In fact it was easily evaded, apparently, as it turned out, with the British government's knowledge. As a result, faced by demands for the use of force from black Africa and indeed from some of his left wing supporters in Britain, and aware that effective pressure on Rhodesia could not be applied by Britain alone, he sought from the United Nations a series of resolutions to impose worldwide economic and political sanctions against the intransigent African nation. It was after the second UN resolution on this subject, passed in April, 1968, that the House of Lords vetoed the orders required for its implementation. (The Lords relented on 18 July and allowed the measure to go into effect.)

The inability to reform either the government at Salisbury or at Westminster hurt the Wilson adminstration again. It consumed huge amounts of ministerial time, including the Prime Minister's, who met Smith twice, in 1966 and 1968. It strained relations with the black African Commonwealth and with his own party. It destroyed the all-party approach to the reform of Parliament and worst, it never succeeded in bringing Rhodesia either back under British control or in forcing liberalization of the white government. The result in the next decade was the appearance of black terrorism in Central Africa and the advent of civil war.

Even though the problem of Rhodesia remained unsolved and apparently insolvable and despite the humiliation of the devaluation, the Industrial Relations Bill, the Common Market, and the House of Lords, all of which were underlined by low public opinion poll ratings and disastrous by-election and local election results, toward the end of the decade some light began to appear. After an interval during which speculation against the pound continued, the effect of the devaluation began to show in export statistics and by 1969 the balance of payments was solidly in Britain's favour. This provided an opportunity for the new Chancellor of the Exchequer, Roy Jenkins, to announce in his budget statement in 1969 that statutory price and wage controls, which like much else the government had done were unpopular with the unions and did not work well anyway, would be allowed to expire at the end of the year. But a certain result of decontrol would be an increase in prices, which increases would be made worse by the cheaper pound as the rising cost of imports moved through the economy. With severe inflation probably within a year, it would be well, as the Cabinet knew, to hold an election soon, even though dissolution meant that much important legislation already before Parliament would have to be dropped. (The runaway inflation of the seventies began on schedule with a dramatic increase in wages of over 12 per cent in 1970 while prices went up 6.4 per cent in the same year.) After some anxiety that an election might conflict with the World Cup matches, the polling date was set, unusually for Labour, for mid-June and dissolution was announced on 18 May 1970. Another factor in the decision to hold a quick election was the sudden rise in the spring of 1970 of Labour's dismal standing in the public opinion polls and a swing toward Labour in local elections, all of which were reinforced by a clear and continuing dislike of the Conservative leader, Edward Heath. Labour after having suffered cruel unpopularity since 1966 seemed, briefly at least, to be in a position to win.

The campaign, like the previous one in 1966, was publicly a contest between party leaders. Wilson tried to avoid the subject of devaluation and pointed to the economic progress the nation had made under his administration, the nationalization of the steel industry and the enfranchisement of 18-year-olds. Heath reminded the voters of rising prices and of the unruliness of the trade unions. Again, as the polls made clear, Wilson was the greatest asset the Labour party possessed, even among those not prepared to vote for the party, while scarcely anyone, 5 per cent, suggested that he supported the Conservatives because of Edward Heath.

In the face of the unanimous finding among the polls to the contrary, the Conservatives won handily in the voting on 18 June 1970, electing 330 Members of Parliament to Labour's 288. The swing to the Conservatives was 4.7 per cent, a greater turnover than the Tories had enjoyed at any time since 1931. Evidently a number of the defectors who had voted Liberal in 1964 returned to the fold. Of the 13 seats held by the Liberals at the time of the dissolution, the party lost seven of which five went to the Conservatives. On 19 June Edward Heath became Prime Minister.

CHAPTER EIGHT

The Seventies

The new Prime Minister was born in 1916, only three months after the man he replaced and like him Heath had grown up in modest middle-class circumstances, had graduated from Oxford University, and had served for a time in the Civil Service before entering the House of Commons. He shared also Wilson's interest in music. But there the similarity ended. In debate Wilson was witty; Heath was heavily earnest. Before television Heath was often embarrassingly awkward while Wilson had a decade-old reputation as a genial master-performer. Heath seemed to be rigid, humourless, unfriendly and uncompromising. Few people questioned his competence—his choice as a party leader had been dictated partly by the belief that he would be able to deal with Wilson in the complex world of economics—but he did not inspire, nor indeed did he invite, popularity either in the party or in the electorate.

During the general election the Tory campaign had turned, above all, on economic growth. Labour, it was asserted, had failed to revive Britain's productive energy. This Heath—like Wilson, an economist—intended to accomplish. In January, 1970, before the election, Conservative leaders had met at the Selsdon Park Hotel near Croydon and there in a glare of publicity formulated the party's economic philosophy. The platform called for more competition, lower taxes, freedom for wages and prices, the elimination of subsidies so that firms unable to compete would be allowed to close, and in general for a freer economic environment. Included also were promises to regulate trade union activity, to enforce the law and maintain public order and to take Britain into the European Economic Community. But public interest settled on what seemed to be the sharp lurch to the right in Tory economic thinking. In office the Tories looked forward to at least a couple of years of breathing time. They inherited a healthy balance of payments surplus from Labour's devaluation and hoped generally to use the shield of a strong pound as protection behind which the government could dismantle economic controls. With any luck, the party expected, increased output and improved productivity would counterbalance the inflationary pressures and the rise of imports that inevitably would follow decontrol.

But the pressure of events, the inheritance of past decisions and. compromises, frustrated Heath's intentions. The so-called 'dash for growth' proved as difficult to realize as had been Wilson's technological revolution. Although manufacturing and investment leapt up early in the decade these indices soon began to subside while inflation grew rapidly, pushed ahead by a continued growth in consumer, and above all in government, expenditure. By 1971 the comparative advantage conferred on British exports by the devaluation was rapidly being eroded by inflation and the surge of imports, born also of the wage explosion that had begun in 1969, promised that the payments surplus would not last long. Average prices nearly doubled between 1970 and 1975 while wages and salaries more than doubled. On 23 June 1972 the Treasury announced that efforts to maintain the pound at a fixed value were at an end. (The pound has 'floated' ever since which means it has pretty constantly sunk in terms of the strongest European currencies, although not in relation to the dollar.) The dash for growth which the Conservatives had publicized as the slogan for their tenure of office stalled in mid-course. With the pressure of accumulated consumer demand and the ever rising expectations for a better standard of living left over from the sixties, and given the new militancy in leadership among the big unions, the engineers, the transport workers and the miners, it is difficult to see how it ever could have succeeded. But Heath went down to defeat after little more than three-and-a-half years in office less because of his failure to expand the economy—no one seemed to be able to do that—than because he could neither control, nor learn to live with, the power of the trade unions.

THE INDUSTRIAL RELATIONS ACT

For the Conservatives the central issue in the general election had been Labour's economic stewardship and the heart of this question was trade union irresponsibility. How, it was asked, does the modern industrial state deal with a large but not well organized group within itself which on the one hand is unable to control its own members but which on the other hand can intimidate the government, which is exempt, unlike any other institution, from the civil law, but which has at the same time the power to bring economic life to a standstill? Heath's problem with the trade unions would turn out to be the same as Wilson's and indeed, for that matter, as James Callaghan's when he succeeded Wilson. The unions seemed to care only marginally more for the welfare of a Labour government than for a Conservative one. Union members would support their leaders when the organization as a whole was threatened politically. But they refused to honour their leaders' promises made in negotiation and at the very basic level, on the shop floor, they refused to recognize that in taking industrial action they had any responsibility for the economy as a whole. They could not be disciplined and would not discipline themselves.

Heath had said many times that a Conservative government would bring the unions within the purview of the law and by the time Parliament assembled in December, 1970, the cabinet had ready the so-called Industrial Relations Bill. The story of this measure and of its eventual failure and repeal by Labour in 1974, provides a central theme of British domestic history in the decade of the seventies.

The Conservative Industrial Relations Bill went far beyond Labour's modest proposals in *In Place of Strife*. In general the Conservative bill can be divided into two parts. One part consisted of a reaffirmation of the rights of the unions to organize workers and to conduct strikes. These would take place under the supervision of an Industrial Relations Commission which also had the responsibility of overseeing bargaining agent elections, refereeing jurisdictional disputes, protecting the industrial worker's rights, supervising union rules, searching for unfair labour practices, and offering arbitration services. In this way the bill would establish a body of statutory procedures in an area so far untouched by law.

The other part of the act however removed the immunity from suits by employers that unions had enjoyed since 1906 and stipulated further that the rights established for organizing activities were available only to unions which registered and submitted their rules to the registrar. An Industrial Relations Court, of the rank of the High Court, would be established to hear cases of breach of contract and unfair labour practices defined by the act. Unions which refused to register would lose the rights granted under the act but could nevertheless be sued by employers who, in the case of unregistered unions, would not be restrained in the amount of awards such as was stipulated for registered unions.

The Industrial Relations Bill finally became law on 5 August 1971 after evoking almost unprecedented violence within Parliament from the Labour party and outside from unions, which protested with strikes and demonstrations. The next year, 1972, saw the number of days lost through strikes rise to 24,000,000, double the number of 1971 and more than four times the average of the 1960s. Unions refused to register under the act—indeed the Trades Union Congress announced it would expel any union that registered—and employers showed a marked reluctance to use their new right of taking unions to court.

The fact was that the Industrial Relations Act never worked. Instead of introducing regulation and order into union affairs, it made industrial action more than ever a confrontation between organized labour and government. The results of this in British politics were almost wholly bad. Heath, although denounced as a reactionary by the unions, was essentially a moderate in the Macmillan tradition but the failure of his policy of balance strengthened the right wing of the Tories. Conversely, Labour in opposition moved closer to the unions. It became even more difficult for the second Wilson government to oppose demands for new union privileges, to refuse the government grants necessary to keep obsolete plants in production, or to arrange the consolidation of industry and the introduction of new technology. In effect Wilson found himself unable to do most of the things with which he had hoped to make his mark in political life.

The rising inflation and the growing uncompetitiveness of many British manufactures forced Heath also to abandon much of the Selsdon programme, which had pointed toward a freer economy. Increasing unemployment for instance made it impossible to cut government expenditure. At the same time the bankruptcy, first of Rolls Royce in February, 1971 (not precisely the result of industrial inefficiency but of a promise to produce an engine for the Lockheed Aircraft Corporation at an uneconomic price) and of the Upper Clyde Shipbuilders in June, required the government to enter the business of bailing out ailing companies for which the Tories had denounced Labour only a few years before. Finally, in 1972 with the Industry Act, the Conservatives took the government formally into the financing and supervising of big industrial firms. And at last, in November, 1972 after nine months of fruitless and acrimonious discussion with the TUC in search of a voluntary incomes policy, the Conservatives threw overboard the last vestiges of Selsdon and established comprehensive controls on prices and wages.

Everything seemed to go wrong. Prices and unemployment rose together so that by 1972 the raw figure for persons out of work was approaching one million, close to the rate of the terrible twenties and thirties. Labour was in revolt against both wage restraint in a time of inflation and the Industrial Relations Act. By the end of 1973 the declining value of the new floating pound had begun so to raise the cost of imported goods that the healthy surplus of international payments enjoyed at the beginning of the decade had evaporated and Britain was again in a trade deficit while, at the same time, the resulting higher prices for imported food and raw material were pushing the inflation rate toward 10 per cent.

But worse still was to come. On 6 October 1973 Egypt attacked Israel and two days later the Organization of Petroleum Exporting Countries (OPEC) announced the first of several increases in price of crude petroleum which would in the next three months raise the price of oil to about four times what it had been before. Meanwhile, early in November, the OPEC countries announced in addition a 24 per cent cut in the shipment of oil to western nations. The world, to be sure not only Britain, was suddenly confronted by a new foreign policy conundrum, one which it has not yet solved, the politics of oil.

In the midst of the oil crisis the coal miners, on 12 November 1973 demanding pay increases for some workers running as high as 47 per cent, began industrial action by banning overtime. The effect of the miners' slowdown was reinforced by work-to-rule decisions among the electrical power station workers and by one of the railway unions. All of this threatened electricity supplies and since the middle of November the government had been ordering progressively more stringent steps to save electricity. Finally on New Years Day, 1974, the nation's manufacturing and business establishments were ordered to use electric power only three days per week. On 9 February 1974, with coal stocks already critically short, the miners stopped work altogether.

Heath had fought the National Union of Mineworkers (NUM) before. On 9 January 1972, in their first national strike since the stoppage that had begun the General Strike of 1926, the miners, in pursuit of a 30 per cent wage increase, had forbade not only the digging of the coal but also the delivery to power stations of coal already above ground. This action affected electricity supplies almost immediately and by the beginning of February 1972 electricity reductions were in force and causing widespread unemployment. Within three weeks the government capitulated. Now, fewer than two years later, the miners were exercising their economic leverage again.

The crucial factor in the political revolution that was approaching, which made February 1974 perhaps the most important general election since 1945, was the popular esteem enjoyed by British coal miners. The NUM was not simply another trade union and coal miners were, and are, not simply another form of industrial worker. Rather they are heroes of the labour tradition. Even though by the 1970s the miners were not nearly the largest British union, (with a membership of about 250,000 as compared to 900,000 in 1920) many citizens who had never seen a coal mine felt a sentimental attachment to the blackened men who worked underground at great personal risk to raise the coal that for a century and a half had provided the power for Britain's industrial pre-eminence. Thus, even in February, 1974 the miners were a powerful enemy for any government. Paradoxically, as the three-day work week continued, sympathy for the miners increased. The British Institute of Public Opinion found that in January 44 per cent of the population professed to support the miners as opposed to 30 per cent supporting their employers, but in February the figures were 52 per cent and 24 per cent. Even more dangerous for the Heath government however was the astonishing reversal of public opinion in response to the question of whether the miner should be treated as a 'special case' for purposes of the incomes policy. In January, 55 per cent of those questioned thought they should not and 38 per cent believed they should. In February the figures were almost precisely reversed: 56 per cent replied that the government should give in to the miners' claims with 38 per cent saying that it should not.

At about the time these disturbing figures were compiled, on 7 February, Heath announced that Parliament would be dissolved the next day and that the general election would be held on 28 February. The electoral campaign that followed in the next three weeks was of almost unprecedented signficance. On the surface Heath was responding in perfectly legitimate terms to a constitutional impasse as, for instance, Asquith had done twice in 1910 during the struggle with the House of Lords. But in 1910 the debate had centred upon whether an ancient and fully recognized branch of the government had the right to tamper with certain parts of the legislative process and the voters were being consulted as to whether a constitutional adjustment should be made. Moreover the peers, for all their wealth, could not throttle the national economy. The contest was entirely political. But in 1974 the government was faced by an organized group in pursuit of money for itself who because of the peculiar nature of its work, could bring, indeed were bringing, British commerce and industry to a stop. The miners were demanding, in effect, a form of ransom. The question in the election, never clearly stated, was first whether the taxpayers, who would in the end have to find the sums necessary, should submit. But secondly, a larger question than simply that of the miners' dispute, was how in the future British society should handle similar threats from any of several unions who could, by industrial action, disrupt economic life. This form of tribute, or danegeld, was essentially open-ended. Indeed one success almost certainly would provoke another.

Heath always argued against the notion that the electoral issue was 'Who Governs Britain?' He was quite correct. Neither the miners nor any other union wished to govern Britain. Nor, more important, did they accept responsibility as governments must do, for the economic consequences of their actions upon the nation as a whole. The issue in the election was the curbing of trade union power. Would the unions, the miners in 1974, other groups later, be allowed indefinitely to coerce the population at large through the withholding of vital services?

The Conservatives, to their disadvantage, never made clear during the election how they would handle the miners should they win, while Labour insisted that the three-day week hurt Britain far more than the concessions they intended to make to the miners. The campaign, conducted in an atmosphere of almost unrelieved gloom, never really focused on the question of the place of independent trade unions within a national framework. Rather it turned on the issue of whether the miners' hardship was great enough to entitle them to be treated as a special case under the terms of the pay policy. In the event British voters decided, unenthusiastically, that the miners should have their way. The voting on 28 February returned 301 Labour members to 297 Conservatives although the Conservatives received 225,000 more votes than Labour. The Liberals were disappointed. They had hoped that the obvious disenchantment with the major parties would drive voters toward them. They made a considerable effort, running more candidates than at any time since the party broke up and collecting a greater percentage of votes than in any election since 1929, but they seated only 14 members.

Nevertheless they held the balance of power in the House of Commons and Heath negotiated briefly for a coalition, on the wisdom of which both Conservatives and Liberals were divided. But nothing came of it and after a week of confusion, while coal stocks grew ever lower, Harold Wilson took office for a second time on 5 March.

BRITAIN AND THE COMMON MARKET

During a largely luckless administration which had been attempting to manage a nation buffeted by forces from abroad that no government could control and whose every project seemed doomed from its inception, Heath had a piece of good fortune. In April 1969, while Wilson was still in power, over a bit of domestic politics which to foreign observers has always seemed strangely insignificant in proportion to the gigantic events it set in train, Charles DeGaulle retired as President of the French Republic. The greatest obstacle to Britain's entry into the European Economic Community had disappeared and in the election of June, 1970, both Labour and the Conservatives stressed renewed commitment to the Common Market. In January, 1970, Labour had in fact committed Britain to a new round of negotiations with the EEC, also to be attended by Ireland, Norway, and Denmark, which were set to begin on 30 June 1970. When the Conservatives took office Heath, whose commitment to unity with Europe was virtually absolute, sent a strong delegation to Brussels. The negotiations proceeded smoothly and culminated in July 1971 with the publication of a White Paper setting out the terms under which Britain would enter the Common Market. There would be special rights of access to the EEC for Commonwealth food products, which concessions would be gradually eliminated over a period of six years. Britain's payments to the community budget and to the Common Agricultural Fund would increase over a similar period and domestic subsidies for agriculture would be phased out. On 18 October 1971, in a free vote, Parliament approved the terms of the White Paper. The Treaty of Accession was signed in Brussels on 22 January 1972. The necessary enabling legislation to make the treaty part of British law finally received the royal assent on 17 October 1972. Two and one half months later, on 1 January 1973, Britain entered the European Economic Community.

This recitation of the fairly rapid progression of events which took Britain into the Common Market conceals the really dangerous political dislocations that the entry caused in both major parties. In 1970 both Conservative and Labour parties contained a group of intractable MPs opposed to the EEC, even though the front benches on both sides were committed to joining. Had Labour won in June, 1970, there can be no doubt that a delegation headed by George Thomson would have attended the negotiations that the Labour government had arranged to begin that month and would have returned with a set of terms that Parliament could have been expected to accept. However, the Common Market turned out to be not a Labour, but a Conservative, project and as such received the accumulated odium that Labour felt for Heath's economic policy and for the Industrial Relations Bill which was making its way through Parliament at the same time. Wilson himself, ignoring charges of inconsistency and dishonesty, attacked Heath's handling of the arrangements. The former Prime Minister was to be sure, roundly criticized by a substantial group of pro-marketeers in his own party led by Roy Jenkins and George Brown, two of his most important lieutenants in the previous administration. But Wilson argued forcefully that while he welcomed the approach to Europe he would have insisted on terms of entry more favourable to Britain. In all of this the former Prime Minister was certainly representing the wishes of the majority of the Labour party in the country and of the leadership of the trade union movement, which through the last months of 1970 and the early months of 1971 moved from lukewarm support for the EEC to active hostility.

Wilson's position was delicate. He knew, as an economist, that Britain had no future outside Europe and so he never allowed himself to be trapped into outright opposition by the left wing trade union leadership or radical party intellectuals who wished to see the country retire to an economic cocoon dependent upon domestically generated resources and a managed economy. Yet as a politician who was contemptuous of Edward Heath and all his works, who could see powerful sections of the party which he was determined to lead swinging against the Common Market, and who knew that public opinion by the end of 1970 had turned heavily against participation in Europe, his change in position was almost inevitable. (Strangely, in view of the later referendum, the BIPO found the Common Market to be consistently unpopular. Only 16 per cent of the population approved entry in December 1970 as opposed to 61 per cent against. In fact, except for a few months after October 1967, just before DeGaulle's veto, when the ratio of approval to disapproval of the

Market was 46 per cent to 34 per cent there had never been a majority in favour of joining.)

He took therefore a peculiarly Wilsonian form of middle ground. He attacked Heath's terms of entry into the Common Market, gathering around himself all the now exploding anti-market sentiment in the party and channelling off onto the EEC proposals the violent resentment against all Conservative measures. But at the same time he reserved the option of taking up the Market again, terms and dates always unspecified. From this position he allowed himself to be pushed by the anti-marketeers in March, 1972 into agreeing that when Labour returned to power the party would insist upon the renegotiation of the terms of entry and would then refer the package to an advisory referendum of the national electorate. He thus turned the Common Market issue away from one of approval or disapproval of the EEC and made it instead a question of being for or against the referendum. It was difficult to argue against consulting the people.

The referendum, of course, was opposed by most of Labour's pro-marketeers, led by Roy Jenkins. Not only did they fear the apparrent state of public opinion in which the Common Market would lose in any national vote. They argued also that it contradicted a fundamental tenet of the British constitution, the supremacy of a lawful Parliament, that it was a clumsy perversion of the legislative process, and that in the past demands for public referenda had come most frequently from the extreme right in attempts to block innovative measures. Altogether a referendum was a dangerous precedent for a socialist party to provide as indeed it turned out to be. In Wilson's defence it must be argued that what seemed to be simple opportunism in fact allowed the party leader to avoid what might have been an irreconcilable breach among his followers.

Renegotiation and referendum were, accordingly, a part of Labour's manifesto during the February 1974 election and almost immediately after taking office James Callaghan, the new Foreign Secretary, began discussions with the council of the EEC. The revisions Britain desired were in some cases almost symbolic—the rejection of a fixed parity for sterling and slightly more favourable terms for agricultural products from New Zealand—but they included also changes in the formula for determining Britain's contribution to the community budget. (These modifications as it turned out did not go far enough.) On the whole the other members of the EEC, fully aware of Labour's difficulties at home and anxious to see Britain remain a part of the Common Market, were conciliatory. In mid-March 1975, with the negotiations complete, the cabinet voted 16 to seven to recommend approval of the new terms of Britain's membership. The poll was set for 5 June.

The cabinet vote on the Common Market symbolized the split within the Labour party. The committed socialist left led by Tony Benn and Michael Foot were opposed to the Market while the moderates, represented by the Prime Minister and James Callaghan, supported the committed Europeans, Roy Jenkins and Shirley Williams. (Adding to the constitutional innovations represented by the referendum itself, the cabinet agreed that its members could take sides publicly on the issue in the subsequent campaign.)

The Conservatives were more united. The only prominent party member who opposed the Community, if indeed he counted as a party member since February, 1974, when he said he might vote for the Labour party, was Enoch Powell, the apostle of free enterprise and an all-white Britain. In effect the opponents of the Common Market, as they had been in the fifties, were the men of the far left and the far right while the pro-marketeers represented the moderates of both parties.

Nevertheless the question remains, in view of its repeatedly documented unpopularity in the nation at large, how did the Common Market win so decisively in the referendum. Probably the most important factor in the affirmative vote was the undebatable proposition that Britain was already in the EEC. Hence the average uncommitted, cautious, voter-citizen, whose reaction to difficult questions was likely to be negative, found himself in this case to be asked to vote for a change by voting no. This he was reluctant to do. Those opposed to the Market thus were at the disadvantage of having to oppose a fact with a hypothesis. The practical British voter will usually prefer a reality to a promise, especially when the nature of the promise was uncertain.

Beside being unclear about what would follow Britain's withdrawal, the anti-marketeers were never united about the reasons for their resistance. They were, as has been pointed out, a diverse group of advanced ideological socialists who knew that the achievement of their dreams would be impossible within the Community, and nostalgic nationalists who distrusted Europe on principle and feared for ties with the Empire. The anti-marketeers were, in addition, among the most controversial figures in their respective parties and by taking the positions they held were contradicting their own leadership. Unquestionably the anti-Common Market campaign suffered from the nature of the men who were its advocates while the pro-marketeers benefited for the same reason. It seemed that all the solid citizens were on one side and all the cranks and crackpots on the other. As a result, on 5 June 1975 Wilson's gamble paid off handsomely. Even though as late as February the BIPO had found the Common Market ratio of approval to disapproval in the proportion of 39 per cent to 45 per cent, the renegotiated terms (which no one understood and did not figure in the campaign) were supported by 67 per cent of those who voted. Nowhere except in Shetland and in the Western Isles of Scotland did a majority of voters approve withdrawal. The Prime Minister thus had discredited the anti-marketeer left wing of his own party both in and out of Parliament (using the victory to replace Anthony Wedgwood Benn at the Department of Industry where his behaviour had driven the British business world into near hysteria), had strengthened his own leadership, and best of all had gained from Heath some of the credit for taking the nation into Europe. (Constitutionally the referendum was only advisory to Parliament but Wilson had announced that the government would abide by its results.)

IRELAND AGAIN

Perhaps the most tragic and invincible problem in the United Kingdom in the period of this study, a conundrum that seems not only without solution but without hope, is the civil war in Northern Ireland. Even as astute a politician as Lloyd George had been unable to solve it, only to sweep it under the rug. Lloyd George's unstable compromise in 1921, had meant surrender to the Protestants of the North while giving disguised independence—in effect the right to claim independence—to 26 counties of the South. He had abandoned the landowning unionist magnates of the South who had destroyed his attempts at settlement after the Easter Rebellion. But in order to gain Tory support for this sacrifice, a bargain the party had been unwilling to make either in 1914 or 1916, he was forced to institutionalize Protestant ascendancy in the North. The Better Government of Ireland Act, the Fourth Home Rule Act, gave the power not to the inhabitants of six of the nine counties of Ulster but to a party machine which for nearly 50 years held unquestioned control of the Northern Irish administration. Politics in the North ignored the overriding issues of the rest of the United Kingdom, unemployment, welfare, capital and labour—even though the area suffered devastating unemployment—and centred entirely on the matter, as it was put, of 'maintaining the constitution'. Northern Irish politics were consistent if not stable. In the 47 years between 1921 and 1968, during which Britain experienced 14 changes of Prime Minister, Northern Ireland had four, all of the same party. Of these four, two presided for a period of 39 years. There were many similarities to post-reconstruction one-party rule in the American South.

Like the American South also, Northern Ireland was a segregated society in which the lines dividing Protestant and Catholic extended far beyond religion, into housing, schooling and commerce. Each side enshrined its own peculiar sort of atavistic tribalism in secret organizations, public ceremonies and commemorations of past victories, a form of living history. With political power firmly in the hands of the two-thirds of the population who were Protestant there was plenty of evidence of discrimination against Catholics in school financing, employment, and gerrymandering of local government districts and having provided adequate grievances, the Protestants could justifiably argue that the Catholic population of Northern Ireland was less than entirely loyal to the settlement of 1920. There were continual provocations to disturbance on each side and serious riots in 1935 with lesser ones in 1959.

Briefly the advent of the fourth Prime Minister in Northern Ireland's history, Captain Terence O'Neill in 1963, and of Harold Wilson in Britain in 1964, offered hope of reconciliation between Protestants and Catholics. Public opinion polls even suggested that a large number of Catholics were willing to accept the constitutional division of Ireland and to work for better conditions for themselves within the existing framework. At the same time there were signs of friendliness between the governments at Dublin and Belfast. O'Neill was the first Northern Irish Prime Minister not of the generation of the Troubles and the treaty. In January and February 1965 the Prime Ministers of North and South made much publicized calls at each other's capitals and in 1966 Wilson returned the remains of Roger Casement who had been hanged in Pentonville Prison following the Easter Rebellion 50 years before.

There was at last some movement. But as many historians have noted, oppression seems most unendurable when the possibility for its amelioration appears. Moreover there was from the United States the exemplary success of the civil rights movement which brought much improvement to the condition of the blacks in the American

South. In the middle-sixties a coalition of moderate Catholics, some liberal Protestants, and a substantial number of students from Queens University, had formed the North Ireland Civil Rights Association. The Association goals were constitutional, securing an end to gerrymandering of local authority districts, equal funding for Catholic housing and school projects, and countering the rhetoric of Protestant extremists. Particularly violent among these was the Free Presbyterian Minister, Ian Paisley, who had already begun to speak out against the rather mild reforms that Captain O'Neill had proposed since taking office.

The story of the present tragic stalemate in North Ireland falls easily into three phases. The first extended from June 1968, when the Civil Rights Association undertook its first large public demonstration in Dungannon, typically over· housing, to January 1969. During this period Catholic moderates demonstrated in most major Ulster towns and were generally opposed by Protestant hard-liners whose spokesman, and usually also leader, was Ian Paisley. Police intervention was limited to occasional arrests and beatings of Catholics. The issues however were only those of civil and economic discrimination against Catholics and violence, so far, was not lethal.

The second phase began on 1 January 1969 with vicious attacks by Protestant thugs upon marchers who had set out to walk from Belfast to Londonderry. By the time the demonstrators, many seriously hurt, reached Londonderry, a city which itself was virtually a Northern Irish Protestant shrine, the community was in an uproar. The badly disorganized police were attacking the Catholic Bogside section of the town while the citizens in the Bogside defended themselves with rocks, petrol bombs, and barricades. During this period, which lasted until the autumn of 1969, the entire character of the struggle changed from a demand for Catholic equality carried forward by young, largely middle-class demonstrators, to a general war between Catholic and Protestant working classes of the larger towns in which the issues changed to simple racial hatred combined with a fairly consistent demand for the unification of North and South, in effect for British withdrawal from the North. The second phase saw also the breakdown of political control, the hardening of public opinion against Prime Minister O'Neill's moderate policies, and the demoralization of the Royal Ulster Constabulary who lost any semblance of power over the Protestant mobs with whom, in any case, they usually sympathized. The result, in August 1969, was the replacement of the Royal Ulster Constabulary for peacekeeping purposes by the British Army. Three months earlier, in May 1969, O'Neill had resigned.

As heavy reinforcements of British troops arrived in Northern Ireland to strengthen the three battalions already there, a shift in authority from Belfast to London took place. The manifest impotence of the police to protect Catholics, which had made the introduction of troops necessary in the first place, revealed to all the weakness of Northern Ireland's government. On 1 April 1972, direct rule from London superseded the authority of the Stormont Parliament which had governed Ireland since 1921.

However, well before the introduction of direct rule, by the end of 1969, the third phase had begun. Northern Ireland had become, as it is to this day, a battleground between British troops and a sinister new force, the professional terrorists of the Provisional Wing of the Irish Republican Army. The Provisionals of the seventies traced their ancestry back to DeValera's anti-treaty forces of 1922, that is to the portion of the original Irish Republican Army of the Troubles which had refused to accept the partition treaty brought back from London in December 1921 by Arthur Griffith and Michael Collins and which in 1922 had risen against the government of the new Irish Free State. For half a century after their defeat the IRA remained an illegal but visible conspiracy, devoted to the unification of the island, denouncing the governments of both North and South, and committing from time to time acts of terrorism in both Ireland and Britain. The Provisionals in the North represented yet another breakaway group which had seceded from the 'official' IRA based in Dublin when the latter turned more and more toward Marxist political agitation while giving up violence.

The present phase of Northern Ireland's civil war, then, continues to be the battle between the Provisionals and the British troops whose appearance at first had been welcomed by the Catholic ghettos. Undoubtedly the IRA was present during the early civil rights marches but attained ascendancy only by taking advantage of attacks of Protestants on peaceful demonstrators and later, after the Londonderry march, by helping to resist Protestant invasions of Catholic housing areas. As such they were able to present themselves as the only protectors of the Catholic population and to replace the demand for civil rights within the context of a Northern Ireland with the ancient cry of United Ireland. By the beginning of the decade of the seventies civil rights for Catholics, if it meant recognition by Catholics of the separation of North and South, had virtually disappeared as a demand and with it had gone, unhappily, any possibility of the peaceful reconciliation which had seemed briefly possible in the sixties. The Protestants refused to discuss civil rights if it meant discussing also the unification of North and South and the Catholics would discuss nothing else.

The termination of Home Rule and the imposition of direct government from London carried with it the implication that Northern Ireland was incapable of governing itself. Consequently, even though one may suspect that many North Irish Protestants cared little whether the Parliament at Stormont sat or not, demands for a return to local self-government began to be heard among politicians almost immediately. Britain's problem was that it could not simply return power to the exclusively Protestant political machine that had run Northern Ireland for half a century. Somehow Catholic participation would have to be insured. But since 1969 no Catholic politician could survive in the North who did not recognize the sentiment among his constituents for some sort of political connection with the South, a topic upon which Protestants were immovable.

Among the several of Edward Heath's failed initiatives was the attempt, beginning in the spring of 1973, to reconstruct the Northern Irish administration with the statutory inclusion (power sharing) of Catholics, at all levels of government while providing also for the formation of at least an embryonic Council of Ireland which would recognize the unity of the island. Although an assembly and an executive council were in fact elected they were unable to function and the Protestants of Northern Ireland on 15 May 1974, proclaimed a general strike which virtually paralyzed the six counties. As a result power was reclaimed by the Wilson government. Britain has been caught in the vice on one side of intransigent Protestantism which sees the English connection first of all as the symbol of freedom from Catholic domination and on the other side of an IRA terrorism which will accept nothing but total unification. (Not surprisingly, like the Protestant militants, the Provisional IRA also rejected the tentative power sharing proposals and the Council of Ireland.) Between these two poles lies surely the majority of the population of both North and South, which may favour privately either separation or unification but which most of all wants to see the killing stopped. Meanwhile on the sidelines exists a hapless Irish government in Dublin, well aware that the IRA gunmen represent in the long run as grave a threat to itself as to the British, but which is unable to take action against them without seeming to favour partition.

Thus for over a decade violence and disorder have been the rule in Northern Ireland, arrests by British soldiers are countered by bombings of troop carriers and sniping, with occasional outrages in Great Britain and most recently by the murder of Earl Mountbatten. The tragedy in the situation seems to be that for the political authorities in Britain there are no options. Proposals for concessions to the Catholics in the North break against the hard wall of the Northern Irish Protestant siege mentality. On the other hand the Provisional IRA has no interest in a stable and contented Irish population within the present Northern Irish constitutional framework. Negotiations among the few remaining moderate leaders, Catholic or Protestant, are repudiated by the rank and file, as occurred in the power sharing experiments of 1973–74 and in the constitutional convention of 1975–76. And in ten years a generation has grown up in civil war with new sacrifices to celebrate and a new calendar of saints and devils to revere and hate.

THE DEVOLUTION OF POWER

Harold Wilson could fairly claim, both to his party and to the opposition, that his return to power in March 1974 represented a vindication of his behaviour in his previous administration and of his assertions that his was the only way to handle both the economy and the unions. Yet for the historian, the Wilson/Callaghan government of the last half of the decade of the seventies seems to have been weaker, less purposeful, and less interesting than the first Wilson ministry. At least at that time the Prime Minister, whether or not he was successful, knew what he wanted to accomplish. In the second administration the centre of attention was not really within Westminster Palace nor within Whitehall or Downing Street. Rather one senses a scattering of political power centres. Efficient governmental decisions for Britain seem to have been made elsewhere, in conclaves at the TUC headquarters in Great Russell Street, or by Jack Jones at Transport House, or by the Board of Governors of the International Bank in Washington, DC or by the ordinary voter in referenda. To be sure, no government, democracy or dictatorship, at any time has a total monopoly of power; it must always deal with forces it cannot control. But in Britain after the election of 1974 Her majesty's ministers seem to be more than usually the recipients, rather than the makers, of decisions.

The election of February 1974 had turned upon the basic constitutional point of whether one group in the nation was to be allowed to use its coercive power, unmolested by the ordinary guarantors of civil peace, to bring economic activity to a stop. The British nation determined that it would rather pay than fight. During the election Wilson announced, not clearly but repeatedly, that Labour's formula for controlling inflation—which by February was over 20 per cent on a yearly basis—would be price and dividend controls coupled with an understanding with the trade unions for moderation in wage demands. In support of this the TUC stated that they would not regard a generous miners' settlement as a model for wage agreements in other industries.

This 'social contract' which Wilson said he had negotiated in February, 1973, became the symbol or the banner, of the 1974–79 Labour government. It was never certain whether the social contract was a written document or a form of spiritual communion with the union leaders, among whom Jack Jones of the Transport and General Workers was the most powerful. But in tone it seemed to suggest that the Labour administration had taken the unions as partners into the business of governing. Cooperation, Wilson explained, would replace confrontation.

The first item of ministerial business was the settlement of the coal strike, which immediately ended virtually on the miners' terms, and the first large piece of parliamentary business was the repeal of the Industrial Relations Act by a new statute, The Trade Unions and Labour Relations Act. This measure, drawn up in close cooperation with union leadership, not only swept away all vestiges of legal control over labour but granted also specific new rights in the direction of enforcing union membership upon all workers in a firm and in permitting secondary boycotts. The act, indeed, would have done more, but Labour was restrained by the thinness of its majority. In fact the opposition succeeded in diluting the force of a few provisions which were, however, restored after Labour achieved a firmer hold on the House of Commons in the second general election of October 1974.

Although they occupied much parliamentary time, these concessions to labour and the dramatically increased taxes on incomes and capital transfers that presumably were also a part of the social contract, do not seem in retrospect to count for much in the story of Great Britain in the last half of the decade of the seventies. In fact not much political history was being made at Westminster Palace. The important forces were outside it. Increasing inflation meant rising costs for all government services while stagnant and unprofitable industry reduced the yield of even higher taxes. The result was the rise in the public borrowing requirement and an increasing money supply resulting in still more inflation and more wage demands. This necessitated government payments to make up deficits, not only of nationalized industries but of private ones as well where, as in British Leyland, the government possessed an equity interest through the newly created National Enterprise Board. Consequently the first years of the second Wilson government, 1974, 1975, 1976, saw at once unprecedented price inflation, well into double digits each year and over 20 per cent in 1975, record international payment deficits, and a decline in the value of the pound from about $2.40 in the beginning of 1974 to a little more than a $1.60 by autumn 1976. All of this was accompanied by an apparent drop in the real standard of living, with of course wide variations among different economic groups.

Yet there was little the government could do to change this course of affairs except to arrange for ever larger international loans. Nor indeed, when international payment stability returned in 1977 with the large scale production of oil from the North Sea, could the government take much credit. The critical factor in off-shore petroleum development was the rapid increase in the price of crude oil set by the OPEC cartel beginning at the end of 1973. Without the increases in oil prices from about $3.00 a barrel in 1973 to nearly $40 on the spot market by the end of 1979, North Sea oil, although proven to exist in exploitable quantities since 1969, would not have been economically feasible to develop. But with rapid drilling in 1974 and 1975, by 1977 Britain was receiving nearly half her domestic consumption of fuels from areas under her own control and by the end of the year the balance of payments for the first time since 1972, was in surplus.

Unquestionably North Sea oil and the general economic malaise of the seventies were responsible for another movement toward the dilution of central power in Britain, the growth of nationalist sentiment in Scotland, and to a lesser extent in Wales. Neither was a new phenomenon. Separation from England in varying forms had been a feature of politics in both countries well back in the nineteenth century, while the modern Scottish Nationalists and Plaid Cymru, the Welsh nationalist party, had been founded in 1934 and 1925 respectively. But except for R.D. McIntyre, who sat for Motherwell from April to June, 1975, capturing the seat during the wartime electoral truce, neither party had ever put a member into Parliament when Harold Wilson first took office. However, in July, 1966, Gwynfor Evans won Megan Lloyd George's old seat in Carmarthenshire for the Welsh nationalists and in November, 1967, the Scottish Nationalists candidate, Mrs Winifred Ewing, carried Glasgow Pollok. Both of these seats were lost in 1970, but elsewhere the Scottish Nationalists won an unexpected victory in a safe Labour seat in the Western Isles.

The Scottish Nationalists showed increasing strength in by-elections and local authority elections during the Heath administration, nearly always against Labour, and succeeded in winning a second parliamentary seat in Glasgow Gowan in November, 1973. But few people were prepared for the sensational triumph of seven Scottish Nationalists and two Welsh in February 1974. In addition the Scottish Nationalists won nearly 22 per cent of the vote in that kingdom. Still worse was to come. In the October general election, the Scots carried 11 seats with over 30 per cent of the total vote and the Welsh increased their delegation to three.

The question for Westminster politicians and the nationalists alike remains: what exactly did regional nationalism mean? The nationalists never seemed sure whether they wanted total independence, home rule on the Irish model, or some amount of devolution of administrative and legislative powers from London. All of these points of view had supporters and nationalist leaders in each country were frequently vague in their demands. The rhetoric of the movement centred on the English exploitation and gave little indication of how the political, and above all the economic, problems attendant upon separation would be solved. Of course for many in Scotland, North Sea oil, 'Scotland's oil,' provided the all-purpose answer to any question of how Scotland could get along without England's help.

In Wales, without even the pretence of a claim to oil and without Scotland's visible evidence of a national being in courts and law, an established church, currency, banking, education and health systems, the nationalist programme was still more unclear. The movement thus devoted its energy to a revival of the declining Cymric language and culture, painting out English signs, and pestering the government for widest possible use of the Welsh language in television, the courts and government publications.

Labour usually proclaimed itself a friend of nationalist causes. (Wilson had established the cabinet post of Secretary of State for Wales when he took office in 1964 and made the Welsh language legal for use in courts and government business in 1967.) In 1969 the government had appointed a Royal Commission on the Constitution to examine the relationship among the various nations within the United Kingdom. But the Labour party could never forget that any measure for the sort of Home Rule Ireland had once claimed, would, in equity, require a reduction of Scottish and Welsh seats at Westminster, most of which were currently held by loyal Labour MPs. For Wilson's government, therefore, and for James Callaghan when he succeeded to the Prime Ministership in April 1976, regional nationalism was a ticking bomb that could neither be defused nor thrown away. Even after the October 1974 election, Labour's majority over all parties was only three. The party needed, and usually received, the support of the Scots and Welsh. But a measure of Home Rule adequate to satisfy ardent nationalists would inevitably entail the loss of seats, while anything less, the devolution of a few administrative powers, many of which were already handled in Edinburgh and Cardiff, and the establishment of some kind of a glorified county council, would jeopardize the nationalist support at Westminster. Meanwhile, according to the polls, the English public, with its attention focused on trade union problems and the balance of payments, remained profoundly uninterested.

Not surprisingly, the government moved slowly. A White Paper on devolution in September, 1974 was followed by a promise of legislation in the Queen's speech only in October, 1975. No bills appeared until late in 1976 by which time Labour had lost its overall majority in the House of Commons. As a result the leadership in the cabinet now headed by James Callaghan was unable to control the debate timetable and although most of the 1976–77 session was devoted to a single devolution bill for both Scotland and Wales, Tory filibustering made completion of all its stages impossible. The issue was taken up again in the next session with separate bills for the two countries and the two finally became law on 31 July 1978. However, the opposition had forced upon the government a vital amendment, based on Labour's own precedent provided in the Common Market struggle, requiring a referendum in each country in which 40 per cent of the electorate was required to show approval of devolution if the bills were to take effect.

In the subsequent campaign, the question of the devolution seriously divided Labour party leadership which foresaw the loss of its control of Scottish politics if the Scottish Nationalists won, but which anticipated revenge at Westminster if they did not. In the event, when the referenda took place on 1 March 1979, Scotland voted 52 per cent to 48 per cent for an assembly, but the Nationalists failed to win the required approval of 40 per cent of the electorate. In Wales, the more restrictive administrative devolution offered was heavily defeated, 20 per cent to 80 per cent. At Westminster the Scottish and Welsh struck back swiftly. Four weeks later, on 28 March they supported a motion of no confidence which was carried against the Labour government 311 to 310. Thus for the first time since October 1924, when a combination of Conservatives and Liberals also had combined to turn out Ramsay MacDonald's original Labour government, an administration fell as a result of a formal vote of no confidence. Callaghan immediately dissolved Parliament and announced elections for 3 May which were won by the Conservatives under the leadership of Margaret Thatcher who had succeeded Edward Heath as party leader in February 1975.

The parliamentary story of the seventies offers only gloomy reflections for an admirer of Britain and its constitution. Not only the House of Commons, but the cabinet itself, seem to be evolving into dignified rather than efficient parts of the governmental system. The use of referenda (putting the most difficult questions to those least equipped to answer them), the internationalization of fiscal control (not a new difficulty, but now a greater problem as Britain's economic leverage declines), the willingness of trade union leaders to use coercive powers against the government—indeed to treat it as a foreign, not too friendly nation so making it virtually impossible for government to control the nation's economic plant—and the recent Labour party proposals to destroy the independence of the parliamentary party, all tell the story of increasing impotence at Westminster. It is no longer the seat of power, only one among many.

Liberal government presumes, and depends upon, individual restraint, as the Victorians well-understood. What has been missing in Britain has been not only the sense of moderation in political and civic deportment that maintains the balance between freedom and authority, but also the sense of participation in the national enterprise. Somewhere along the way between the Armistice and the election of Margaret Thatcher Britain has fallen into pieces. It is no longer Her Majesty's Realm but a collection of large and small competing, sometimes overlapping, power centres situated on one and a half small islands off the coast of Europe, a new feudal state. It has a government (the civil service of which constitutes one of the feudatories) which administers the law still with some effectiveness, but which makes less and less of it that is important. The really significant departure of the 1964–1979 period, the only measure that both went into effect and remains on the books, the entry into the European Economic Community, had to be approved by referendum before all the power centres in the country accepted it. The verdict of a lawful Parliament is no longer final.

This new fractured loyalty, call it incivility—not to be sure a problem only of Britain—is the most disturbing inheritance of the last quarter of the twentieth century. As men have found that government can do little to alter or improve the conditions under which they live and work, their loyalties have been transferred elsewhere, to their union or their region, or occasionally to some form of political activist group. Meanwhile the conventional political parties suffer declining membership and support. Those who are totally dependent upon the old institutions of government, which used to be called the welfare state, now suffer most.

All this is not to say that the New Feudalism need be permanent. Nevertheless while it lasts the dilution of civil propriety upon which organized society depends cannot make the resolution of Britain's productive and fiscal problems easier. The story of the last sixty years is at once reassuring in the recollection of the strength of national will that held together Britain's social fabric in times of emergency and frightening in its demonstration of how easily fecklessness can revive. Resolution in adversity is no doubt a measure of greatness but the survival of democracy in the modern world may depend more upon personal restraint than upon great national sacrifice.

Bibliography

Among the general histories of the inter-war period, probably the first comprehensive one, C. L. Mowet, *Britain Between the Wars, 1918–1940,* Chicago, 1955 is still the best. A. J. P. Taylor's *English History, 1914–1945,* Oxford, 1965 is more controversial, less objective but better reading. For the student, Alfred Havighurst's *Britain in Transition,* Chicago, 1979 is an excellent introduction to the entire period since the Boer War. One immensely readable treatise dealing with the period between 1918 and 1939, not to be neglected by anyone interested in social history, is Robert Graves and Alan Hodge, *The Long Weekend, A Social History of Great Britain, 1918–1939,* New York, 1941.

Until the last few years, full-scale histories of Britain in the post-1945 period were scarce. Recently, however, several have been published. Among the most useful are C. J. Bartlett, *A History of Postwar Britain, 1945–1974,* London, 1977 which is crammed with information but contains too little analysis and is rather like reading research notes. On a more elementary level is Mary Proudfoot, *British Politics and Government, 1951–1970,* London, 1974. An excellent book, at the moment unfortunately out of print, is Vernon Bogdanor and Robert Skidelsky, (eds)., *The Age of Affluence,* London, 1970. For sheer entertainment one should read, Bernard Levin, *The Pendulum Years, Britain and the Sixties,* London, 1970.

Worthwhile biographies of the major political figures of the period are only now beginning to appear in any number although Robert Blakes life of Andrew Bonar Law *The Unknown Prime Minister,* London, 1955 is an exception and Keith Filing's *The Life of Neville Chamberlain,* London, 1947 and Iain Macleod, *Neville Chamberlain,* London, 1961 should not be neglected. Probably the former is to be preferred.

Keith Middlemas and James Barnes, *Stanley Baldwin*, London, 1969 is not fully satisfactory but is a great improvement on G. M. Young's earlier attempt. David Marquand, *Ramsay MacDonald*, London, 1977, is excellent. Martin Gilbert, of course, is at work on a massive multi-volume study of Winston Churchill that is a monument of scholarship if, like other such works, sometimes unreadable. In the meantime the student should consult Henry Pelling, *Winston Churchill*, London, 1974. Since 1970 there have been a large number of excellent works on Lloyd George although as yet no fully satisfactory biography. There are however a number of important special studies. For the period covered by this book the student should consult John Campbell, *Lloyd George, the Goat in the Wilderness, 1922–1931*, London, 1977, not only for information on the man himself but for a full picture of British politics in the twenties and for a good short survey see also Kenneth Morgan, *David Lloyd George*, Cardiff, 1963. Lord Beaverbrook's *The Decline and Fall of Lloyd George*, New York, 1963 is less valuable now that many of the previously unobtainable letters printed in it are available. For the same period no reader should neglect Maurice Cowling, *The Impact of Labour, 1920–24*, London, 1970.

The secondary figures are also being studied, although here an immense amount of work remains to be done. Among the earlier ones are Alan Bullock, *The Life and Times of Ernest Bevin*, 3 Volumes, London, 1960–67; John Wheeler Bennet, *John Anderson, Viscount Waverley*, New York, 1962; Roy Harrod, *The Life of John Maynard Keynes*, New York, 1951; A. J. P. Taylor, *Beaverbrook*, London, 1972; Michael Foot, *Aneurin Bevan*, 2 Volumes, London, 1962-3; Jose Harris, *William Beveridge*, Oxford, 1977. These are full-scale scholarly biographies. There are many more that are not.

The last two decades have been exceptionally rich in publication of diaries, memoirs and autobiographies. Among the more important are Anthony Eden, *Memoirs*, 3 Volumes, London, 1960–65; Lord Dalton, *Memoirs*, London, 1953–62. These two count as politician's apologies. Far better is Harold Macmillan's *Memoirs*, 6 Volumes, London, 1966–73. Among the diaries no one should miss Harold Nicolson, *Diaries*, 3 Volumes, 1966–68; Thomas Jones, *Whitehall Diary*, 3 Volumes, London, 1969–71 which cover the period 1916–1930 and supplements his *Diary with Letters, 1931–50*, New York, 1954. For the war period the scholar should note Arthur Bryant's two-volume study of Lord Alanbrooke, *The Turn of the Tide*, New York, 1957, and *Triumph in the West*, New York, 1959. This is not really a biography but rather a stitching together of Alanbrooke's diaries and as such is useful as a supplement to Winston Churchill's six-volume history of the Second World War. Also on the war, for dates, time of day, and immediate reactions the *Diaries of Sir Alexander Cadogan, 1938–1945,* New York, 1972 should not be ignored. Perhaps the most important of all modern political diaries of the rank of Greville and Pepys and a mine of information for any scholar of the contemporary British constitution, is Richard Crossman, *The Diaries of a Cabinet Minister,* 3 Volumes, London, 1975–77 covering the years of the first Wilson government.

The fascination of Crossman's account is heightened when read in conjunction with Harold Wilson's *A Personal Record, The Labour Government, 1964–70,* London, 1971 in which Wilson gives another, sometimes contradictory, side of the same story. Wilson's memoirs are almost certainly written from a diary which scholars can only hope the world will one day see. Another account also of the same period, written by a minor cabinet official and economist and extremely useful, is Michael Stewart, *The Jekyll and Hyde Years, Politics and Economic Policy Since 1964,* London, 1977, which deals with the period between 1964 and 1975. An excellent Conservative commentary on the same period is Robert Rhodes James, *Ambitions and Realities, British Politics, 1964–1970,* London, 1972.

For histories of special topics and events there is Carl Brand, *The British Labour Party,* Stanford, 1964; Robert Skidelsky, *Politicians and the Slump,* London, 1967; Henry Pelling, *Britain and the Second World War,* London, 1970; Angus Calder, *The People's War,* London, 1969; Michael Sissons and Philip French, (eds), *The Age of Austerity,* London, 1963; and Harry Hopkins, *The New Look, A Social History of the Forties and Fifties,* Boston, 1964. For economics the best survey, now revised, remains Sidney Pollard, *The Development of the British Economy, 1914–1967,* London, 1969. The classic survey of foreign policy is William N. Medlicott, *British Policy Since Versailles, 1919–1963,* London, 1968 which is usefully supplemented with Elizabeth Monroe, *Britain's Moment in the Middle East,* London, 1963. On the EEC negotiations and referendum see Anthony King, *Britain Says Yes,* Washington, 1977.

Graphs of Unemployment, Construction of Dwellings and Bank Rate—1918–1976

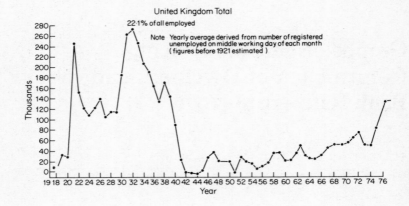

United Kingdom Total

22·1% of all employed

Note   Yearly average derived from number of registered
unemployed on middle working day of each month
(figures before 1921 estimated)

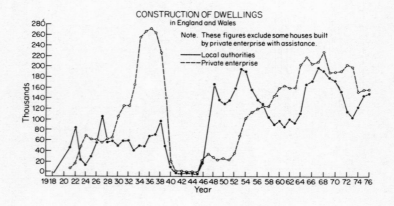

CONSTRUCTION OF DWELLINGS
in England and Wales

Note. These figures exclude some houses built
by private enterprise with assistance.

——— Local authorities
- - - - Private enterprise

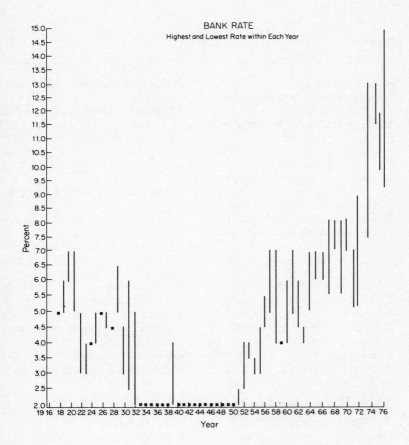

BANK RATE
Highest and Lowest Rate within Each Year

Index

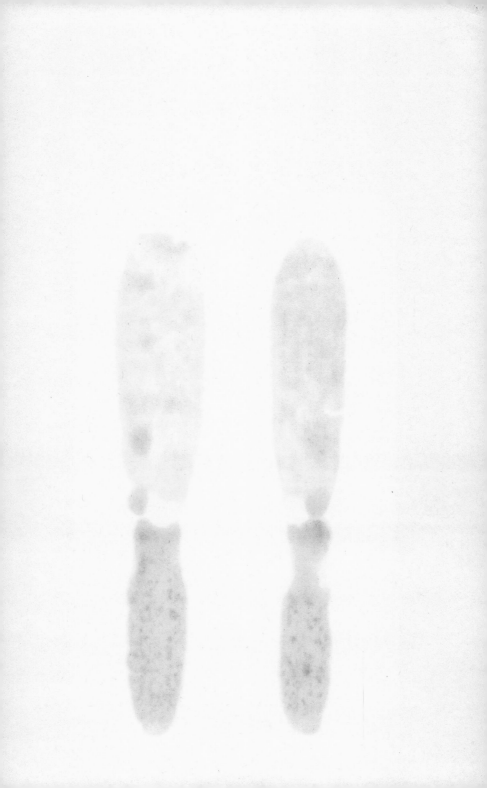

DATE DUE	
MAR 19 1996	

GAYLORD   PRINTED IN U.S.A.